# Prayers for the School Year

# Prayers for the School Year

Rosanna E. Golino

© 2005 Novalis, Saint Paul University, Ottawa, Canada

Cover artwork: Lynne McIlvride Evans

Cover design: Yasher Hassan, Studio Bubble

Layout: Martin Roy (Novalis)

Business Office:

Novalis

49 Front Street East, 2nd Floor

Toronto, Ontario, Canada

M5E 1B3

Phone: 1-800-387-7164

Fax: 1-800-204-4140

E-mail: cservice@novalis-inc.com

www.novalis.ca

Library and Archives Canada Cataloguing in Publication

Golino, Rosanna

Prayers for the school year / Rosanna Golino.

ISBN 2-89507-484-4

1. Schools–Prayers.  2. Devotional calendars–Catholic Church.

I. Title.

BV283.S3G64 2005          264'.02          C2005-901531-4

Printed in Canada.

We acknowledge the financial support of the Government of Canada through the Book Publishing Industry Development Program (BPIDP) for our publishing activities.

5 4 3 2 1    09 08 07 06 05

*This book is dedicated to*
*the teachers and students of*

*Saint Margaret Mary School,*
*Hamilton, Ontario,*

*who willingly prepared and prayed this work*
*during the school years*
*1998–1999 and 1999–2000,*
*and to principal Jack O'Neill*
*who, in his words,*
*"twisted my arm to become an author."*

*This book is also dedicated to*
*God the Holy Spirit,*
*without whose guidance and inspiration*
*this work could never have been written.*

# TABLE OF CONTENTS

## Acknowledgments

The teachers and students of St. Margaret Mary School, Hamilton, Ontario, piloted this program, which they received on what became known as the "instalment plan." I am indebted to them for their patience and understanding as I prayed and wrote these prayers for them, in the hope that it would be helpful to the children and staff in all the schools of our system.

I also owe a debt of thanks to Dr. Anthony Cuschieri for his support and suggestions, and to my colleagues and friends who have encouraged me as this work progressed.

Special thanks go to Father Don Sanvido and Father Wayne Lobsinger, for their support and reassurance when I felt unsure about what I had written.

*Rosanna E. Golino*

# How to Use This Book

*Prayers for the School Year* follows the Canadian *Liturgical Calendar* and uses readings from the *Weekday Lectionary* (both these resources are published by the Canadian Conference of Catholic Bishops). It is divided into the liturgical seasons of Advent, Christmas, Lent, Easter and Ordinary Time.

The prayer services may be used as a whole or in sections throughout the day, over the P.A. system or in each classroom. Children are encouraged to proclaim the readings and lead the prayers.

While the services are aimed at students in grades 4 and up, they have been used successfully in primary to intermediate schools. High-school teachers could incorporate these prayers into their religion programs, or use them to begin their classes. Students of all ages who have special needs can of course enjoy and participate in the services, too. As each prayer service is thematic, often with reflection questions incorporated into the introduction, they can be used as discussion starters.

Scripture references are listed at the end of each day's prayer. The prayers can supplement the religion program when specific Scripture passages are being taught, as the course materials often contain background information related to the passage in question. The closing prayer offers a good ending to the lesson covering that particular passage, as the prayer summarizes the Scripture reading and the introduction. An index at the end of the book will help you find specific passages.

Things happen in daily life and in classrooms that teachers need to address; specific prayers can be used to reinforce these aspects of Christian living, of what it means to be a faithful follower of Jesus. These prayers will remind students that following Jesus is not "out there" but within them; it is a way of life, with lessons to be learned to help them grow and develop.

This book demonstrates liturgical continuity with the official prayers of the Church. The readings are introduced in the same way as they are heard in the Church's liturgy (especially the Mass), and students respond in that same way, too. You are welcome to use the prayers to create other liturgies for your class or school. Be creative in sharing the Good News of God's word!

Although *Prayers for the School Year* is based on the liturgical year, it is not date-specific and therefore can be used every year, no matter when the various feasts and seasons are celebrated on the calendar. Each section of the Church year is clearly marked: Ordinary Time, Advent, Christmas Season, Lent, Easter Season, and Feast Days. Also included are the First Week of School, Last Week of School, and Special Occasions.

Use the tables in Appendix 4 – Table of Moveable Dates and Weeks in Ordinary Time – to find the dates of the calendar year and the corresponding liturgical date.

The Feast Days section is the only calendar-dated section – for example, September 8, Nativity of Mary. If it is a feast day, turn to the Feast Days section in this book to see if there is a special prayer service for that particular feast. Not all feasts have a prayer for that day. Always check the dates.

The weekday cycle of readings is different from the readings for Sundays and Solemnities. The weekday cycle consists of a first reading and psalm which, in Ordinary Time, follows a two-year cycle (Year I and Year II). The gospel passage in most cases remains the same every year. For the other liturgical seasons, the first reading, psalm, and gospel are almost always the same every year. Readings that were best suited for students in grades 1 to 8 were chosen from these options. Some readings have been shortened where appropriate.

During the month of November, reference is made to the Book of Remembrance. Students and staff are invited to write on special sheets of paper the names of people they know who have died. The sheets are then placed in a book (a nice-looking binder works well). The book becomes part of the November display in the front hall of the school, and these people are prayed for as a part of the prayer each day.

Praying together as a school community or class every day is a wonderful way to stay focused on our faith journey. May the Holy Spirit guide your prayer celebrations, lead you closer to God and encourage you to be faithful followers of Jesus!

# The Church Year

## Advent

The word *Advent* derives from the Latin word that means *coming* or *arrival*. The season of Advent begins the Church Year on the fourth Sunday before Christmas, on the Sunday closest to the feast of St. Andrew (November 30); thus, it falls between November 27 and December 3.

The season of Advent is not considered today to be penitential in tone, nor was it ever considered in the history of the Church to be a time for the solemn reconciliation of penitents, as Lent has been.

Advent is a time that reflects the joy of anticipation, and the expectation, of Jesus' first coming when he appeared on earth; his second coming at the end of time; and, for believers, his current presence in the hearts of all the faithful.

Advent is a time of preparation, and as such becomes a time of desire, longing and expectancy. The spiritual hunger that these three states inspire is satisfied by the ways the Church prepares us for the coming of Jesus. It does this in a three-fold manner:

1. Through the *Old Testament* – in particular, through the prophet Isaiah, and the many prophecies about the messiah. Our longing for the Redeemer increases as we see how God is revealed in these Scriptures.

2. Through *John the Baptist*, the herald and forerunner of Jesus' Advent in history. John shows us that Advent is a time of conversion, of turning back to God.

3. Through *Mary*. God chose to work through a woman, as our salvation is built on a human framework. Mary, who was immaculately conceived, became the Mother of God.

Until the last seven days of Advent, the emphasis is on the coming of Jesus at the end of time. On December 17, the theme switches to the coming of Jesus as a baby in Bethlehem. The great prayers of longing, known as the *O Antiphons*, are prayed from December 17 to 23.

Advent helps us to recognize the presence of God in our midst today, awakens a deeper longing for the second coming of Christ, and encourages us to get rid of worldly preoccupations in order to prepare for a fuller celebration of Christmas.

## Christmas

The feast of the Nativity of our Lord on December 25 commemorates the redemptive mystery of the entrance of Jesus into this world. This solemnity is characterized by the celebration of three Masses: during the night, at dawn and during the day. The Mass during the day is the oldest of the three; it was first celebrated in the Basilica of St. Peter in Rome around 336 AD. The Mass at dawn, which developed next, was celebrated at St. Peter's from the end of that same century. The Mass during the Night, commonly known as Midnight Mass, was inaugurated by Pope Sixtus III in the middle of the fifth century.

We celebrate the following events at Christmas:

- *the eternal birth* of the Word of God in the heart of the eternal Father – the Word who is, was and always will be;

- *the temporal birth* of Jesus as a human being at a particular time and place;

- *the final return* of Jesus on the day of judgment.

## Christmas Season

Christmas Season begins with Christmas Eve and ends with the Feast of the Baptism of Our Lord.

The Octave of Christmas extends the feast of Christmas for eight days, ending on January 1, the Solemnity of Mary, Mother of God. The octave includes the feasts of St. Stephen, St. John the Evangelist and the Holy Innocents, all of whom have a direct link to the Nativity of Christ being celebrated. It also includes the Feast of the Holy Family, which is celebrated on the Sunday between Christmas Day and January 1, or on December 30 when Christmas and New Year's Day fall on a Sunday.

The Solemnity of Epiphany, which has been moved to the Sunday following January 1 in Canada, and the days following until the Feast of the Baptism of Our Lord, are also included in the Christmas Season: the mystery of our salvation is not static, or something that happened two thousand years ago. It is something present. Even though the Incarnation took place then, the effects are present today in the lives of all who believe. Jesus, the Word made flesh, born in a stable to simple working people, helps us see that God is not a stranger to the human condition. God is also one of us.

# Lent

Lent is a penitential season of prayer, fasting and almsgiving. It begins with the reception of ashes on Ash Wednesday and ends when the Mass of the Lord's Supper begins on Holy Thursday. Lent is a time for us to prepare well for the feast of the Resurrection. It lasts for forty days (not including Sundays: fasting never takes place on this day, as Sunday is considered a celebration of the Resurrection). The time period recalls the forty days Jesus spent praying in the desert before he began his public ministry.

The penitential aspect of Lent is primarily and originally seen as a period of fasting. Ash Wednesday and Good Friday are days of both fasting and abstinence for the Universal Church. (Fasting is binding for those who are in good health between the ages of 18 and 59; abstinence is binding from the age of 14.) In Canada, the other Fridays of Lent are still to be observed as penitential days. Penitential practices are not only internal, but also social and external, as in almsgiving and other practices of charity. The privileged forms of penance, based on the teaching of the gospels (fasting, prayer, almsgiving, works of mercy) are encouraged during Lent to express conversion in relation to oneself, God and others. Penances of traditional value, such as abstinence from meat on Fridays, are also encouraged.

Fasting has full meaning when we deprive ourselves of food in order to be more open for prayer, to share more in the suffering of those who are hungry, and to save money to give to the poor. As a penitential discipline, it is intended to open our hearts to God and to others. Through fasting we seek purification and spiritual liberation, and witness to the depth of our faith.

In the early Church, preparing for baptism was a key activity during Lent. We have returned to this practice today with the restoration of the Rite of Christian Initiation of Adults (RCIA) and the scrutinies and rites that it calls for during this season. The Lenten liturgy calls us to remember our identity as baptized people, and to deepen our commitment to Jesus by following him more closely. This prepares those of us who are baptized to recall and renew our baptismal promises during the Easter vigil and on Easter Sunday.

Lent is a time of penance and renewal for the entire Church, the body of Christ. It is not enough for individuals to make a commitment to personal reform and renewal: we must act. After listening and reflecting, we respond and put into practice what we have learned. By doing and responding, we experience inner conversion to God, which is the key purpose of this season.

# Triduum

The Triduum is celebrated from the beginning of the Mass of the Lord's Supper on Holy Thursday to Evening Prayer on Easter Sunday. During the *Triduum*, or three days, the suffering, death and resurrection of Jesus are celebrated. They are the most holy and solemn days of the entire Church Year.

# Easter

Easter is the yearly celebration of the Resurrection of Jesus. The oldest and most solemn Christian feast, it is the centre of the liturgical year. Easter is also called *Pasch*, after the Jewish feast of Passover, which commemorates the Israelites' exodus from Egypt. During Jesus' last celebration of Passover, he instituted the sacrament of the Eucharist. We celebrate this event on Holy Thursday. Other feasts of the Church depend on the date of Easter, which is always the first Sunday following the first full moon after the spring equinox. (That is why the date of Easter changes from year to year.)

Easter is characterized by the Paschal candle, the symbol that Christ, the light of the world, is risen, and by the frequent reiteration of the *Alleluia*, the ancient liturgical acclamation of jubilation, which is not said or sung during Lent.

On Easter morning, we give thanks to God for the new life given to us by Christ's Resurrection on this day, and for his victory over sin and death. We renew our baptismal promises during the liturgies of Easter Sunday. Each Sunday of the year is considered to be a continuation of Easter.

## Easter Season

Easter Season begins after Evening Prayer on Easter Sunday and ends after Evening Prayer on the Feast of Pentecost.

This season, which lasts for fifty days, is characterized by joy, which is expressed in the readings from Scripture and the Mass prayers. The gospel readings are taken from the gospel of John, and focus on the message of Jesus in the light of Easter. The first readings are all taken from the Acts of the Apostles, which gives us the history of the early Church. These texts from Acts emphasize the joy and fervour of the early Christians that flowed from Christ's resurrection.

## Ordinary Time

*Ordinary Time* is the name given to the part of the liturgical year that does not fall within one of the major seasons listed above. (It is called "Ordinary" from the word "ordinal," because it is time that is numbered.) It does not observe any specific aspect of the mystery of Christ. It numbers 33 or 34 weeks, depending on the date of Easter, and is assigned to two periods of the year:

> • from the day after the feast of the Baptism of the Lord to the Tuesday before Ash Wednesday, and

> • from the Monday after Pentecost to the eve of the first Sunday of Advent.

The Church continues to celebrate the Resurrection of Jesus during Ordinary Time, but emphasizes how it applies to our daily lives. The time after the Feast of the Baptism of Our Lord deals with Jesus' baptism, the beginning of his preaching and the call of his disciples. The time after Pentecost covers Jesus' public ministry of healing and preaching.

In Ordinary Time, there are no particular celebrations (except for feasts, a few of which take precedence over the regular Sunday liturgy). It is characterized by two themes: Sunday and the Church. Every Sunday is a weekly Easter, the day we celebrate with great joy and faith the victory of Jesus through his cross. Jesus gathers us around him, for he is present among us as we gather to listen to his Word and celebrate the Eucharist. This is a time when we become filled with the desire for Jesus' final coming in glory – a foretaste of the life that will be ours when we are united with God in heaven.

Ordinary Time introduces us into the mystery of the Church, which was born on Pentecost and built up over the ages in our history. With the help of the Holy Spirit, this is a time for all of us to grow in faith.

# The School Year

# FIRST DAY OF SCHOOL*

✠ In the name of the Father, and of the Son, and of the Holy Spirit. Amen.

Introduction: Today is the first day of school! We ask God to bless our new school year, that we will learn and grow in many ways this year.

Today's reading talks about the importance of wisdom. The writer prayed for this gift, and it was given to him. Like him, let us ask God for the gifts of wisdom and understanding.

A reading from the book of Wisdom

I prayed, and understanding was given me;
I called on God,
and the spirit of wisdom came to me.
I preferred her to sceptres and thrones,
and I accounted wealth as nothing
in comparison with her.
Neither did I liken to her any priceless gem,
because all gold is but a little sand
in her sight,
and I chose to have her rather than light,
because her radiance never ceases.
For it is an unfailing treasure for mortals;
those who get it
obtain friendship with God,
commended for the gifts
that come from instruction.

The word of the Lord.
**Thanks be to God.**

Let us pray:
Dear God,
you are the source
of all wisdom and holiness.
Bless each one of us
as we begin this new school year.
Help us to grow
in wisdom and love.
We ask this through Christ our Lord.
**Amen.**

Let us pray the prayer that Jesus taught us:
**Our Father, who art in heaven,**
**hallowed be thy name;**
**thy kingdom come;**
**thy will be done on earth as it is in heaven.**
**Give us this day our daily bread;**
**and forgive us our trespasses**
**as we forgive those**
**who trespass against us;**
**and lead us not into temptation,**
**but deliver us from evil.**
**Amen.****

✠ In the name of the Father, and of the Son, and of the Holy Spirit. Amen.

* If the first day of school falls on September 8, the Feast of the Nativity of Mary, point out in the introduction that today we remember and celebrate Mary's birthday. Pray the Hail Mary together at the end of your prayer time.

**Hail Mary, full of grace,**
**the Lord is with you.**
**Blessed are you among women**
**and blessed is the fruit of your womb, Jesus.**
**Holy Mary, Mother of God,**
**pray for us sinners,**
**now and at the hour of our death.**
**Amen.**

** If you wish, you may pray the doxology after the Our Father throughout the year, as we do at Mass:

For the kingdom, the power and the glory are yours, now and forever.

Note: Today's reading is Wisdom 7:7b-9a,10b,14.

# WEDNESDAY OF THE FIRST WEEK OF SCHOOL

✠ In the name of the Father, and of the Son, and of the Holy Spirit. Amen.

Introduction: When Jesus was a boy, he learned many things. He learned how to make things out of wood from Joseph, to pray with the men and boys of Nazareth, and to follow the customs of the Jewish people.

Each year he went with Joseph and Mary to Jerusalem, to celebrate the Passover festival. When he was 12, he stayed behind in Jerusalem, to learn from the teachers there.

A reading from the holy gospel according to Luke
**Glory to you, Lord.**

After three days they found Jesus
in the temple, sitting among the teachers,
listening to them
and asking them questions.
And all who heard him were amazed
at his understanding and his answers.
Then he went down with them
and came to Nazareth,
and was obedient to them.
And Jesus increased in wisdom and in years,
and in divine and human favour.

The gospel of the Lord.
**Praise to you, Lord Jesus Christ.**

Let us pray:
Dear God,
your beloved Son, Jesus,
listened to the teachers carefully
and asked them questions,
eager to learn more and more.
As we begin this school year,
grant that we may be like Jesus,
listening and learning,
and doing our best at all times.
We ask this through Christ our Lord.
**Amen.**

Let us pray the prayer that Jesus taught us:
**Our Father...**

✠ In the name of the Father, and of the Son, and of the Holy Spirit. Amen.

Note: Today's reading is Luke 2:46, 47, 51a, 52.

# THURSDAY OF THE FIRST WEEK OF SCHOOL

✠ In the name of the Father, and of the Son, and of the Holy Spirit. Amen.

Introduction: As a young boy, Jesus would have been taught the importance of wisdom and knowledge by the rabbis or Jewish teachers. Here is one passage about wisdom that Jesus might have heard when he was young.

A reading from the book of Proverbs

Happy are those who find wisdom,
and those who get understanding,
for her income is better than silver,
and her revenue better than gold.
She is more precious than jewels,
and nothing you desire
can compare with her.
Long life is in her right hand;
in her left hand are riches and honour.
Her ways are ways of pleasantness,
and all her paths are peace.
She is a tree of life
to those who lay hold of her;
those who hold her fast are called happy.

The word of the Lord.
**Thanks be to God.**

Let us pray:
Dear God,
send us your Spirit
that we may always seek wisdom
and those things
you wish us to learn and understand.
We ask this through Christ our Lord.
**Amen.**

Let us pray the prayer that Jesus taught us:
**Our Father...**

✠ In the name of the Father, and of the Son, and of the Holy Spirit. Amen.

Note: Today's reading is Proverbs 3:13-18.

# FRIDAY OF THE FIRST WEEK OF SCHOOL

✠ In the name of the Father, and of the Son, and of the Holy Spirit. Amen.

Introduction: In school we learn a lot of important things. One of them is how to treat others in a kind and loving way. St. Paul tells us how to do this.

A reading from the letter of Paul to the Colossians

As God's chosen ones, holy and beloved, clothe yourselves with compassion, kindness, humility, meekness, and patience. Bear with one another and, if anyone has a complaint against another, forgive each other; just as the Lord has forgiven you, so you also must forgive. Above all, clothe yourselves with love, which binds everything together in perfect harmony.

The word of the Lord.
**Thanks be to God.**

After each prayer, please respond:
**Lord, hear and help us.**

That we will always be kind to one another, we pray…
**Lord, hear and help us.**

That we will learn to be loving and understanding, we pray…
**Lord, hear and help us.**

That we will learn to forgive one another, we pray…
**Lord, hear and help us.**

That we will learn to be patient with one another, we pray…
**Lord, hear and help us.**

That we may learn your wisdom and your ways, we pray…
**Lord, hear and help us.**

That our school year may be one filled with many graces and blessings, we pray…
**Lord, hear and help us.**

Let us pray the prayer that Jesus taught us:
**Our Father…**

✠ In the name of the Father, and of the Son, and of the Holy Spirit. Amen.

Note: Today's reading is Colossians 3:12-14.

## MONDAY

✠ **In the name of the Father, and of the Son, and of the Holy Spirit. Amen.**

Introduction: In our reading today, we see Jesus in Nazareth, his hometown, on the Sabbath; he went to the synagogue, as usual, and was invited to read. He was given the scroll of the prophet Isaiah. Jesus read a portion from the book of the prophet Isaiah, and then explained what it meant. At first, they were surprised at his knowledge and wisdom.

Then they remembered who he was: Joseph's son, who had grown up among them – they knew him, and they could not accept his message and his work.

People do grow and change – and sometimes that is very hard to accept. Are we willing to accept that the people we know can grow and change? Are we open to that change in others, and in ourselves?

A reading from the holy gospel according to Luke
**Glory to you, Lord.**

When Jesus came to Nazareth,
where he had been brought up,
he went to the synagogue
on the sabbath day,
as was his custom.
He stood up to read,
and the scroll of the prophet Isaiah
was given to him.
He unrolled the scroll and found the place
where it was written: "The Spirit of the Lord
is upon me, because he has anointed me
to bring good news to the poor.
He has sent me to proclaim release to the
captives and recovery of sight to the blind,
to let the oppressed go free,
to proclaim the year of the Lord's favour."
Then he began to say to them,

"Today this scripture has been fulfilled
in your hearing."
All spoke well of him and were amazed
at the gracious words
that came from his mouth.
They said, "Is not this Joseph's son?"
And he said, "Truly I tell you,
no prophet is accepted in the prophet's
hometown."
When they heard this,
all in the synagogue
were filled with rage.

The gospel of the Lord.
**Praise to you, Lord Jesus Christ.**

Let us pray:
Most loving God,
the people of Nazareth
did not accept Jesus' words and teachings
because they thought they knew him.
Help us to accept growth and change
in others and in ourselves.
We ask this through Christ our Lord.
**Amen.**

Let us pray the prayer that Jesus taught us:
**Our Father...**

✠ **In the name of the Father, and of the Son, and of the Holy Spirit. Amen.**

Note: Today's reading is Luke 4:16-19, 21-22, 24, 28.

# TWENTY-SECOND WEEK OF ORDINARY TIME

## TUESDAY

✠ In the name of the Father, and of the Son, and of the Holy Spirit. Amen.

Introduction: In our reading today, St. Paul tells us that we have received the Spirit of God to help us understand spiritual things, the things that God has given us. St. Paul reminds us to ask the Spirit to help us understand and to welcome God's gifts.

A reading from the first letter of Paul to the Corinthians

These things God has revealed to us
through the Spirit;
for the Spirit searches everything,
even the depths of God.
For what human being knows
what is truly human
except the human spirit that is within?
So also no one comprehends
what is truly God's
except the Spirit of God.
Now we have received
not the spirit of the world,
but the Spirit that is from God,
so that we may understand
the gifts bestowed on us by God.

The word of the Lord.
**Thanks be to God.**

Let us pray:
Most holy and gracious God,
in your goodness you gave us your Spirit
to help us understand
the truths about you.
Help us to remember
to always ask the Spirit
to guide us and help us
in our understanding.
We ask this through Christ our Lord.
**Amen.**

Let us pray the prayer that Jesus taught us:
**Our Father…**

✠ In the name of the Father, and of the Son, and of the Holy Spirit. Amen.

Note: Today's reading is 1 Corinthians 2:10-12.

## WEDNESDAY

✠ In the name of the Father, and of the Son, and of the Holy Spirit. Amen.

Introduction: In today's reading, Jesus is just beginning his work; he has been to Nazareth and is now in Capernaum. This is where Simon, the one whom Jesus will later rename "Peter," lives.

Simon's mother-in-law is sick. When Jesus visits Simon's house, he heals her. The news spreads quickly, and people bring others to Jesus to be healed.

Jesus showed care and concern for all the people of Capernaum, not just for his friends. Jesus shows care and concern for all of us, too. We can bring those we know who are sick to Jesus in our prayers.

A reading from the holy gospel according to Luke
**Glory to you, Lord.**

After leaving the synagogue
Jesus entered Simon's house.
Now Simon's mother-in-law was suffering
from a high fever,
and they asked him about her.
Then he stood over her
and rebuked the fever, and it left her.
Immediately she got up
and began to serve them.
As the sun was setting,
all those who had any who were sick
with various kinds of diseases
brought them to him;
and he laid his hands on each of them
and cured them.

The gospel of the Lord.
**Praise to you, Lord Jesus Christ.**

Let us pray:
God in heaven,
your beloved Son, Jesus,
healed the sick who were brought to him.
We ask you to heal those we know
who are sick.
Help us to remember
that you love each of us very much.
We ask this through Christ our Lord.
**Amen.**

Let us pray the prayer that Jesus taught us:
**Our Father…**

✠ In the name of the Father, and of the Son, and of the Holy Spirit. Amen.

Note: Today's reading is Luke 4:38-40.

## THURSDAY

✠ **In the name of the Father, and of the Son, and of the Holy Spirit. Amen.**

Introduction: Today we hear the story of Jesus calling his first disciples. Jesus is at the shore of Lake Gennesaret, also known as the Sea of Galilee. Simon and his partners had fished all night and had caught nothing. Jesus uses Simon's boat to teach the people. When he finishes talking, he tells Simon to let down the nets for a catch. There are so many fish, the nets almost tear. Jesus tells them that instead of catching fish, they will soon be catching people.

As followers of Jesus, we are not only "caught," but we are also called to do the catching. The nets we use are made of our words and actions. Are our nets mended and whole, made of kind words and good deeds, or are they ripped and torn? If they are ripped, how can we mend them?

A reading from the holy gospel according to Luke
**Glory to you, Lord.**

Once while Jesus was standing beside
the lake of Gennesaret,
and the crowd was pressing in on him
to hear the word of God,
he saw two boats there
at the shore of the lake;
the fishermen had gone out of them
and were washing their nets.
He got into one of the boats,
the one belonging to Simon,
and asked him to put out
a little way from the shore.
Then he sat down and taught the crowds
from the boat.
When he had finished speaking,
he said to Simon,
"Put out into the deep water
and let down your nets for a catch."

Simon answered,
"Master, we have worked all night long
but have caught nothing. Yet if you say so,
I will let down the nets."
When they had done this,
they caught so many fish
that their nets were beginning to break.
So they signalled their partners
in the other boat to come and help them.
And they came and filled both boats,
so that they began to sink.
Then Jesus said to Simon, "Do not be afraid;
from now on you will be catching people."
When they had brought their boats
to shore,
they left everything and followed him.

The gospel of the Lord.
**Praise to you, Lord Jesus Christ.**

Let us pray:
Heavenly Father,
those first disciples did
what Jesus asked them to do right away,
and became his followers.
Help us to obey your will
and immediately do what you ask.
We ask this through Christ our Lord.
**Amen.**

Let us pray the prayer that Jesus taught us:
**Our Father…**

✠ **In the name of the Father, and of the Son, and of the Holy Spirit. Amen.**

---

Note: Today's reading is Luke 5:1-7, 10b-11.

## FRIDAY

✠ In the name of the Father, and of the Son, and of the Holy Spirit. Amen.

Introduction: In our reading today, some people ask Jesus why he and his disciples do not fast (go without food for a certain time as a way of honouring God). It bothers them that Jesus and his friends do not seem to follow the rules of religion; to them, you weren't religious unless you followed the rules. Some of the Pharisees, who were Jewish teachers, made sure everyone knew that they were fasting.

But Jesus tells them he did not come to enforce the rules, but to teach the spirit of the Law, which is love. He does not want to put burdens on people. Jesus is the bridegroom mentioned in this reading; in an indirect way, he is telling them that he will be taken away. Then it will be time to fast.

Do we do things because we want people to think we are a good person, to impress them, or because it is the right thing to do?

A reading from the holy gospel according to Luke
**Glory to you, Lord.**

Then they said to Jesus, "John's disciples,
like the disciples of the Pharisees,
frequently fast and pray,
but your disciples eat and drink."
Jesus said to them,
"You cannot make wedding guests fast
while the bridegroom is with them,
can you?
The days will come when the bridegroom
will be taken away from them,
and then they will fast in those days."

The gospel of the Lord.
**Praise to you, Lord Jesus Christ.**

Let us pray:
Most holy and gracious God,
your beloved Son, Jesus,
is the bridegroom of his Church.
Help us to be joyful
because Jesus is with us always.
Help us to show your love to all we meet.
We ask this through Christ our Lord.

Let us pray the prayer that Jesus taught us:
**Our Father…**

✠ In the name of the Father, and of the Son, and of the Holy Spirit. Amen.

Note: Today's reading is Luke 5:33-35.

## MONDAY

✠ **In the name of the Father, and of the Son, and of the Holy Spirit. Amen.**

Introduction: In today's reading, Jesus heals a man with a paralyzed hand on the Sabbath, the day of rest. According to Jewish law, healing was work, and was not to be done on the Sabbath, unless there was danger of death. This man was not dying. The Pharisees and teachers of the Law watched to see if Jesus would heal on the Sabbath. Jesus did a good deed by healing the man.

Jesus got into trouble because he did what he knew was right, even though it was against Jewish law. Are we willing to do what is right, what God wants, even if we might get into trouble for doing so?

A reading from the holy gospel according to Luke
**Glory to you, Lord.**

On another sabbath Jesus entered the
synagogue and taught,
and there was a man there
whose right hand was withered.
The scribes and the Pharisees watched him
to see whether he would cure
on the sabbath,
so that they might
find an accusation against him.
Even though he knew
what they were thinking,
he said to the man
who had the withered hand,
"Come and stand here."
He got up and stood there.
Then Jesus said to them, "I ask you,
is it lawful to do good or to do harm
on the sabbath, to save life or to destroy it?"

After looking around at all of them,
he said to him, "Stretch out your hand."
He did so, and his hand was restored.
But they were filled with fury
and discussed with one another
what they might do to Jesus.

The gospel of the Lord.
**Praise to you, Lord Jesus Christ.**

Let us pray:
Most loving God,
your Son, Jesus, knew that he would be
in trouble with the authorities
if he healed the man with the paralyzed
hand on the Sabbath.
Help us always to do
what is right in your eyes,
even though it might get us into trouble
sometimes.
We ask this through Christ our Lord.
**Amen.**

Let us pray the prayer that Jesus taught us:
**Our Father…**

✠ **In the name of the Father, and of the Son, and of the Holy Spirit. Amen.**

Note: Today's reading is Luke 6:6-11.

## TUESDAY

✠ In the name of the Father, and of the Son, and of the Holy Spirit. Amen.

Introduction: In our reading today, we see Jesus spending a whole night in prayer. Then he calls his disciples together and chooses twelve of them, calling them apostles.

Jesus has an important decision to make, and so he spends the whole night praying, talking to his Father in heaven. In the gospels, especially Luke's gospel, we hear about Jesus going off by himself to pray, often through the night.

How often do we pray? Do we ask for God's help when we need to make a decision? Do we seek God's advice?

A reading from the holy gospel according to Luke

**Glory to you, Lord.**

Now during those days
Jesus went out to the mountain to pray;
and he spent the night in prayer to God.
And when day came, he called his disciples
and chose twelve of them,
whom he also named apostles:
Simon, whom he named Peter,
and his brother Andrew,
and James, and John, and Philip,
and Bartholomew, and Matthew,
and Thomas,
and James son of Alphaeus,
and Simon, who was called the Zealot,
and Judas son of James,
and Judas Iscariot, who became a traitor.

The gospel of the Lord.

**Praise to you, Lord Jesus Christ.**

Let us pray:
Most holy God,
your Son often spent time in prayer
to learn your will,
what you wanted him to do.
Help us to be people of prayer,
always seeking your will and your wisdom,
as Jesus did.
We ask this through Christ our Lord.
**Amen.**

Let us pray the prayer that Jesus taught us:
**Our Father…**

✠ In the name of the Father, and of the Son, and of the Holy Spirit. Amen.

---

Note: Today's reading is Luke 6:12-16.

## WEDNESDAY

✠ In the name of the Father, and of the Son, and of the Holy Spirit. Amen.

Introduction: Today we hear Luke's version of the beatitudes: Jesus' teaching on how to live as God asks.

He challenges us to set our hearts on God and to help build the kingdom of heaven, beginning here on earth. Often, following God means doing the opposite of what the world values.

As followers of Jesus, do we set our hearts on God and the kingdom of heaven?

A reading from the holy gospel according to Luke
**Glory to you, Lord.**

Then Jesus looked up at his disciples and said: "Blessed are you who are poor,
for yours is the kingdom of God.
Blessed are you who are hungry now,
for you will be filled.
Blessed are you who weep now,
for you will laugh.
Blessed are you when people hate you,
and when they exclude you, revile you,
and defame you on account of
the Son of Man.
Rejoice in that day and leap for joy,
for surely your reward is great in heaven;
for that is what their ancestors did
to the prophets.

But woe to you who are rich,
for you have received your consolation.
Woe to you who are full now,
for you will be hungry.
Woe to you who are laughing now,
for you will mourn and weep.
Woe to you when all speak well of you,
for that is what their ancestors did
to the false prophets."

The gospel of the Lord.
**Praise to you, Lord Jesus Christ.**

Let us pray:
Most merciful God,
you keep a great reward in heaven
for the poor, the hungry, the sad,
and all who set their hearts on you
and the values of your kingdom.
Help us to follow your ways,
making you our heart's deepest desire.
We ask this through Christ our Lord.
**Amen.**

Let us pray the prayer that Jesus taught us:
**Our Father…**

✠ In the name of the Father, and of the Son, and of the Holy Spirit. Amen.

Note: Today's reading is Luke 6:20-26.

## THURSDAY

✠ In the name of the Father, and of the Son, and of the Holy Spirit. Amen.

Introduction: In today's reading, Jesus issues many challenges to us. What he tells us to do is not easy, yet it is central to the life of a Christian, someone who believes in and follows Jesus.

A reading from the holy gospel according to Luke
**Glory to you, Lord.**

Jesus said, "I say to you that listen,
Love your enemies,
do good to those who hate you,
bless those who curse you,
pray for those who abuse you.
Give to everyone who begs from you;
and if anyone takes away your goods,
do not ask for them again.
Do to others
as you would have them do to you.
But love your enemies, do good, and lend,
expecting nothing in return.
Your reward will be great,
and you will be children of the Most High;
for he is kind to the ungrateful
and the wicked.
Be merciful, just as your Father is merciful.
Do not judge, and you will not be judged;
do not condemn,
and you will not be condemned.
Forgive, and you will be forgiven;
give, and it will be given to you.
A good measure, pressed down,
shaken together,
running over, will be put into your lap;
for the measure you give
will be the measure you get back."

The gospel of the Lord.
**Praise to you, Lord Jesus Christ.**

Let us pray:
Most loving and merciful God,
Jesus tells us how to treat others
in a loving way.
Help us to listen to his words
with open hearts and open minds,
and do what he asks,
even when it is not easy.
Help us to do all things with love.
We ask this through Christ our Lord.
**Amen.**

Let us pray the prayer that Jesus taught us:
**Our Father…**

✠ In the name of the Father, and of the Son, and of the Holy Spirit. Amen.

Note: Today's reading is Luke 6:27, 28, 30, 31, 35-38.

# TWENTY-THIRD WEEK OF ORDINARY TIME

## FRIDAY

✠ In the name of the Father, and of the Son, and of the Holy Spirit. Amen.

Introduction: In our reading today, Jesus gives us some good advice.

All of us tend to criticize or find fault with others, and ignore the things we do that are wrong. It is easier to see other people's mistakes than it is to admit our own mistakes. Starting today, can we be more gentle when others do something wrong? Can we admit when we do something wrong and try to do better?

A reading from the holy gospel according to Luke
**Glory to you, Lord.**

Jesus said,
"Why do you see the speck
in your neighbour's eye,
but do not notice the log in your own eye?
Or how can you say to your neighbour,
'Friend, let me take out
the speck in your eye,'
when you yourself
do not see the log in your own eye?
You hypocrite,
first take the log out of your own eye,
and then you will see clearly
to take the speck
out of your neighbour's eye."

The gospel of the Lord.
**Praise to you, Lord Jesus Christ.**

Let us pray:
Merciful God,
Jesus tells us to correct our own faults
before we criticize others
and try to correct them.
Help us to speak and act kindly,
helping others instead of hurting them.
We ask this through Christ our Lord.
**Amen.**

Let us pray the prayer that Jesus taught us:
**Our Father…**

✠ In the name of the Father, and of the Son, and of the Holy Spirit. Amen.

Note: Today's reading is Luke 6:41-42.

## MONDAY

✠ In the name of the Father, and of the Son, and of the Holy Spirit. Amen.

Introduction: In our reading today, St. Paul gives a young Christian named Timothy some advice on praying – whom to pray for, what to pray for, and even how to pray. Timothy became a companion and assistant to St. Paul in his missionary work.

Do we follow St. Paul's advice when we pray? How does the way we pray need to grow and deepen?

A reading from the first letter of Paul to Timothy

First of all, then,
I urge that supplications, prayers,
intercessions, and thanksgivings
be made for everyone,
for kings and all who are in high positions,
so that we may lead
a quiet and peaceable life
in all godliness and dignity.
This is right and is acceptable
in the sight of God our Saviour,
who desires everyone to be saved
and to come to the knowledge of the truth.
For there is one God;
there is also one mediator
between God and humankind, Christ Jesus,
himself human,
who gave himself a ransom for all.
I desire, then, that in every place
the men should pray,
lifting up holy hands
without anger or argument.

The word of the Lord.
**Thanks be to God.**

Let us pray:
Most loving God,
you hear and answer all our prayers
when we offer them to you
with sincerity and humility.
Help us to remember
to pray for one another,
and for the intentions we have
deep within our hearts.
We ask this through Christ our Lord.
**Amen.**

Let us pray the prayer that Jesus taught us:
**Our Father...**

✠ In the name of the Father, and of the Son, and of the Holy Spirit. Amen.

_____

Note: Today's reading is 1 Timothy 2:1-6a, 8.

## TUESDAY

✠ In the name of the Father, and of the Son, and of the Holy Spirit. Amen.

Introduction: In our reading today, Jesus raises the young man from Nain from the dead, because he felt sorry for his mother, who was a widow. At the time of Jesus, children took care of their parents when they grew old. This mother had no one else to look after her; the young man was her only son. Without him, she would have been very poor.

How do we show care for those who have no one to help them? How can we help those who are very poor?

A reading from the holy gospel according to Luke
**Glory to you, Lord.**

Soon afterwards Jesus went to a town
called Nain,
and his disciples and a large crowd
went with him.
As he approached the gate of the town,
a man who had died was being carried out.
He was his mother's only son,
and she was a widow;
and with her was a large crowd
from the town.
When the Lord saw her,
he had compassion for her and said to her,
"Do not weep."
Then he came forward and touched the bier,
and the bearers stood still.
And he said, "Young man, I say to you, rise!"
The dead man sat up and began to speak,
and Jesus gave him to his mother.
Fear seized all of them;
and they glorified God, saying,

"A great prophet has risen among us!"
and "God has looked favourably on his
people!"
This word about him spread throughout
Judea and all the surrounding country.

The gospel of the Lord.
**Praise to you, Lord Jesus Christ.**

Let us pray:
Merciful God,
our world is full of people
who are poor, sick or lonely.
Help us remember to reach out to them
and share our blessings and love with them.
We ask this through Christ our Lord.
**Amen.**

Let us pray the prayer that Jesus taught us:
**Our Father...**

✠ In the name of the Father, and of the Son, and of the Holy Spirit. Amen.

---

Note: Today's reading is Luke 7:11-17.

# TWENTY-FOURTH WEEK OF ORDINARY TIME

## WEDNESDAY

✠ **In the name of the Father, and of the Son, and of the Holy Spirit. Amen.**

Introduction: Today St. Paul talks to us about the gift of love. When we live by these words, and love as Jesus loves, we show that we are true followers of Jesus.

How can we strive for the amazing gift of love?

A reading from the first letter of Paul to the Corinthians

Strive for the greater gifts.
Love is patient; love is kind;
love is not envious or boastful
or arrogant or rude.
It does not insist on its own way;
it is not irritable or resentful;
it does not rejoice in wrongdoing,
but rejoices in the truth.
It bears all things, believes all things,
hopes all things, endures all things.
Love never ends.

The word of the Lord.
**Thanks be to God.**

Let us pray:
Creator God,
you showed your great love for us
by sending your Son, Jesus,
to teach us and to save us.
Help us to be good disciples of Jesus,
following his example
of showing love and respect to all we meet.
We ask this through Christ our Lord.
**Amen.**

Let us pray the prayer that Jesus taught us:
**Our Father…**

✠ **In the name of the Father, and of the Son, and of the Holy Spirit. Amen.**

Note: Today's reading is 1 Corinthians 12:31a, 13:4-8a.

## THURSDAY

✠ In the name of the Father, and of the Son, and of the Holy Spirit. Amen.

Introduction: In today's reading, St. Paul gives some good advice to his friend Timothy and to all young people. Youth have an important role to play in building up God's kingdom on earth.

A reading from the first letter of Paul to Timothy

Let no one despise your youth,
but set the believers an example
in speech and conduct,
in love, in faith, in purity.
Until I arrive, give attention to
the public reading of scripture,
to exhorting, to teaching.
Do not neglect the gift that is in you.
Put these things into practice,
devote yourself to them,
so that all may see your progress.

The word of the Lord.
**Thanks be to God.**

Let us pray:
Most holy and loving God,
help us, your children,
to show our love and our faith
by the way we speak and act,
and by doing what you ask of us.
We ask this through Christ our Lord.
**Amen.**

Let us pray the prayer that Jesus taught us:
**Our Father…**

✠ In the name of the Father, and of the Son, and of the Holy Spirit. Amen.

Note: Today's reading is 1 Timothy 4:12-14a, 15.

## FRIDAY

✠ **In the name of the Father, and of the Son, and of the Holy Spirit. Amen.**

Introduction: Today St. Paul tells Timothy how he, as a good Christian, is to act. We can learn a lot from his words, too. How can we show through our actions that we are people of God?

A reading from the first letter of Paul to Timothy

As for you, man of God, shun all this;
pursue righteousness, godliness, faith, love,
endurance, gentleness.
Fight the good fight of the faith;
take hold of the eternal life,
to which you were called
and for which you made the good
confession
in the presence of many witnesses.

The word of the Lord.
**Thanks be to God.**

Let us pray:
Most loving God,
help us to be loving, patient,
faithful and gentle.
We want to do our best
to run our best in the race of faith
towards eternal life.
Help us always to keep our eyes on Jesus
so we can stay on track.
We ask this through Christ our Lord.
**Amen.**

Let us pray the prayer that Jesus taught us:
**Our Father…**

✠ **In the name of the Father, and of the Son, and of the Holy Spirit. Amen.**

Note: Today's reading is 1 Timothy 6:11-12

32

## MONDAY

✠ In the name of the Father, and of the Son, and of the Holy Spirit. Amen.

Introduction: In our reading today, the lit lamp is the light of our faith. Jesus reminds us that everything hidden will eventually be brought into the light. He asks us to listen well to his words so we will learn and grow each day. If we stay still, what we have already learned will be lost. In today's language, this could be expressed in this way: Use it or lose it.

A reading from the holy gospel according to Luke
**Glory to you, Lord.**

Jesus said,
"No one after lighting a lamp
hides it under a jar,
or puts it under a bed,
but puts it on a lampstand,
so that those who enter may see the light.
For nothing is hidden
that will not be disclosed,
nor is anything secret
that will not become known
and come to light.
Then pay attention to how you listen;
for to those who have, more will be given;
and from those who do not have,
even what they seem to have
will be taken away."

The gospel of the Lord.
**Praise to you, Lord Jesus Christ.**

Let us pray:
Creator God,
you sent Jesus to us
to teach us about you.
Help us to let our light of faith
shine for all to see.
Help us also to be good listeners –
to you, to Jesus, to the Holy Spirit,
and to one another –
so that we may grow in wisdom,
grace and love.
We ask this through Christ our Lord.
**Amen.**

Let us pray the prayer that Jesus taught us:
**Our Father…**

✠ In the name of the Father, and of the Son, and of the Holy Spirit. Amen.

Note: Today's reading is Luke 8:16-18.

## TUESDAY

✠ **In the name of the Father, and of the Son, and of the Holy Spirit. Amen.**

Introduction: In today's reading, Jesus tells us whom he counts as his family – those who hear God's word and put it into practice. This is what we are to do as followers of Jesus.

How can we put God's word into practice at home, at school and in our community?

A reading from the holy gospel according to Luke
**Glory to you, Lord.**

Then his mother and his brothers
came to Jesus,
but they could not reach him
because of the crowd.
And he was told,
"Your mother and your brothers
are standing outside, wanting to see you."
But Jesus said to them,
"My mother and my brothers
are those who hear the word of God
and do it."

The gospel of the Lord.
**Praise to you, Lord Jesus Christ.**

Let us pray:
Most Holy and gracious God,
your beloved Son, the Word made Flesh,
teaches us that it is not only important
to hear your word
but also to practise it.
Grant that we may listen carefully,
not only with our ears,
but also with our hearts,
and put into practice your word,
following your laws and ways.
We ask this through Christ our Lord.
**Amen.**

Let us pray the prayer that Jesus taught us:
**Our Father…**

✠ **In the name of the Father, and of the Son, and of the Holy Spirit. Amen.**

Note: Today's reading is Luke 8:19-21.

## WEDNESDAY

✠ **In the name of the Father, and of the Son, and of the Holy Spirit. Amen.**

Introduction: In our reading today, Jesus calls the twelve disciples together and sends them out to preach the Good News and to heal those who are sick. This is the first mission he gives them.

Jesus sends us out to preach the Good News of the kingdom of God, too. We do this by our actions and words.

Are our words and actions the kind Jesus would use?

A reading from the holy gospel according to Luke
**Glory to you, Lord.**

Then Jesus called the twelve together
and gave them power and authority
over all demons and to cure diseases,
and he sent them out
to proclaim the kingdom of God
and to heal.
He said to them,
"Take nothing for your journey,
no staff, nor bag, nor bread, nor money –
not even an extra tunic.
Whatever house you enter, stay there,
and leave from there.
Wherever they do not welcome you,
as you are leaving that town
shake the dust off your feet
as a testimony against them."

They departed and went through the villages,
bringing the good news
and curing diseases everywhere.

The gospel of the Lord.
**Praise to you, Lord Jesus Christ.**

Let us pray:
Most holy and gracious God,
Jesus, your Son,
sent the disciples out to preach
the Good News of your kingdom.
Help us follow their example
and bring the Good News to all we meet.
We ask this through Christ our Lord.
**Amen.**

Let us pray the prayer that Jesus taught us:
**Our Father…**

✠ **In the name of the Father, and of the Son, and of the Holy Spirit. Amen.**

---

Note: Today's reading is Luke 9:1-6.

## THURSDAY

✠ **In the name of the Father, and of the Son, and of the Holy Spirit. Amen.**

Introduction: King Herod had heard about the work Jesus was doing, and had received different reports about who Jesus was. Herod was confused. We know more than King Herod did – we know, and believe, that Jesus is the Son of God, the promised one.

A reading from the holy gospel according to Luke
**Glory to you, Lord.**

Now Herod the ruler
heard about all that had taken place,
and he was perplexed,
because it was said by some
that John had been raised from the dead,
by some that Elijah had appeared,
and by others that one of the ancient
prophets had arisen.
Herod said, "John I beheaded;
but who is this
about whom I hear such things?"
And he tried to see him.

The gospel of the Lord.
**Praise to you, Lord Jesus Christ.**

Let us pray:
Most loving God,
King Herod was confused
about who Jesus was.
Help us to grow in our belief
in your beloved Son, Jesus,
and in our love of you.
We ask this through Christ our Lord.
**Amen.**

Let us pray the prayer that Jesus taught us:
**Our Father…**

✠ **In the name of the Father, and of the Son, and of the Holy Spirit. Amen.**

Note: Today's reading is Luke 9:7-9.

## FRIDAY

✠ **In the name of the Father, and of the Son, and of the Holy Spirit. Amen.**

Introduction: In our reading today, Jesus asks his disciples who the people think he is. They give various answers. When Jesus asks them who they think he is, Peter answers for them: "You are God's Messiah."

If someone asks us, "Who do you say Jesus is?" what would we answer?

A reading from the holy gospel according to Luke
**Glory to you, Lord.**

Once when Jesus was praying alone,
with only the disciples near him,
he asked them,
"Who do the crowds say that I am?"
They answered,
"John the Baptist; but others, Elijah;
and still others,
that one of the ancient prophets has arisen."
He said to them,
"But who do you say that I am?"
Peter answered, "The Messiah of God."
He sternly ordered and commanded them
not to tell anyone.

The gospel of the Lord.
**Praise to you, Lord Jesus Christ.**

Let us pray:
Gracious God,
Peter recognized that your Son, Jesus,
was sent into the world to save us.
Help us to be faithful followers of Jesus,
and know, deep within our hearts,
that he is also our Messiah,
our Lord and Saviour.
We ask this through Christ our Lord.
**Amen.**

Let us pray the prayer that Jesus taught us:
**Our Father...**

✠ **In the name of the Father, and of the Son, and of the Holy Spirit. Amen.**

---

Note: Today's reading is Luke 9:18-21.

## MONDAY

✠ In the name of the Father, and of the Son, and of the Holy Spirit. Amen.

Introduction: In our reading today, Jesus says something surprising: that the one who is least among us is the greatest! To God, everyone, no matter how great or small, is important. And those who welcome everyone, great or small, welcome God.

A reading from the holy gospel according to Luke
**Glory to you, Lord.**

An argument arose among them
as to which one of them was the greatest.
But Jesus, aware of their inner thoughts,
took a little child and put it by his side,
and said to them,
"Whoever welcomes this child in my name
welcomes me, and whoever welcomes me
welcomes the one who sent me;
for the least among all of you
is the greatest."

The gospel of the Lord.
**Praise to you, Lord Jesus Christ.**

Let us pray:
Most gentle and loving God,
you sent your Son, Jesus,
to show us how to love.
Send your Holy Spirit upon us,
so that we may treat others
the way you treat them.
We ask this through Christ our Lord.
**Amen.**

Let us pray the prayer that Jesus taught us:
**Our Father…**

✠ In the name of the Father, and of the Son, and of the Holy Spirit. Amen.

Note: Today's reading is Luke 9:46-48.

## TUESDAY

✠ **In the name of the Father, and of the Son, and of the Holy Spirit. Amen.**

Introduction: In our reading today, we hear that Jesus was not welcome in one of the villages of Samaria, so he went to another village.

Sometimes we do not welcome Jesus into our hearts, our friendships, our families, our school, our world. How can we make Jesus feel welcome every day?

A reading from the holy gospel according to Luke
**Glory to you, Lord.**

When the days drew near for Jesus
to be taken up,
he set his face to go to Jerusalem.
And he sent messengers ahead of him.
On their way they entered
a village of the Samaritans
to make ready for him;
but they did not receive him,
because his face was set toward Jerusalem.
Then they went on to another village.

The gospel of the Lord.
**Praise to you, Lord Jesus Christ.**

Let us pray:
Most loving God,
you sent your beloved Son, Jesus,
to help us learn more about you
and your ways.
Grant that we may always welcome him
with joy and love
into our hearts.
Help us to be faithful followers of Jesus.
We ask this through Christ our Lord.
**Amen.**

Let us pray the prayer that Jesus taught us:
**Our Father…**

✠ **In the name of the Father, and of the Son, and of the Holy Spirit. Amen.**

---

Note: Today's reading is Luke 9:51-53, 56.

## WEDNESDAY

✠ In the name of the Father, and of the Son, and of the Holy Spirit. Amen.

Introduction: In our reading today, a man tells Jesus that he would like to follow him. Jesus replies that to be his follower is not easy. People who choose to follow him have to give up some of the things they are used to.

Jesus' words also challenge us. When we say to Jesus that we would like to be his disciple, are we truly willing to do what he asks?

A reading from the holy gospel according to Luke
**Glory to you, Lord.**

As they were going along the road,
someone said to Jesus,
"I will follow you wherever you go."
And Jesus said to him,
"Foxes have holes,
and birds of the air have nests;
but the Son of Man
has nowhere to lay his head."

The gospel of the Lord.
**Praise to you, Lord Jesus Christ.**

Let us pray:
Most merciful God,
the man in our gospel story today
wants to be a follower of Jesus.
Grant us the grace to be his disciple,
even when it isn't easy.
We ask this through Christ our Lord.
**Amen.**

Let us pray the prayer that Jesus taught us:
**Our Father…**

✠ In the name of the Father, and of the Son, and of the Holy Spirit. Amen.

Note: Today's reading is Luke 9:57-58.

## THURSDAY

✠ **In the name of the Father, and of the Son, and of the Holy Spirit. Amen.**

Introduction: In our reading today, Jesus is talking about a harvest: not a harvest of food, but of people!

The workers he describes are those who help us learn more about the kingdom of God. Not just bishops, priests, deacons, those in consecrated life* and lay leaders of the Church, but all of us – students and teachers, children and parents, are called to be workers in the harvest.

A reading from the holy gospel according to Luke
**Glory to you, Lord.**

After this the Lord appointed seventy others
and sent them on ahead of him in pairs
to every town and place
where he himself intended to go.
He said to them,
"The harvest is plentiful,
but the labourers are few;
therefore ask the Lord of the harvest
to send out labourers into his harvest."

The gospel of the Lord.
**Praise to you, Lord Jesus Christ.**

Let us pray:
Most holy and gracious God,
your Son, Jesus,
asked us to pray for more workers
to gather in his harvest.
Grant that your people
will hear your call to serve,
and answer with open and generous hearts.
We ask this through Christ our Lord.
**Amen.**

Let us pray the prayer that Jesus taught us:
**Our Father…**

✠ **In the name of the Father, and of the Son, and of the Holy Spirit. Amen.**

* Consecrated life includes religious priests, brothers, sisters, monks, nuns (i.e., cloistered sisters), hermits, consecrated virgins (the oldest form of consecrated life in the Church) and members of secular institutes.

Note: Today's reading is Luke 10:1-2. The full gospel reading for today is Luke 10:1-12.

## FRIDAY

✠ **In the name of the Father, and of the Son, and of the Holy Spirit. Amen.**

Introduction: In our reading today, Jesus is angry. He names towns where people would not listen to him or believe in his message.

One of the towns mentioned is Capernaum, where Simon Peter lived. Jesus warns the people there how badly things will go for them. He says that if we reject him, we reject God, who sent him.

A reading from the holy gospel according to Luke
**Glory to you, Lord.**

Jesus said, "Woe to you, Chorazin!
Woe to you, Bethsaida!
For if the deeds of power done in you
had been done in Tyre and Sidon,
they would have repented long ago,
sitting in sackcloth and ashes.
But at the judgment it will be more tolerable
for Tyre and Sidon than for you.
And you, Capernaum,
will you be exalted to heaven?
No, you will be brought down to Hades.
Whoever listens to you listens to me,
and whoever rejects you rejects me,
and whoever rejects me
rejects the one who sent me."

The gospel of the Lord.
**Praise to you, Lord Jesus Christ.**

Let us pray:
Most holy and merciful God,
you sent Jesus into the world
to show us the ways that lead to you.
Grant that we may always have
a firm faith and belief in you,
in your divine Son,
and in what he teaches us.
We ask this through Christ our Lord.
**Amen.**

Let us pray the prayer that Jesus taught us:
**Our Father...**

✠ **In the name of the Father, and of the Son, and of the Holy Spirit. Amen.**

---

Note: Today's reading is Luke 10:13-16.

## MONDAY

✠ **In the name of the Father, and of the Son, and of the Holy Spirit. Amen.**

Introduction: In our reading today, we hear about a person who wanted to know what he must do to enter the kingdom of heaven. Listen carefully to find out what Jesus told him to do.

A reading from the holy gospel according to Luke
**Glory to you, Lord.**

Just then a lawyer stood up to test Jesus.
"Teacher," he said,
"what must I do to inherit eternal life?"
He said to him, "What is written in the law?
What do you read there?"
He answered,
"You shall love the Lord your God
with all your heart,
and with all your soul,
and with all your strength,
and with all your mind;
and your neighbour as yourself."
And he said to him,
"You have given the right answer;
do this, and you will live."

The gospel of the Lord.
**Praise to you, Lord Jesus Christ.**

Let us pray:
Creator God,
you love each of us very much
and call us your children.
Send us your Holy Spirit
to help us to love you always
with all our heart, with all our soul,
with all our mind, and with all our strength.
Help us to love our neighbour
as we love ourselves.
We ask this through Christ our Lord.
**Amen.**

Let us pray the prayer that Jesus taught us:
**Our Father…**

✠ **In the name of the Father, and of the Son, and of the Holy Spirit. Amen.**

---

Note: Today's reading is Luke 10:25-28.

## TUESDAY

✠ In the name of the Father, and of the Son, and of the Holy Spirit. Amen.

Introduction: In today's gospel, Jesus is visiting some friends. One friend is busy working. The other is busy listening. Which one is doing the better thing?

How we make guests feel welcome in our home is important. We need to get things ready and serve them, but we also need to spend time listening to them and being with them.

A reading from the holy gospel according to Luke
**Glory to you, Lord.**

Now as they went on their way,
Jesus entered a certain village,
where a woman named Martha
welcomed him into her home.
She had a sister named Mary,
who sat at the Lord's feet
and listened to what he was saying.
But Martha was distracted
by her many tasks;
so she came to him and asked,
"Lord, do you not care that my sister
has left me to do all the work by myself?
Tell her then to help me."
But the Lord answered her,
"Martha, Martha,
you are worried and distracted
by many things;
there is need of only one thing.
Mary has chosen the better part,
which will not be taken away from her."

The gospel of the Lord.
**Praise to you, Lord Jesus Christ.**

Let us pray:
Most holy and loving God,
help us always to remember
what is important,
and to take the time to listen to Jesus' words
and live by them.
We ask this through Christ our Lord.
**Amen.**

Let us pray the prayer that Jesus taught us:
**Our Father...**

✠ In the name of the Father, and of the Son, and of the Holy Spirit. Amen.

Note: Today's reading is Luke 10:38-42.

# TWENTY-SEVENTH WEEK OF ORDINARY TIME

## WEDNESDAY

✠ **In the name of the Father, and of the Son, and of the Holy Spirit. Amen.**

Introduction: In our reading today, the disciples of Jesus watched him as he was praying. Then they asked Jesus to teach them to pray. The prayer that Jesus taught them is the prayer we call the Our Father, or the Lord's Prayer.

A reading from the holy gospel according to Luke
**Glory to you, Lord.**

Jesus was praying in a certain place,
and after he had finished,
one of his disciples said to him,
"Lord, teach us to pray,
as John taught his disciples."
He said to them, "When you pray,
say: Father, hallowed be your name.
Your kingdom come.
Give us each day our daily bread.
And forgive us our sins,
for we ourselves forgive everyone
indebted to us.
And do not bring us to the time of trial."

The gospel of the Lord.
**Praise to you, Lord Jesus Christ.**

Let us pray:
Most holy and loving God,
your beloved Son, Jesus,
taught us to call you "Father,"
to ask you for all that we need.
He taught us to ask you to forgive our sins
as we forgive those who hurt us.
Help us to pray this prayer
with reverence and love.
We ask this through Christ our Lord.
**Amen.**

Let us pray the prayer that Jesus taught us:
**Our Father…**

✠ **In the name of the Father, and of the Son, and of the Holy Spirit. Amen**

---

Note: Today's reading is Luke 11:1-4.

## THURSDAY

✠ In the name of the Father, and of the Son, and of the Holy Spirit. Amen.

Introduction: In our reading, Jesus tells us to ask God for what we need, seek God's will for us and do it, and knock on the doors of heaven with our prayers. It is important to keep trying, and not to give up: God will always be with us.

A reading from the holy gospel according to Luke
**Glory to you, Lord.**

Jesus said,
"So I say to you,
Ask, and it will be given you;
search, and you will find;
knock, and the door will be opened for you.
For everyone who asks receives,
and everyone who searches finds,
and for everyone who knocks,
the door will be opened."

The gospel of the Lord.
**Praise to you, Lord Jesus Christ.**

Let us pray:
Father in heaven,
your only Son, Jesus, teaches us
to ask you for all that we need,
seek you and your will,
and knock on your door with our prayers.
Give us the courage and patience
to keep asking, seeking and knocking,
and help us remember
that you are always listening.
We ask this through Christ our Lord.
**Amen.**

Let us pray the prayer that Jesus taught us:
**Our Father…**

✠ In the name of the Father, and of the Son, and of the Holy Spirit. Amen.

Note: Today's reading is Luke 11:9-10.

## FRIDAY

✠ **In the name of the Father, and of the Son, and of the Holy Spirit. Amen.**

Introduction: Some people did not believe that Jesus' healing and miracles were done in God's name. They asked for a miracle to show that God approved of Jesus. Jesus knows they are trying to trick him, so instead of performing a miracle he gives them some advice.

Do we work together as Christians, building God's kingdom each day?

A reading from the holy gospel according to Luke
**Glory to you, Lord.**

Others, to test Jesus,
kept demanding from him
a sign from heaven.
But he knew what they were thinking
and said to them,
"Every kingdom divided against itself
becomes a desert, and house falls on house.
Whoever is not with me is against me, and
whoever does not gather with me scatters."

The gospel of the Lord.
**Praise to you, Lord Jesus Christ.**

Let us pray:
Creator God,
you sent Jesus to us
to show us the truth and lead us to you.
Help us to be faithful followers of Jesus,
working with him to gather his harvest.
We ask this through Christ our Lord.
**Amen.**

Let us pray the prayer that Jesus taught us:
**Our Father…**

✠ **In the name of the Father, and of the Son, and of the Holy Spirit. Amen.**

---

Note: Today's reading is Luke 11:16-17, 23.

## MONDAY

✠ In the name of the Father, and of the Son, and of the Holy Spirit. Amen.

Introduction: Some people wanted Jesus to perform a great miracle to prove that he was the anointed one of God. But like Jonah, a prophet who told people to change their ways and become more loving, Jesus himself is the sign of God's love.

Are we waiting for proof, or do we believe that Jesus is God's own Son?

A reading from the holy gospel according to Luke
**Glory to you, Lord.**

When the crowds were increasing,
he began to say,
"This generation is an evil generation;
it asks for a sign,
but no sign will be given to it
except the sign of Jonah.
For just as Jonah became a sign
to the people of Nineveh,
so the Son of Man will be
to this generation.
The people of Nineveh
will rise up at the judgment
with this generation and condemn it,
because they repented
at the proclamation of Jonah, and see,
something greater than Jonah is here!"

The gospel of the Lord.
**Praise to you, Lord Jesus Christ.**

Let us pray:
Most loving God,
you sent your divine Son into the world
as your greatest gift and sign to us
of your love and mercy.
Grant that we believe in Jesus
with all our hearts, minds and souls,
each and every day of our lives.
We ask this through Christ our Lord.
**Amen.**

Let us pray the prayer that Jesus taught us:
**Our Father...**

✠ In the name of the Father, and of the Son, and of the Holy Spirit. Amen.

---

Note: Today's reading is Luke 11:29-30, 32.

## TUESDAY

✠ **In the name of the Father, and of the Son, and of the Holy Spirit. Amen.**

Introduction: In today's reading, St. Paul describes the power of the Good News, the gospel, and reminds us how important it is to have faith.

How do we listen to God's word in the gospel? How do we show that we follow the gospel in our daily lives?

A reading from the letter of Paul to the Romans

I am not ashamed of the gospel;
it is the power of God for salvation
to everyone who has faith,
to the Jew first and also to the Greek.
For in it the righteousness of God
is revealed
through faith for faith; as it is written,
"The one who is righteous will live by faith."

The word of the Lord.
**Thanks be to God.**

Let us pray:
Creator God,
in your word we find life and holiness,
a lamp to light our way.
Send your Spirit to help us love your word
and read it often.
May your word grow in our hearts,
so that we may learn more about you
and your beloved Son, Jesus,
your Word made flesh.
We ask this through Christ our Lord.
**Amen.**

Let us pray the prayer that Jesus taught us:
**Our Father…**

✠ **In the name of the Father, and of the Son, and of the Holy Spirit. Amen.**

---

Note: Today's reading is Romans 1:16-17.

## WEDNESDAY

✠ **In the name of the Father, and of the Son, and of the Holy Spirit. Amen.**

Introduction: In our reading today, St. Paul reminds us to let the Holy Spirit guide us so we will live as God wants. When we do this, we receive many gifts, such as love, joy and peace.

We can ask the Holy Spirit to help us anytime we are not sure what to do. A simple prayer – Holy Spirit, help! – is all we need to say. Then we need to listen for the answer.

A reading from the letter of Paul to the Galatians

Live by the Spirit, I say,
and do not gratify the desires of the flesh.
For what the flesh desires
is opposed to the Spirit,
and what the Spirit desires
is opposed to the flesh;
By contrast, the fruit of the Spirit is
love, joy, peace, patience,
kindness, generosity,
faithfulness, gentleness, and self-control.
There is no law against such things.
If we live by the Spirit,
let us also be guided by the Spirit.
Let us not become conceited,
competing against one another,
envying one another.

The word of the Lord.
**Thanks be to God.**

Let us pray to the Holy Spirit:
Come, Holy Spirit,
fill the hearts of your faithful,
and kindle in them the fire of your love.
Send forth your Spirit
and they shall be created.
And you will renew the face of the earth.
**Amen.**

Let us pray the prayer that Jesus taught us:
**Our Father…**

✠ **In the name of the Father, and of the Son, and of the Holy Spirit. Amen.**

Note: Today's reading is Galatians 5:16-17a, 22, 23, 25, 26.

## THURSDAY

✠ **In the name of the Father, and of the Son, and of the Holy Spirit. Amen.**

Introduction: In our reading today, we hear the beginning of the letter St. Paul wrote to the people of a city called Ephesus, the Ephesians. He is reminding them (and us!) of the great blessings God has given us through his Son, Jesus. God chose us to be his children through Jesus.

St. Paul helps us remember to praise and thank God for God's many gifts to us.

A reading from the letter of Paul to the Ephesians

Blessed be the God and Father
of our Lord Jesus Christ,
who has blessed us in Christ with every
spiritual blessing in the heavenly places,
just as he chose us in Christ
before the foundation of the world
to be holy and blameless before him in love.
He destined us for adoption as his children
through Jesus Christ,
according to the good pleasure of his will,
to the praise of his glorious grace
that he freely bestowed on us
in the Beloved.
In him we have redemption through his
blood,
the forgiveness of our trespasses,
according to the riches of his grace
that he lavished on us.

The word of the Lord.
**Thanks be to God.**

Let us pray:
Most loving and gracious God,
through your beloved Son, Jesus,
you called us and made us your children.
Grant that we may always have
humble and grateful hearts,
praising and thanking you
for the great gifts and blessings
you have given us.
We ask this through Christ our Lord.
**Amen.**

Let us pray the prayer that Jesus taught us:
**Our Father…**

✠ **In the name of the Father, and of the Son, and of the Holy Spirit. Amen.**

Note: Today's reading is Ephesians 1:3-8.

## FRIDAY

✠ **In the name of the Father, and of the Son, and of the Holy Spirit. Amen.**

Introduction: Today's reading has some surprising news: God knows all God's creatures, even the sparrows! God has counted all the hairs on our heads! That shows how well God knows us, and how much love and care God has for us.

Each of us is called by our name, is loved, and is precious to God.

A reading from the holy gospel according to Luke
**Glory to you, Lord.**

Meanwhile, when the crowd gathered
by the thousands,
so that they trampled on one another,
Jesus began to speak first to his disciples,
"Are not five sparrows sold for two pennies?
Yet not one of them is forgotten
in God's sight.
But even the hairs of your head
are all counted.
Do not be afraid;
you are of more value than many sparrows."

The gospel of the Lord.
**Praise to you, Lord Jesus Christ.**

Let us pray:
Most loving God,
your love for us is beyond measure.
We are so precious and important to you
that you even know how many hairs
there are on our heads!
Help us to be grateful
for your unending love,
and know, deep within our hearts,
how much we are truly loved.
We ask this through Christ our Lord.
**Amen.**

Let us pray the prayer that Jesus taught us:
**Our Father...**

✠ **In the name of the Father, and of the Son, and of the Holy Spirit. Amen.**

Note: Today's reading is Luke 12:1a, 6-7.

## MONDAY

✠ **In the name of the Father, and of the Son, and of the Holy Spirit. Amen.**

Introduction: Each of us has been created by God, in God's image and likeness. God loves each one of us so much, it cannot be measured. We are all special in God's eyes; there is only one of us. We are one of a kind, like a painting or a sculpture! God has chosen each of us to do a special job that only we can do.

A reading from the letter of Paul to the Ephesians

For we are what he has made us,
created in Christ Jesus for good works,
which God prepared beforehand
to be our way of life.

The word of the Lord.
**Thanks be to God.**

Let us pray:
Creator God,
in your great love for us
you give us all we need.
Help us to do what is right every day.
Send us the gift of the Holy Spirit
to guide and inspire us,
so we can show the world
that we are your work of art.
We ask this through Christ our Lord.
**Amen.**

Let us pray the prayer that Jesus taught us:
**Our Father…**

✠ **In the name of the Father, and of the Son, and of the Holy Spirit. Amen.**

---

Note: Today's reading is Ephesians 2:10.

## TUESDAY

✠ In the name of the Father, and of the Son, and of the Holy Spirit. Amen.

Introduction: In our reading today, Jesus tells us that we must be ready at all times. Ready for what? For Jesus to return. As we wait, we work to build God's kingdom day by day, being kind to others and preparing our hearts for Jesus.

A reading from the holy gospel according to Luke
**Glory to you, Lord.**

Jesus said,
"Be dressed for action
and have your lamps lit;
be like those who are waiting
for their master
to return from the wedding banquet,
so that they may open the door for him
as soon as he comes and knocks.
Blessed are those slaves
whom the master finds alert when he comes;
truly I tell you,
he will fasten his belt
and have them sit down to eat,
and he will come and serve them.
If he comes during the middle of the night,
or near dawn, and finds them so,
blessed are those slaves."

The gospel of the Lord.
**Praise to you, Lord Jesus Christ.**

Let us pray:
Most holy God,
how happy you are
when you find us ready
to do what you ask of us!
Help us to prepare for Jesus
as we build your kingdom on earth.
We ask this through Christ our Lord.
**Amen.**

Let us pray the prayer that Jesus taught us:
**Our Father...**

✠ In the name of the Father, and of the Son, and of the Holy Spirit. Amen.

Note: Today's reading is Luke 12:35-38.

## WEDNESDAY

✠ **In the name of the Father, and of the Son, and of the Holy Spirit. Amen.**

Introduction: God loves us and always comes to help us when we ask; we need to trust God always. We must remember to thank God for all that he does for us, and to tell others of God's great deeds for us.

A reading from the book of the prophet Isaiah

Surely God is my salvation;
I will trust, and will not be afraid,
for the Lord God is my strength
and my might;
he has become my salvation.
Give thanks to the Lord, call on his name;
make known his deeds among the nations;
proclaim that his name is exalted.
Sing praises to the Lord,
for he has done gloriously;
let this be known in all the earth.
Shout aloud and sing for joy, O royal Zion,
for great in your midst
is the Holy One of Israel.

The word of the Lord.
**Thanks be to God.**

Let us pray:
Most holy and gracious God,
you do great things for us,
and sometimes
we don't even notice!
Help us to see what you do for us,
and to always be grateful.
We ask this through Christ our Lord.
**Amen.**

Let us pray the prayer that Jesus taught us:
**Our Father…**

✠ **In the name of the Father, and of the Son, and of the Holy Spirit. Amen.**

---

Note: Today's reading is Isaiah 12:2, 4b-6.

## THURSDAY

✠ **In the name of the Father, and of the Son, and of the Holy Spirit. Amen.**

Introduction: Today's reading contains a beautiful prayer describing Jesus' great love for us. This love is bigger than anything we can imagine!

A reading from the letter of Paul to the Ephesians

For this reason I bow my knees
before the Father,
from whom every family
in heaven and on earth
takes its name.
I pray that,
according to the riches of his glory,
he may grant that you may be strengthened
in your inner being with power
through his Spirit,
and that Christ may dwell in your hearts
through faith,
as you are being rooted and grounded
in love.
I pray that you
may have the power to comprehend,
with all the saints,
what is the breadth and length
and height and depth,
and to know the love of Christ
that surpasses knowledge,
so that you may be filled
with all the fullness of God.

Now to him who by the power at work
within us
is able to accomplish abundantly far more
than all we can ask or imagine,
to him be glory in the church
and in Christ Jesus to all generations,
forever and ever. Amen.

The word of the Lord.
**Thanks be to God.**

Let us pray:
Most loving and gracious God,
help us to be rooted and grounded
in the love of Jesus.
Help us to be open to you
and to place all our trust in you,
so your power may work within us.
We ask this through Christ our Lord.
**Amen.**

Let us pray the prayer that Jesus taught us:
**Our Father…**

✠ **In the name of the Father, and of the Son, and of the Holy Spirit. Amen.**

Note: Today's reading is Ephesians 3:14-20.

## FRIDAY

✠ In the name of the Father, and of the Son, and of the Holy Spirit. Amen.

Introduction: Today we continue to hear God's word in St. Paul's letter to the Ephesians. St. Paul was in prison when he wrote this letter. He was put into prison because he was teaching others about Jesus. He tells us how to treat others, and how we must work together to be one in the Spirit.

Do we act in the way St. Paul recommends in this reading?

A reading from the letter of Paul to the Ephesians

I therefore, the prisoner in the Lord,
beg you to lead a life worthy of the calling
to which you have been called,
with all humility and gentleness,
with patience,
bearing with one another in love,
making every effort to maintain the unity
of the Spirit in the bond of peace.
There is one body and one Spirit,
just as you were called
to the one hope of your calling,
one Lord, one faith, one baptism,
one God and Father of all,
who is above all and through all and in all.

The word of the Lord.
**Thanks be to God.**

Let us pray:
Father in heaven,
help us always to treat others
as we would like to be treated,
and to remember that all of us
belong to the one family of God,
united in and through Jesus.
We ask this through Christ our Lord.
**Amen.**

Let us pray the prayer that Jesus taught us:
**Our Father…**

✠ In the name of the Father, and of the Son, and of the Holy Spirit. Amen.

Note: Today's reading is Ephesians 4:1-6.

## MONDAY

✠ In the name of the Father, and of the Son, and of the Holy Spirit. Amen.

Introduction: In today's reading, St. Paul gives us some more good advice on how to treat others. How can we be true friends – at school, at home and in our communities – even with people who are hard to like?

A reading from the letter of Paul to the Ephesians

Be kind to one another, tenderhearted,
forgiving one another,
as God in Christ has forgiven you.
Therefore be imitators of God,
as beloved children,
and live in love,
as Christ loved us
and gave himself up for us.

The word of the Lord.
**Thanks be to God.**

Let us pray:
Most holy and gracious God,
we are your children.
Help us to be true friends,
kind, tender-hearted and forgiving,
even when it is hard,
just as Jesus did.
We ask this through Christ our Lord.
**Amen.**

Let us pray the prayer that Jesus taught us:
**Our Father…**

✠ In the name of the Father, and of the Son, and of the Holy Spirit. Amen.

Note: Today's reading is Ephesians 4:32–5:2a.

# THIRTIETH WEEK OF ORDINARY TIME

## TUESDAY

✠ In the name of the Father, and of the Son, and of the Holy Spirit. Amen.

Introduction: Today we hear two parables. Jesus compares the kingdom of God to two very small things that can make a big difference. The parables remind us that by acting as children of the kingdom, doing what God wants, we can make a big difference – even though we are only one person.

A reading from the holy gospel according to Luke
**Glory to you, Lord.**

Jesus said,
"What is the kingdom of God like?
And to what should I compare it?
It is like a mustard seed
that someone took and sowed in the garden;
it grew and became a tree,
and the birds of the air
made nests in its branches."
And again he said,
"To what should I compare the
kingdom of God?
It is like yeast that a woman took
and mixed in with three measures of flour
until all of it was leavened."

The gospel of the Lord.
**Praise to you, Lord Jesus Christ.**

Let us pray:
Most holy and loving God,
you sent your Son, Jesus,
to teach us about the kingdom of God.
Help us to be good citizens
of your kingdom,
realizing that we can do good
even though we are just one person.
We ask this through Christ our Lord.
**Amen.**

Let us pray the prayer that Jesus taught us:
**Our Father…**

✠ In the name of the Father, and of the Son, and of the Holy Spirit. Amen.

---

Note: Today's reading is Luke 13:18-21.

## WEDNESDAY

✠ **In the name of the Father, and of the Son, and of the Holy Spirit. Amen.**

Introduction: In our reading today, St. Paul tells us why we must respect and obey our parents. Parents, too, are given some advice on raising children. Parents and children are to follow Jesus' example, living and acting out of love and respect.

A reading from the letter of Paul to the Ephesians

Children, obey your parents in the Lord,
for this is right.
"Honour your father and mother" –
this is the first commandment
with a promise:
"so that it may be well with you
and you may live long on the earth."
And, fathers,
do not provoke your children to anger,
but bring them up in the discipline
and instruction of the Lord.

The word of the Lord.
**Thanks be to God.**

Let us pray:
Creator God,
your Son, Jesus,
taught us to call you "Abba,"
which means "Daddy."
Help us to obey you and our parents;
give them the grace they need
to raise us in our faith.
Help us to obey our teachers, too;
give them the wisdom,
grace and insight they need
to teach us and help us grow in your ways.
We ask this through Christ our Lord.
**Amen.**

Let us pray the prayer that Jesus taught us:
**Our Father…**

✠ **In the name of the Father, and of the Son, and of the Holy Spirit. Amen.**

Note: Today's reading is Ephesians 6:1-4.

## THURSDAY

✠ In the name of the Father, and of the Son, and of the Holy Spirit. Amen.

Introduction: In our reading today, St. Paul tells us how powerful is God's love for us – nothing can come between us and God's love.

A reading from the letter of Paul to the Romans

If God is for us, who is against us?
He who did not withhold his own Son,
but gave him up for all of us,
will he not with him
also give us everything else?
Who will bring any charge
against God's elect?
It is God who justifies.
Who is to condemn?
It is Christ Jesus, who died,
yes, who was raised,
who is at the right hand of God,
who indeed intercedes for us.
Who will separate us
from the love of Christ?
Will hardship, or distress, or persecution,
or famine, or nakedness, or peril, or sword?
For I am convinced that
neither death, nor life,
nor angels, nor rulers,
nor things present, nor things to come,
nor powers, nor height, nor depth,
nor anything else in all creation,
will be able to separate us
from the love of God
in Christ Jesus our Lord.

The word of the Lord.
**Thanks be to God.**

Let us pray:
Most holy and eternal God,
how wonderful you are!
Your love for us is so great,
nothing can separate us from it.
May we always remember to be grateful
for this gift.
Send us your Holy Spirit
to help us grow in holiness
so that we may reflect your love in our lives.
We ask this through Jesus Christ our Lord.
**Amen.**

Let us pray the prayer that Jesus taught us:
**Our Father…**

✠ In the name of the Father, and of the Son, and of the Holy Spirit. Amen.

Note: Today's reading is Romans 8:31b-35, 38-39.

## FRIDAY

✠ **In the name of the Father, and of the Son, and of the Holy Spirit. Amen.**

Introduction: In today's reading, we hear part of the letter St. Paul and St. Timothy sent to the Philippians, who lived in the city of Philippi. They are encouraging the people and thanking them for their faith in Jesus, and for their help.

If St. Paul and St. Timothy wrote a letter to our class today, would they say the same about us?

A reading from the letter of Paul to the Philippians

Paul and Timothy, servants of Christ Jesus,
To all the saints in Christ Jesus
who are in Philippi,
with the bishops and deacons:
Grace to you and peace
from God our Father
and the Lord Jesus Christ.
I thank my God every time I remember you,
constantly praying with joy
in every one of my prayers for all of you,
because of your sharing in the gospel
from the first day until now.
I am confident of this,
that the one who began a good work
among you
will bring it to completion
by the day of Jesus Christ.
It is right for me to think this way
about all of you,
because you hold me in your heart,
for all of you share in God's grace with me,
both in my imprisonment
and in the defence
and confirmation of the gospel.

For God is my witness,
how I long for all of you
with the compassion of Christ Jesus.
And this is my prayer,
that your love may overflow more and more
with knowledge and full insight
to help you to determine what is best.

The word of the Lord.
**Thanks be to God.**

Let us pray:
God our Father,
help us to grow in love and knowledge
of Jesus, your beloved Son.
Help us to share his love
and the Good News of your kingdom.
We ask this through Christ our Lord.
**Amen.**

Let us pray the prayer that Jesus taught us:
**Our Father…**

✠ **In the name of the Father, and of the Son, and of the Holy Spirit. Amen.**

---

Note: Today's reading is Philippians 1:1-7a, 8-10a.

## MONDAY

✠ **In the name of the Father, and of the Son, and of the Holy Spirit. Amen.**

Introduction: In our reading today, Jesus tells us to look at our motive for doing things. We are to do things for others not because of what they might give us in return, but out of love. We will receive our reward at the end of time. And that is a reward that cannot be bought with money!

Can we love without wanting something in return?

A reading from the holy gospel according to Luke
**Glory to you, Lord.**

Jesus said also to the one
who had invited him,
"When you give a luncheon or a dinner,
do not invite your friends or your brothers
or your relatives or rich neighbours,
in case they may invite you in return,
and you would be repaid.
But when you give a banquet,
invite the poor, the crippled,
the lame, and the blind.
And you will be blessed,
because they cannot repay you,
for you will be repaid
at the resurrection of the righteous."

The gospel of the Lord.
**Praise to you, Lord Jesus Christ.**

Let us pray:
Most loving and merciful God,
your Son, Jesus,
tells us to do things out of love,
without expecting payment in return.
Help to follow his example
today and every day.
We ask this through Christ our Lord.
**Amen.**

Let us pray the prayer that Jesus taught us:
**Our Father...**

During the month of November, add:
Let us pray for all those whose names are
written in our Book of Remembrance:
Eternal rest grant unto them, O Lord,
and let perpetual light shine upon them.
May they rest in peace.
**Amen.**

✠ **In the name of the Father, and of the Son, and of the Holy Spirit. Amen.**

---

Note: Today's reading is Luke 14:12-14.

## TUESDAY

✠ In the name of the Father, and of the Son, and of the Holy Spirit. Amen.

Introduction: St. Paul tells us that we all form one body: the body of Christ. Each of us is important, and each of us has something to add. If a part of our body is missing, we are not complete. So it is with the body of Christ.

A reading from the letter of Paul to the Romans

For as in one body we have many members,
and not all the members
have the same function,
so we, who are many,
are one body in Christ,
and individually we are members
one of another.
We have gifts that differ
according to the grace given to us:
prophecy, in proportion to faith;
ministry, in ministering;
the teacher, in teaching;
the exhorter, in exhortation;
the giver, in generosity;
the leader, in diligence;
the compassionate, in cheerfulness.
Let love be genuine;
hate what is evil, hold fast to what is good;
love one another with mutual affection;
outdo one another in showing honour.
Do not lag in zeal, be ardent in spirit,
serve the Lord.
Rejoice in hope, be patient in suffering,
persevere in prayer.

The word of the Lord.
**Thanks be to God.**

Let us pray:
Eternal God,
in your word you teach us to act;
you gave us your Son, Jesus,
to show us how to live.
Give us the grace we need
to act in ways that are pleasing to you.
We ask this through Christ our Lord.
**Amen.**

Let us pray the prayer that Jesus taught us:
**Our Father…**

During the month of November, add:
Let us pray for all those whose names are written in our Book of Remembrance:
Eternal rest grant unto them, O Lord,
and let perpetual light shine upon them.
May they rest in peace.
**Amen.**

✠ In the name of the Father, and of the Son, and of the Holy Spirit. Amen.

Note: Today's reading is Romans 12:4-12.

## WEDNESDAY

✠ **In the name of the Father, and of the Son, and of the Holy Spirit. Amen.**

Introduction: In our reading today, St. Paul tells us that the most important thing we can do is love. All the commandments are summed up in this one command: love one another.

Do we truly love others? How can we love our neighbour as we love ourselves?

A reading from the letter of Paul to the Romans

Owe no one anything,
except to love one another;
for the one who loves another
has fulfilled the law.
The commandments,
"You shall not commit adultery;
You shall not murder;
You shall not steal;
You shall not covet";
and any other commandment,
are summed up in this word,
"Love your neighbour as yourself."
Love does no wrong to a neighbour;
therefore, love is the fulfilling of the law.

The word of the Lord.
**Thanks be to God.**

Let us pray:
Most loving and holy God,
you are the source of all goodness,
life, love and holiness.
Help us to love one another,
treating others as we would
like to be treated
and following the example of Jesus.
We ask this through Christ our Lord.
**Amen.**

Let us pray the prayer that Jesus taught us:
**Our Father…**

During the month of November, add:
Let us pray for all those whose names are
written in our Book of Remembrance:
Eternal rest grant unto them, O Lord,
and let perpetual light shine upon them.
May they rest in peace.
**Amen.**

✠ **In the name of the Father, and of the Son, and of the Holy Spirit. Amen.**

---

Note: Today's reading is Romans 13:8-10.

## THURSDAY

✠ In the name of the Father, and of the Son, and of the Holy Spirit. Amen.

Introduction: The Scribes and Pharisees, who were Jewish teachers and leaders, are complaining that Jesus welcomed and ate with sinners and tax collectors. Jesus tells them two parables about finding something that was lost – just as Jesus found and welcomed sinners who felt they had lost their way to God.

The first parable was about a lost sheep. This one is about a lost coin.

A reading from the holy gospel according to Luke
**Glory to you, Lord.**

Jesus told them this parable:
"What woman having ten silver coins,
if she loses one of them,
does not light a lamp,
sweep the house,
and search carefully until she finds it?
When she has found it,
she calls together her friends and
neighbours, saying,
'Rejoice with me,
for I have found the coin that I had lost.'
Just so, I tell you,
there is joy in the presence
of the angels of God
over one sinner who repents."

The gospel of the Lord.
**Praise to you, Lord Jesus Christ.**

Let us pray:
Most merciful and forgiving God,
the angels in heaven rejoice
when those who have sinned repent
and find their way back to you.
Help us to turn back to you
when we have sinned,
and to ask forgiveness
from you and from those we have hurt.
We ask this through Christ our Lord.
**Amen.**

Let us pray the prayer that Jesus taught us:
**Our Father…**

During the month of November, add:
Let us pray for all those whose names are
written in our Book of Remembrance:
Eternal rest grant unto them, O Lord,
and let perpetual light shine upon them.
May they rest in peace.
**Amen.**

✠ In the name of the Father, and of the Son, and of the Holy Spirit. Amen.

Note: Today's reading is Luke 15:8-10.

## FRIDAY

✠ **In the name of the Father, and of the Son, and of the Holy Spirit. Amen.**

Introduction: St. Paul tells the Romans that they are full of goodness, but he reminds them of things that would help them be good followers of Jesus. For Paul, the only thing that is worth being proud of is his work of spreading the Gospel to the Gentiles (people who are not Jewish), because it is Jesus who works through him, not himself.

Do we allow Jesus to work through us? Do we spread the Good News to others?

A reading from the letter of Paul to the Philippians

I myself feel confident about you,
my brothers and sisters,
that you yourselves are full of goodness,
filled with all knowledge,
and able to instruct one another.
Nevertheless on some points
I have written to you rather boldly
by way of reminder,
because of the grace given me by God
to be a minister of Christ Jesus
to the Gentiles
in the priestly service of the gospel of God,
so that the offering of the Gentiles
may be acceptable,
sanctified by the Holy Spirit.
In Christ Jesus, then,
I have reason to boast of my work for God.
For I will not venture to speak of anything
except what Christ has accomplished
through me to win obedience
from the Gentiles, by word and deed
by the power of signs and wonders,
by the power of the Spirit of God,
so that from Jerusalem
and as far around as Illyricum

I have fully proclaimed
the good news of Christ.
Thus I make it my ambition
to proclaim the good news,
not where Christ has already been named,
so that I do not build
on someone else's foundation,
but as it is written,
"Those who have never been told of him
shall see,
and those who have never heard of him
shall understand."

The word of the Lord.
**Thanks be to God.**

Let us pray:
Most holy God,
Jesus is your greatest gift to us.
Help us to put him first in our lives
as we follow your ways.
We ask this through Christ our Lord.
**Amen.**

Let us pray the prayer that Jesus taught us:
**Our Father...**

During the month of November, add:
Let us pray for all those whose names are
written in our Book of Remembrance:
Eternal rest grant unto them, O Lord,
and let perpetual light shine upon them.
May they rest in peace.
**Amen.**

✠ **In the name of the Father, and of the Son, and of the Holy Spirit. Amen.**

Note: Today's reading is Romans 15:14-21.

# THIRTY-SECOND WEEK OF ORDINARY TIME

## MONDAY

✠ In the name of the Father, and of the Son, and of the Holy Spirit. Amen.

Introduction: Our reading today tells us how to search for God and for true wisdom. Wisdom does not stay near those who are deceitful, sinful or foolish.

Do we invite wisdom to come to us? Do we pay attention to what she has to say?

A reading from the book of Wisdom

Love righteousness, you rulers of the earth,
think of the Lord in goodness
and seek him with sincerity of heart;
because he is found by those
who do not put him to the test,
and manifests himself
to those who do not distrust him.
For perverse thoughts
separate people from God,
and when his power is tested,
it exposes the foolish;
because wisdom will not enter
a deceitful soul,
or dwell in a body enslaved to sin.
For a holy and disciplined spirit
will flee from deceit,
and will leave foolish thoughts behind,
and will be ashamed
at the approach of unrighteousness.
For wisdom is a kindly spirit,
but will not free blasphemers
from the guilt of their words;
because God is witness
of their inmost feelings,
and a true observer of their hearts,
and a hearer of their tongues.

Because the spirit of the Lord
has filled the world,
and that which holds all things together
knows what is said.

The word of the Lord.
**Thanks be to God.**

Let us pray:
God, source of all wisdom,
help us to grow in your wisdom and ways,
and always be faithful to you
and your divine Son, Jesus.
We ask this through Christ our Lord.
**Amen.**

Let us pray the prayer that Jesus taught us:
**Our Father...**

During the month of November, add:
Let us pray for all those whose names are
written in our Book of Remembrance:
Eternal rest grant unto them, O Lord,
and let perpetual light shine upon them.
May they rest in peace.
**Amen.**

✠ In the name of the Father, and of the Son, and of the Holy Spirit. Amen.

Note: Today's reading is Wisdom 1:1-7.

## TUESDAY

✠ **In the name of the Father, and of the Son, and of the Holy Spirit. Amen.**

Introduction: In today's reading, we are reminded that if we do what is right, follow God's law, and love God, the rewards will be great. God will help us along the way.

A reading from the book of Psalms

Trust in the Lord, and do good;
so you will live in the land,
and enjoy security.
Take delight in the Lord,
and he will give you
the desires of your heart.
Our steps are made firm by the Lord,
when he delights in our way;
though we stumble,
we shall not fall headlong,
for the Lord holds us by the hand.
Depart from evil, and do good;
so you shall abide forever.
For the Lord loves justice;
he will not forsake his faithful ones.
The righteous shall be kept safe forever.

The word of the Lord.
**Thanks be to God.**

Let us pray:
Gracious and holy God,
your love for us is unending.
You love what is right
and will always help us, your children,
to follow you and do good.
We ask this through Christ our Lord.
**Amen.**

Let us pray the prayer that Jesus taught us:
**Our Father…**

During the month of November, add:
Let us pray for all those whose names are
written in our Book of Remembrance:
Eternal rest grant unto them, O Lord,
and let perpetual light shine upon them.
May they rest in peace.
**Amen.**

✠ **In the name of the Father, and of the Son, and of the Holy Spirit. Amen.**

---

Note: Today's reading is Psalm 37:3, 4, 23, 24, 27, 28.

# THIRTY-SECOND WEEK OF ORDINARY TIME

## WEDNESDAY

✠ **In the name of the Father, and of the Son, and of the Holy Spirit. Amen.**

Introduction: In our reading today, we hear about the ten lepers who were healed. Only one returned to thank Jesus. Saying "thank you" to others and to God is very important – it shows that we appreciate what they do for us.

Do we remember to thank God and others for what they do for us?

A reading from the holy gospel according to Luke
**Glory to you, Lord.**

On the way to Jerusalem
Jesus was going through the region
between Samaria and Galilee.
As he entered a village,
ten lepers approached him.
Keeping their distance,
they called out, saying,
"Jesus, Master, have mercy on us!"
When he saw them, he said to them,
"Go and show yourselves to the priests."
And as they went,
they were made clean.
Then one of them,
when he saw that he was healed,
turned back, praising God with a loud voice.
He prostrated himself at Jesus' feet
and thanked him. And he was a Samaritan.
Then Jesus asked,
"Were not ten made clean?
But the other nine, where are they?

Was none of them found to return
and give praise to God
except this foreigner?"
Then he said to him,
"Get up and go on your way;
your faith has made you well."

The gospel of the Lord.
**Praise to you, Lord Jesus Christ.**

Let us pray:
Most holy and gracious God,
only one of the ten lepers thanked Jesus
for healing him.
Help us to remember to thank you for all
your gifts,
and to thank those who do things for us.
We ask this through Christ our Lord.
**Amen.**

Let us pray the prayer that Jesus taught us:
**Our Father…**

During the month of November, add:
Let us pray for all those whose names are
written in our Book of Remembrance:
Eternal rest grant unto them, O Lord,
and let perpetual light shine upon them.
May they rest in peace.
**Amen.**

✠ **In the name of the Father, and of the Son, and of the Holy Spirit. Amen.**

Note: Today's reading is Luke 17:11-19.

## THURSDAY

✠ **In the name of the Father, and of the Son, and of the Holy Spirit. Amen.**

Introduction: In today's reading, the writer talks about Wisdom. Wisdom means more than being smart and knowing a lot of facts; it means having good sense, judgment, insight and learning. Wisdom is holy and a reflection of God's activity and goodness.

Do we use good sense, judgment and insight as we learn? Are we becoming wise as well as smart? Is our wisdom holy, reflecting God's activity and goodness?

A reading from the book of Wisdom

There is in her a spirit
that is intelligent, holy,
unique, manifold, subtle,
mobile, clear, unpolluted,
distinct, invulnerable,
loving the good, keen, irresistible,
beneficent, humane,
steadfast, sure, free from anxiety,
all-powerful, overseeing all.
For wisdom is more mobile
than any motion;
because of her pureness
she pervades and penetrates all things.
For she is a breath of the power of God,
and a pure emanation
of the glory of the Almighty.
For she is a reflection of eternal light,
a spotless mirror of the working of God,
and an image of his goodness.

The word of the Lord.
**Thanks be to God.**

Let us pray:
Most holy and gracious God,
in your goodness
you gave us your Wisdom
to give light to our minds
and to teach our hearts.
Help us always to seek your wisdom,
so that we may grow
in holiness and understanding.
We ask this through Christ our Lord.
**Amen.**

Let us pray the prayer that Jesus taught us:
**Our Father…**

During the month of November, add:
Let us pray for all those whose names are written in our Book of Remembrance:
Eternal rest grant unto them, O Lord,
and let perpetual light shine upon them.
May they rest in peace.
**Amen.**

✠ **In the name of the Father, and of the Son, and of the Holy Spirit. Amen.**

---

Note: Today's reading is Wisdom 7:22b-23a, 24-25a, 26.

## FRIDAY

✠ **In the name of the Father, and of the Son, and of the Holy Spirit. Amen.**

Introduction: Today we continue to hear from the book of Wisdom. It is talking about the wonder and beauty of creation. We hear that some people do not recognize the Creator, who is God.

A reading from the book of Wisdom

For all people who were ignorant of God
were foolish by nature;
and they were unable
from the good things that are seen
to know the one who exists;
but they supposed that either
fire or wind or swift air,
or the circle of the stars, or turbulent water,
or the luminaries of heaven
were the gods that rule the world.
If through delight
in the beauty of these things
people assumed them to be gods,
let them know how much better than these
is their Lord,
for the author of beauty created them.
And if people were amazed at their power
and working,
let them perceive from them
how much more powerful
is the one who formed them.
For from the greatness and beauty
of created things
comes a corresponding perception
of their Creator.

The word of the Lord.
**Thanks be to God.**

Let us pray:
Creator of the Universe,
you made the earth, the heavens
and all that is in them.
Grant that we may treat your creation
with respect,
taking care of what you have entrusted to us
and praising and thanking you
for these gifts
every day of our lives.
We ask this through Christ our Lord.
**Amen.**

Let us pray the prayer that Jesus taught us:
**Our Father...**

During the month of November, add:
Let us pray for all those whose names are
written in our Book of Remembrance:
Eternal rest grant unto them, O Lord,
and let perpetual light shine upon them.
May they rest in peace.
**Amen.**

✠ **In the name of the Father, and of the Son, and of the Holy Spirit. Amen.**

Note: Today's reading is Wisdom 13:1a, 2-5.

## MONDAY

✠ **In the name of the Father, and of the Son, and of the Holy Spirit. Amen.**

Introduction: In today's reading, we hear the story of the blind beggar who called out to Jesus to cure him. Sometimes we are blind, too – not with our eyes but with our hearts.

Do we have the courage to ask Jesus to help us to see with our hearts – to see with love?

A reading from the holy gospel according to Luke
**Glory to you, Lord.**

As Jesus approached Jericho,
a blind man
was sitting by the roadside begging.
When he heard a crowd going by,
he asked what was happening.
They told him,
"Jesus of Nazareth is passing by."
Then he shouted,
"Jesus, Son of David, have mercy on me!"
Those who were in front
sternly ordered him to be quiet;
but he shouted even more loudly,
"Son of David, have mercy on me!"
Jesus stood still and ordered the man
to be brought to him;
and when he came near, he asked him,
"What do you want me to do for you?"
He said, "Lord, let me see again."
Jesus said to him,
"Receive your sight;
your faith has saved you."

Immediately he regained his sight
and followed him, glorifying God;
and all the people, when they saw it,
praised God.

The gospel of the Lord.
**Praise to you, Lord Jesus Christ.**

Let us pray:
Merciful God,
Jesus cured the blind man
so he could see again.
Help us to see others
with the eyes of our hearts –
the eyes of love.
We ask this through Christ our Lord.
**Amen.**

Let us pray the prayer that Jesus taught us:
**Our Father…**

During the month of November, add:
Let us pray for all those whose names are
written in our Book of Remembrance:
Eternal rest grant unto them, O Lord,
and let perpetual light shine upon them.
May they rest in peace.
**Amen.**

✠ **In the name of the Father, and of the Son, and of the Holy Spirit. Amen.**

---

Note: Today's reading is Luke 18:35-43.

## TUESDAY

✠ In the name of the Father, and of the Son, and of the Holy Spirit. Amen.

Introduction: Today we hear the story of Zacchaeus, a tax collector who made people give him more tax money than they owed. When Zacchaeus meets Jesus, something amazing happens!

A reading from the holy gospel according to Luke
**Glory to you, Lord.**

Jesus entered Jericho
and was passing through it.
A man was there named Zacchaeus;
he was a chief tax collector and was rich.
He was trying to see who Jesus was,
but on account of the crowd he could not,
because he was short in stature.
So he ran ahead
and climbed a sycamore tree
to see him,
because he was going to pass that way.
When Jesus came to the place,
he looked up and said to him,
"Zacchaeus, hurry and come down;
for I must stay at your house today."
So he hurried down
and was happy to welcome him.
Zacchaeus stood there and said to the Lord,
"Look, half of my possessions, Lord,
I will give to the poor;
and if I have defrauded anyone of anything,
I will pay back four times as much."

The gospel of the Lord.
**Praise to you, Lord Jesus Christ.**

Let us pray:
Loving God,
because of Jesus' kindness and love
Zacchaeus had a change of heart.
Help us to be kind, honest and truthful,
treating others with kindness,
respect and courtesy.
We ask this through Christ our Lord.
**Amen.**

Let us pray the prayer that Jesus taught us:
**Our Father...**

During the month of November, add:
Let us pray for all those whose names are
written in our Book of Remembrance:
Eternal rest grant unto them, O Lord,
and let perpetual light shine upon them.
May they rest in peace.
**Amen.**

✠ In the name of the Father, and of the Son, and of the Holy Spirit. Amen.

---

Note: Today's reading is Luke 19:1-6, 8.

## WEDNESDAY

✠ In the name of the Father, and of the Son, and of the Holy Spirit. Amen.

Introduction: At the end of time, everyone on earth and in heaven will praise God for all the wonderful things God has done. We should praise and thank God every day!

How do we praise God for our many blessings?

A reading from the book of Psalms

Praise the Lord!
Praise God in his sanctuary;
praise him in his mighty firmament!
Praise him for his mighty deeds;
praise him according to his
surpassing greatness!
Praise him with trumpet sound;
praise him with lute and harp!
Praise him with tambourine and dance;
praise him with strings and pipe!
Praise him with clanging cymbals;
praise him with loud clashing cymbals!
Let everything that breathes praise the Lord!
Praise the Lord!

The word of the Lord.
**Thanks be to God.**

Let us pray:
Most holy and loving God,
you give us everything we need.
You love us more than anyone –
even our parents!
May we always praise and thank you
for your love and for your help.
We ask this through Christ our Lord.
**Amen.**

Let us pray the prayer that Jesus taught us:
**Our Father…**

During the month of November, add:
Let us pray for all those whose names are
written in our Book of Remembrance:
Eternal rest grant unto them, O Lord,
and let perpetual light shine upon them.
May they rest in peace.
**Amen.**

✠ In the name of the Father, and of the Son, and of the Holy Spirit. Amen.

Note: Today's reading is Psalm 150.

## THURSDAY

☩ In the name of the Father, and of the Son, and of the Holy Spirit. Amen.

Introduction: In today's reading, we hear about the joys and reward that await those who listen to God and do God's will.

Are we one of the faithful ones?

A reading from the book of Psalms

Sing to the Lord a new song,
his praise in the assembly of the faithful.
Let Israel be glad in its Maker;
let the children of Zion
rejoice in their King.
Let them praise his name with dancing,
making melody to him
with tambourine and lyre.
For the Lord takes pleasure in his people;
he adorns the humble with victory.
Let the faithful exult in glory;
let them sing for joy on their couches.
This is glory for all his faithful ones.
Praise the Lord!

The word of the Lord.
**Thanks be to God.**

Let us pray:
Most loving God,
help us always to do your will
to be faithful to you,
and to praise your name.
We ask this through Christ our Lord.
**Amen.**

Let us pray the prayer that Jesus taught us:
**Our Father...**

During the month of November, add:
Let us pray for all those whose names are
written in our Book of Remembrance:
Eternal rest grant unto them, O Lord,
and let perpetual light shine upon them.
May they rest in peace.
**Amen.**

☩ In the name of the Father, and of the Son, and of the Holy Spirit. Amen.

Note: Today's reading is Psalm 149:1, 2, 3, 4, 5, 9b.

# THIRTY-THIRD WEEK OF ORDINARY TIME

## FRIDAY

✠ **In the name of the Father, and of the Son, and of the Holy Spirit. Amen.**

Introduction: In our reading today, Jesus gets angry when he sees people turning the Temple, God's house, into a place where things are bought and sold. He reminds us that God's house is a holy place. Are we respectful in God's house, the church?

Our hearts and bodies are God's temple, too. How can we make sure they are holy places where God dwells?

A reading from the holy gospel according to Luke
**Glory to you, Lord.**

Then Jesus entered the temple
and began to drive out
those who were selling things there;
and he said, "It is written,
'My house shall be a house of prayer';
but you have made it a den of robbers."

The gospel of the Lord.
**Praise to you, Lord Jesus Christ.**

Let us pray:
Creator God,
help us always to respect your church
as a house of prayer,
and our hearts and bodies
as your holy temple.
We ask this through Christ our Lord.
**Amen.**

Let us pray the prayer that Jesus taught us:
**Our Father…**

During the month of November, add:
Let us pray for all those whose names are written in our Book of Remembrance:
Eternal rest grant unto them, O Lord,
and let perpetual light shine upon them.
May they rest in peace.
**Amen.**

✠ **In the name of the Father, and of the Son, and of the Holy Spirit. Amen.**

Note: Today's reading is Luke 19:45-46.

# THIRTY-FOURTH WEEK OF ORDINARY TIME

## MONDAY

✠ **In the name of the Father, and of the Son, and of the Holy Spirit. Amen.**

Introduction: In today's reading, Jesus watches people give money in the Temple of Jerusalem. Some who have a lot give a lot of money; some who have little give only a little. Which gift is worth more?

A reading from the holy gospel according to Luke
**Glory to you, Lord.**

Jesus looked up and saw rich people
putting their gifts into the treasury;
he also saw a poor widow
put in two small copper coins.
He said, "Truly I tell you,
this poor widow has put in more
than all of them;
for all of them have contributed
out of their abundance,
but she out of her poverty
has put in all she had to live on."

The gospel of the Lord.
**Praise to you, Lord Jesus Christ.**

Let us pray:
Most holy and generous God,
the poor widow gave all she had.
Teach us to be as generous with our gifts
as she was.
We ask this through Christ our Lord.
**Amen.**

Let us pray the prayer that Jesus taught us:
**Our Father...**

During the month of November, add:
Let us pray for all those whose names are
written in our Book of Remembrance:
Eternal rest grant unto them, O Lord,
and let perpetual light shine upon them.
May they rest in peace.
**Amen.**

✠ **In the name of the Father, and of the Son, and of the Holy Spirit. Amen.**

Note: Today's reading is Luke 21:1-4.

## TUESDAY

✠ In the name of the Father, and of the Son, and of the Holy Spirit. Amen.

Introduction: Sunday was the Feast of Christ the King, when we celebrate that Jesus will come again at the end of time. Jesus is the King, the Lord of Lords. Our reading today tells us that God is our king, and all creation is to be glad!

A reading from the book of Psalms

Say among the nations,
"The Lord is king!
The world is firmly established;
it shall never be moved.
He will judge the peoples with equity."
Let the heavens be glad,
and let the earth rejoice;
let the sea roar, and all that fills it;
let the field exult, and everything in it.
Then shall all the trees of the forest
sing for joy
before the Lord; for he is coming,
for he is coming to judge the earth.
He will judge the world with righteousness,
and the peoples with his truth.

The word of the Lord.
**Thanks be to God.**

Let us pray:
God our Creator,
you made the earth and all that is on it.
You made the sea and all that is in it.
May we always praise you,
thank you
and love you with all our hearts.
We ask this through Christ our Lord.
**Amen.**

Let us pray the prayer that Jesus taught us:
**Our Father…**

During the month of November, add:
Let us pray for all those whose names are
written in our Book of Remembrance:
Eternal rest grant unto them, O Lord,
and let perpetual light shine upon them.
May they rest in peace.
**Amen.**

✠ **In the name of the Father, and of the Son, and of the Holy Spirit. Amen.**

---

Note: Today's reading is Psalm 96:10-13.

## WEDNESDAY

✠ In the name of the Father, and of the Son, and of the Holy Spirit. Amen.

Introduction: In our reading today, Jesus warns the apostles that it won't be easy to teach others what he has taught them, and to keep believing in him.

This is the cost of discipleship. It is not always easy to be a follower of Jesus and be obedient to God's ways. Life can be hard for us sometimes, too, because we believe in Jesus.

A reading from the holy gospel according to Luke
**Glory to you, Lord.**

Jesus said,
"They will arrest you and persecute you;
they will hand you over
to synagogues and prisons,
and you will be brought before
kings and governors because of my name.
This will give you an opportunity to testify."

The gospel of the Lord.
**Praise to you, Lord Jesus Christ.**

Let us pray:
God in heaven,
you gave the apostles
the strength to tell the Good News
even though they knew
they would sometimes get into trouble.
Help us to be brave disciples
and to do what is right,
even though it is hard at times.
We ask this through Christ our Lord.
**Amen.**

Let us pray the prayer that Jesus taught us for all those who are persecuted because they believe in Jesus and teach the message of the gospel:
**Our Father...**

During the month of November, add:
Let us pray for all those whose names are written in our Book of Remembrance:
Eternal rest grant unto them, O Lord,
and let perpetual light shine upon them.
May they rest in peace.
**Amen.**

✠ In the name of the Father, and of the Son, and of the Holy Spirit. Amen.

Note: Today's reading is Luke 21:12, 13.

# THIRTY-FOURTH WEEK OF ORDINARY TIME

## THURSDAY

✠ In the name of the Father, and of the Son, and of the Holy Spirit. Amen.

Introduction: In our reading today, the Jewish people were in exile in Babylon, and were forbidden to worship God. Three young men who did not obey the law were thrown into a very hot furnace. Instead of giving in, they sang this hymn of praise to God and the fire did not hurt them.

A reading from the book of Daniel

Bless the Lord, sun and moon;
sing praise to him
and highly exalt him forever.
Bless the Lord, stars of heaven;
sing praise to him
and highly exalt him forever.
Bless the Lord, all rain and dew;
sing praise to him
and highly exalt him forever.
Bless the Lord, all you winds;
sing praise to him
and highly exalt him forever.
Bless the Lord, fire and heat;
sing praise to him
and highly exalt him forever.
Bless the Lord, dews and falling snow;
sing praise to him
and highly exalt him forever.
Bless the Lord, nights and days;
sing praise to him
and highly exalt him forever.

The word of the Lord.
**Thanks be to God.**

Let us pray:
Creator of the universe,
our Lord and king,
you made everything in the world.
Help us take good care of our world
as we praise and thank you forever
for creation.
We ask this through Christ our Lord.
**Amen.**

Let us pray the prayer that Jesus taught us:
**Our Father…**

During the month of November, add:
Let us pray for all those whose names are
written in our Book of Remembrance:
Eternal rest grant unto them, O Lord,
and let perpetual light shine upon them.
May they rest in peace.
**Amen.**

✠ In the name of the Father, and of the Son, and of the Holy Spirit. Amen.

---

Note: Today's reading is Daniel 3:63-67, 69-70.

## FRIDAY

✠ In the name of the Father, and of the Son, and of the Holy Spirit. Amen.

Introduction: In our reading today, Jesus is teaching the apostles about things that are going to happen to him: his suffering, death and resurrection. He tells them a parable and reminds them that no matter what happens, his words – his teachings – will live on forever.

A reading from the holy gospel according to Luke
**Glory to you, Lord.**

Then Jesus told them a parable:
"Look at the fig tree and all the trees;
as soon as they sprout leaves
you can see for yourselves
and know that summer is already near.
So also, when you see these things
taking place,
you know that the kingdom of God is near.
Truly I tell you, this generation
will not pass away
until all things have taken place.
Heaven and earth will pass away,
but my words will not pass away."

The gospel of the Lord.
**Praise to you, Lord Jesus Christ.**

Let us pray:
Most loving and holy God,
Jesus taught us about the kingdom of God
and how the people of the kingdom
should act.
Help us to be faithful members
of your kingdom,
following your laws and ways
and bringing the Good News to others.
We ask this through Christ our Lord.
**Amen.**

Let us pray the prayer that Jesus taught us:
**Our Father…**

During the month of November, add:
Let us pray for all those whose names are
written in our Book of Remembrance:
Eternal rest grant unto them, O Lord,
and let perpetual light shine upon them.
May they rest in peace.
**Amen.**

✠ In the name of the Father, and of the Son, and of the Holy Spirit. Amen.

Note: Today's reading is Luke 21:29-33.

# FIRST WEEK OF ADVENT

## MONDAY

✠ **In the name of the Father, and of the Son, and of the Holy Spirit. Amen.**

Introduction: Happy New Year! Yesterday was the first day of the new Church year. We are now in the liturgical season of Advent. Advent is a time to remember Jesus' coming – not only that he came as a baby, but that he will return at the end of time. No one except God knows when that will be, but we are called to be ready for that coming by following God's laws and ways.

Our gospel today tells the story of Jesus healing the Roman officer's servant. The officer believed that all Jesus had to do was to speak, and his servant would be healed. Jesus says that many who are not Jews will be invited to the feast in the kingdom of heaven.

Do we have the kind of faith that the officer had in the healing power of Jesus?

A reading from the holy gospel according to Matthew
**Glory to you, Lord.**

When Jesus entered Capernaum,
a centurion came to him,
appealing to him and saying,
"Lord, my servant is lying at home
paralyzed, in terrible distress."
And he said to him,
"I will come and cure him."
The centurion answered,
"Lord, I am not worthy
to have you come under my roof;
but only speak the word,
and my servant will be healed.
For I also am a man under authority,
with soldiers under me; and I say to one,
'Go,' and he goes, and to another,
'Come,' and he comes, and to my slave,
'Do this,' and the slave does it."

When Jesus heard him, he was amazed
and said to those who followed him,
"Truly I tell you, in no one in Israel
have I found such faith.
I tell you,
many will come from east and west
and will eat with Abraham and Isaac
and Jacob in the kingdom of heaven."

The gospel of the Lord.
**Praise to you, Lord Jesus Christ.**

Let us pray:
God most merciful,
grant that we may be faithful
to your laws and ways
and grow in holiness
during this season of Advent.
Help us to prepare our hearts well
to celebrate the coming of your beloved
Son, Jesus.
We ask this through Christ our Lord.
**Amen.**

Let us pray the prayer that Jesus taught us:
**Our Father…**

✠ **In the name of the Father, and of the Son, and of the Holy Spirit. Amen.**

Note: Today's reading is Matthew 8:5-11.

## TUESDAY

✠ **In the name of the Father, and of the Son, and of the Holy Spirit. Amen.**

Introduction: The people of Israel had been waiting a long time for the Messiah. The prophet Isaiah describes what kind of person the Messiah will be, and the kinds of things he will do. As followers of Jesus, we are called to follow his example.

Do we act as Jesus did? Are we willing to change our ways to become more like Jesus?

A reading from the book of the prophet Isaiah

A shoot shall come out
from the stump of Jesse,
and a branch shall grow out of his roots.
The spirit of the Lord shall rest on him,
the spirit of wisdom and understanding,
the spirit of counsel and might,
the spirit of knowledge
and the fear of the Lord.
His delight shall be in the fear of the Lord.
He shall not judge by what his eyes see,
or decide by what his ears hear;
but with righteousness
he shall judge the poor,
and decide with equity
for the meek of the earth;
he shall strike the earth
with the rod of his mouth,
and with the breath of his lips
he shall kill the wicked.
Righteousness shall be the belt
around his waist,
and faithfulness the belt around his loins.

The word of the Lord.
**Thanks be to God.**

Let us pray:
Most holy and loving God,
in Advent we prepare
for the coming of Jesus, our Saviour.
Help us to prepare our hearts
so that we may be faithful and holy
followers of Jesus.
We ask this through Christ our Lord.
**Amen.**

Let us pray the prayer that Jesus taught us:
**Our Father…**

✠ **In the name of the Father, and of the Son, and of the Holy Spirit. Amen.**

---

Note: Today's reading is Isaiah 11:1-5.

## WEDNESDAY

✠ **In the name of the Father, and of the Son, and of the Holy Spirit. Amen.**

Introduction: In our reading today, we hear about some of the amazing things that will happen when the Messiah, the promised one of God, comes.

A reading from the book of the prophet Isaiah

On this mountain the Lord of hosts
will make for all peoples
a feast of rich food,
a feast of well-matured wines,
of rich food filled with marrow,
of well-matured wines strained clear.
And he will destroy on this mountain
the shroud that is cast over all peoples,
the sheet that is spread over all nations;
he will swallow up death for ever.
Then the Lord God will wipe away
the tears from all faces,
and the disgrace of his people
he will take away from all the earth,
for the Lord has spoken.
It will be said on that day,
Lo, this is our God;
we have waited for him,
so that he might save us.
This is the Lord for whom we have waited;
let us be glad and rejoice in his salvation.

The word of the Lord.
**Thanks be to God.**

Let us pray:
Most Holy One, our God,
through the prophets you told your people
the wonderful things
you have prepared for us when Jesus comes.
Help us to be joyful people,
lights in the darkness of our world.
We ask this through Christ our Lord.
**Amen.**

Let us pray the prayer that Jesus taught us:
**Our Father…**

✠ **In the name of the Father, and of the Son, and of the Holy Spirit. Amen.**

Note: Today's reading is Isaiah 25:6-9.

## THURSDAY

✠ **In the name of the Father, and of the Son, and of the Holy Spirit. Amen.**

Introduction: In today's reading, we hear who will enter the kingdom of heaven – those who hear the words of Jesus, live them and do God's will.

Jesus tells us that if we hear and obey his words, we are like the wise man who built his house on rock. If we do not hear and obey his words, we are like the man who built his house on sand. What do you think happens to each house?

Have we built our house – our faith – on rock or on sand?

A reading from the holy gospel according to Matthew
**Glory to you, Lord.**

Jesus said,
"Not everyone who says to me, 'Lord, Lord,'
will enter the kingdom of heaven,
but only the one who does the will
of my Father in heaven.
Everyone then who hears
these words of mine and acts on them
will be like a wise man
who built his house on rock.
The rain fell, the floods came,
and the winds blew and beat on that house,
but it did not fall,
because it had been founded on rock.
And everyone who
hears these words of mine
and does not act on them
will be like a foolish man
who built his house on sand.
The rain fell, and the floods came,
and the winds blew
and beat against that house, and it fell –
and great was its fall!"

The gospel of the Lord.
**Praise to you, Lord Jesus Christ.**

Let us pray:
Most loving God,
send your Holy Spirit
to help us hear the words of Jesus,
live them,
and always do your will
so that our faith is built on rock.
We ask this through Christ our Lord.
**Amen.**

Let us pray the prayer that Jesus taught us:
**Our Father...**

✠ **In the name of the Father, and of the Son, and of the Holy Spirit. Amen.**

---

Note: Today's reading is Matthew 7:21, 24-27.

## FRIDAY

✠ In the name of the Father, and of the Son, and of the Holy Spirit. Amen.

Introduction: In today's reading, Jesus cures two blind men.

Sometimes, we are blind, too – not with our eyes, but with our hearts. Our hearts are blind when we refuse to see the good in others, when we do not help people in need, when we hurt others, when we do not listen to them.

How can we open our eyes and our hearts to those around us?

A reading from the holy gospel according to Matthew
**Glory to you, Lord.**

As Jesus went on from there,
two blind men followed him, crying loudly,
"Have mercy on us, Son of David!"
When he entered the house,
the blind men came to him;
and Jesus said to them,
"Do you believe that I am able to do this?"
They said to him, "Yes, Lord."
Then he touched their eyes and said,
"According to your faith
let it be done to you."
And their eyes were opened.
Then Jesus sternly ordered them,
"See that no one knows of this."
But they went away
and spread the news about him
throughout that district.

The gospel of the Lord.
**Praise to you, Lord Jesus Christ.**

Let us pray:
Jesus,
you restored sight to the two blind men,
who believed that you could heal them.
Heal the blindness in our hearts,
so that we may see others
as you see them –
as children of God,
our brothers and sisters.
**Amen.**

Let us pray the prayer that Jesus taught us:
**Our Father…**

✠ In the name of the Father, and of the Son, and of the Holy Spirit. Amen.

Note: Today's reading is Matthew 9:27-31.

## MONDAY

✠ In the name of the Father, and of the Son, and of the Holy Spirit. Amen.

Introduction: In our reading today, we hear about the amazing things that will happen in Israel when the Lord comes to save the people. Even the land will rejoice!

A reading from the book of the prophet Isaiah

The wilderness and the dry land
shall be glad,
the desert shall rejoice and blossom;
like the crocus it shall blossom abundantly,
and rejoice with joy and singing.
The glory of Lebanon shall be given to it,
the majesty of Carmel and Sharon.
They shall see the glory of the Lord,
the majesty of our God.
Then the eyes of the blind shall be opened,
and the ears of the deaf unstopped;
then the lame shall leap like a deer,
and the tongue of the speechless
sing for joy.
For waters shall break forth
 in the wilderness,
and streams in the desert;
the burning sand shall become a pool,
and the thirsty ground springs of water;
the haunt of jackals shall become a swamp,
the grass shall become reeds and rushes.

The word of the Lord.
**Thanks be to God.**

Let us pray:
Most holy God,
at your touch everything is made new again:
healed, transformed and strengthened.
Send your Spirit upon us
to transform the deserts of our hearts
into a blooming field,
waiting to receive you with joy
when you come.
We ask this through Christ our Lord.
**Amen.**

Let us pray the prayer that Jesus taught us:
**Our Father…**

✠ In the name of the Father, and of the Son, and of the Holy Spirit. Amen.

---

Note: Today's reading is Isaiah 35:1-2, 5-7. The full reading for today is Isaiah 35:1-10.

## TUESDAY

✠ **In the name of the Father, and of the Son, and of the Holy Spirit. Amen.**

Introduction: In our reading today, God tells Isaiah to comfort his people. They are living far from home, in exile in Babylon, because they had stopped listening to God and following God's ways. Now God tells them that their time of exile from the land of Israel is ending; God will lead them home.

God gathers all of us tenderly into his arms, and feeds us, just like a shepherd cares for sheep. Do we let God hold us and comfort us when we need care?

A reading from the book of the prophet Isaiah

Comfort, O comfort my people,
says your God.
Speak tenderly to Jerusalem,
and cry to her
that she has served her term,
that her penalty is paid,
that she has received from the Lord's hand
double for all her sins.
Get you up to a high mountain,
O Zion, herald of good tidings;
lift up your voice with strength,
O Jerusalem, herald of good tidings,
lift it up, do not fear;
say to the cities of Judah,
"Here is your God!"
See, the Lord God comes with might,
and his arm rules for him;
his reward is with him,
and his recompense before him.

He will feed his flock like a shepherd;
he will gather the lambs in his arms,
and carry them in his bosom,
and gently lead the mother sheep.

The word of the Lord.
**Thanks be to God.**

Let us pray:
Most holy and loving God,
you carry us and hold us close to your heart.
Help us always to reach out for your help
when we feel alone.
We ask this through Christ our Lord.
**Amen.**

Let us pray the prayer that Jesus taught us:
**Our Father...**

✠ **In the name of the Father, and of the Son, and of the Holy Spirit. Amen.**

---

Note: Today's reading is Isaiah 40:1-2, 9-11.

# SECOND WEEK OF ADVENT

## WEDNESDAY

✠ In the name of the Father, and of the Son, and of the Holy Spirit. Amen.

Introduction: In today's reading, we hear comforting words from Jesus. He tells us that when we are tired, and things are becoming almost too much for us, he is there to help us. He invites us to take up the responsibilities of following him. At the same time, he promises that the task he gives us – following him and doing what God asks – is an easy one, if we trust in him.

A reading from the holy gospel according to Matthew
**Glory to you, Lord.**

Jesus said,
"Come to me, all you that are weary
and are carrying heavy burdens,
and I will give you rest.
Take my yoke upon you,
and learn from me;
for I am gentle and humble in heart,
and you will find rest for your souls.
For my yoke is easy, and my burden is light."

The gospel of the Lord.
**Praise to you, Lord Jesus Christ.**

Let us pray:
Merciful God,
you sent your Son, Jesus,
to help us carry
our worries, our sadness, our hurts.
Help us to accept the responsibilities
of following Jesus,
and to become more like him.
We ask this through Christ our Lord.
**Amen.**

Let us pray the prayer that Jesus taught us for those whose burdens are heavy, those who live without hope:
**Our Father…**

✠ In the name of the Father, and of the Son, and of the Holy Spirit. Amen.

Note: Today's reading is Matthew 11:28-30.

## THURSDAY

✠ **In the name of the Father, and of the Son, and of the Holy Spirit. Amen.**

Introduction: In our reading today, God sends a message of hope to the people of Israel, who were in exile in Babylon. Isaiah tells them to continue to believe and hope in God, for God will set them free. God had not abandoned them! We find courage and hope in these words, too.

A reading from the book of the prophet Isaiah

Do not fear, for I am with you,
do not be afraid, for I am your God;
I will strengthen you, I will help you,
I will uphold you
with my victorious right hand.
Do not fear, you worm Jacob,
you insect Israel!
I will help you, says the Lord;
your Redeemer is the Holy One of Israel.
When the poor and needy seek water,
and there is none,
and their tongue is parched with thirst,
I the Lord will answer them,
I the God of Israel will not forsake them.

The word of the Lord.
**Thanks be to God.**

Let us pray:
Most holy and eternal God,
you promised to be with your people.
Help us, your children,
to be children of light and hope,
knowing that all we will ever need
comes from you,
and that you will never leave us.
We ask this through Christ our Lord.
**Amen.**

Let us pray the prayer that Jesus taught us:
**Our Father...**

✠ **In the name of the Father, and of the Son, and of the Holy Spirit. Amen.**

Note: Today's reading is Isaiah 41:10, 14, 17. The full reading for today is Isaiah 41:10, 14-20.

## FRIDAY

✠ In the name of the Father, and of the Son, and of the Holy Spirit. Amen.

Introduction: In our reading today, God says that he is the One who teaches us the way we are to live. He reminds the people of Israel that they are in trouble at this time because they did not listen to him. It is a warning and a reminder for us, too; when we do what is right and follow God's ways, we will have peace in our hearts and we will be at one with God.

A reading from the book of the prophet Isaiah

Thus says the Lord,
your Redeemer, the Holy One of Israel:
I am the Lord your God,
who teaches you for your own good,
who leads you in the way you should go.
O that you had paid attention
to my commandments!
Then your prosperity
would have been like a river,
and your success like the waves of the sea;
your offspring would have been
like the sand,
and your descendants like its grains;
their name would never be cut off
or destroyed from before me.

The word of the Lord.
**Thanks be to God.**

Let us pray:
Most loving and faithful God,
teach us what we need to know
and direct us in the ways we should go.
Help us to be open to you
and to let your Holy Spirit work within us,
so that we may be blessed
like a stream that never goes dry.
We ask this through Christ our Lord.
**Amen.**

Let us pray the prayer that Jesus taught us:
**Our Father…**

✠ In the name of the Father, and of the Son, and of the Holy Spirit. Amen.

Note: Today's reading is Isaiah 48:17-19.

## MONDAY

✠ **In the name of the Father, and of the Son, and of the Holy Spirit. Amen.**

Introduction: Our reading today is from the book of Psalms, which is really a book of songs to God. This psalm of petition asks God to teach us his ways.

A reading from the book of Psalms

Make me to know your ways, O Lord;
teach me your paths.
Lead me in your truth, and teach me,
for you are the God of my salvation;
for you I wait all day long.
Be mindful of your mercy, O Lord,
and of your steadfast love,
for they have been from of old.
According to your steadfast love
remember me,
for your goodness' sake, O Lord!
Good and upright is the Lord;
therefore he instructs sinners in the way.
He leads the humble in what is right,
and teaches the humble his way.

The word of the Lord.
**Thanks be to God.**

Let us pray:
Ever-loving and merciful God,
you teach us your ways and truths,
the path that leads to eternal life.
Help us to follow your guidance
more and more each day
as we prepare to celebrate
the coming of your Son, Jesus.
We ask this through Christ our Lord.
**Amen.**

Let us pray the prayer that Jesus taught us:
**Our Father...**

✠ **In the name of the Father, and of the Son, and of the Holy Spirit. Amen.**

Note: Today's reading is Psalm 25:4-6, 7b-9.

## TUESDAY

✠ In the name of the Father, and of the Son, and of the Holy Spirit. Amen.

Introduction: In today's gospel story, we hear about two sons. One did not want to do what his father asked, but thought about it and decided to do it. The other son said he would, but didn't do what his father asked. Jesus tells his listeners that those who seem to be sinners are not always so. He was speaking to the elders and chief priests at the time, who did not listen to the words of John the Baptist, even though sinners did.

A reading from the holy gospel according to Matthew
**Glory to you, Lord.**

Jesus said to the chief priests
and elders of the people:
"What do you think?
A man had two sons;
he went to the first and said,
'Son, go and work in the vineyard today.'
He answered, 'I will not';
but later he changed his mind and went.
The father went to the second
and said the same; and he answered,
'I go, sir'; but he did not go.
Which of the two did the will of his father?"
They said, "The first."
Jesus said to them, "Truly I tell you,
the tax collectors and the prostitutes
are going into the kingdom of God
ahead of you.
For John came to you
in the way of righteousness
and you did not believe him,
but the tax collectors and the prostitutes
believed him;
and even after you saw it,
you did not change your minds
and believe him."

The gospel of the Lord.
**Praise to you, Lord Jesus Christ.**

Let us pray:
Most merciful God,
in your great love for us
you sent John the Baptist
to prepare the way for Jesus.
Help us always to listen to you
and do what you ask of us right away,
as John the Baptist and Mary did.
We ask this through Christ our Lord.
**Amen.**

Let us pray the prayer that Jesus taught us:
**Our Father…**

✠ In the name of the Father, and of the Son, and of the Holy Spirit. Amen.

Note: Today's reading is Matthew 21:28-32.

## WEDNESDAY

✠ **In the name of the Father, and of the Son, and of the Holy Spirit. Amen.**

Introduction: John the Baptist sent two of his disciples to ask Jesus if he was the one who was to come. Jesus did not say yes or no; instead, he told them to tell John what they had seen and heard. What they had heard and seen was exactly what the promised one, the Messiah, would do.

A reading from the holy gospel according to Luke
**Glory to you, Lord.**

The disciples of John
reported all these things to him.
So John summoned two of his disciples
and sent them to the Lord to ask,
"Are you the one who is to come,
or are we to wait for another?"
When the men had come to him, they said,
"John the Baptist has sent us to you to ask,
'Are you the one who is to come,
or are we to wait for another?'"
Jesus had just then cured many people
of diseases, plagues, and evil spirits,
and had given sight
to many who were blind.
And he answered them, "Go and tell John
what you have seen and heard:
the blind receive their sight,
the lame walk, the lepers are cleansed,
the deaf hear, the dead are raised,
the poor have good news brought to them.
And blessed is anyone
who takes no offence at me."

The gospel of the Lord.
**Praise to you, Lord Jesus Christ.**

Let us pray:
Most holy and loving God,
your Son, Jesus, went about healing
and preaching the Good News.
Help us to hear the Good News
deep in our hearts
and share it with others.
We ask this through Christ our Lord.
**Amen.**

Let us pray the prayer that Jesus taught us:
**Our Father…**

✠ **In the name of the Father, and of the Son, and of the Holy Spirit. Amen.**

Note: Today's reading is Luke 7:18-23.

## THURSDAY

✠ In the name of the Father, and of the Son, and of the Holy Spirit. Amen.

Introduction: In today's reading, Jesus tells the crowds that his cousin, John the Baptist, was sent to prepare the way for Jesus.

As children of God, we are God's messengers on earth.

How are we preparing God's way? Do we listen for what God wants us to do, and then do it?

A reading from the holy gospel according to Luke
**Glory to you, Lord.**

When John's messengers had gone,
Jesus began to speak to the crowds
about John:
"What did you go out into the wilderness
to look at? A reed shaken by the wind?
What then did you go out to see?
Someone dressed in soft robes?
Look, those who put on fine clothing
and live in luxury are in royal palaces.
What then did you go out to see?
A prophet?
Yes, I tell you, and more than a prophet.
This is the one about whom it is written,
'See, I am sending my messenger
ahead of you,
who will prepare your way before you.'
I tell you, among those born of women
no one is greater than John;
yet the least in the kingdom of God
is greater than he."

The gospel of the Lord.
**Praise to you, Lord Jesus Christ.**

Let us pray:
Most holy and loving God,
help us to prepare your way on earth
by obeying your laws
and following your ways,
as Jesus has taught us.
Help us to open our hearts and
prepare them well
to celebrate his coming at Christmas.
We ask this through Christ our Lord.
**Amen.**

Let us pray the prayer that Jesus taught us:
**Our Father...**

✠ In the name of the Father, and of the Son, and of the Holy Spirit. Amen.

Note: Today's reading is Luke 7:24-28.

## FRIDAY

✠ **In the name of the Father, and of the Son, and of the Holy Spirit. Amen.**

Introduction: Today's reading also talks about John the Baptist. This time Jesus compares John to a lamp, burning and shining, but tells the people that the light of his own witness is greater than John's.

What kind of witness do our actions and words provide? Do they show that we are indeed a child of God and a follower of Jesus? Do our words and actions speak of God's love?

A reading from the holy gospel according to John
**Glory to you, Lord.**

Jesus said to the people:
"You sent messengers to John,
and he testified to the truth.
Not that I accept such human testimony,
but I say these things
so that you may be saved.
He was a burning and shining lamp,
and you were willing to rejoice for a while
in his light.
But I have a testimony greater than John's.
The works that the Father has given me
to complete, the very works that I am doing,
testify on my behalf
that the Father has sent me."

The gospel of the Lord.
**Praise to you, Lord Jesus Christ.**

Let us pray:
Loving God,
John the Baptist was a shining lamp
lighting the way for Jesus.
Help us to be like John,
so that our actions may always lead to you
and reflect your love to all we meet.
We ask this through Christ our Lord.
**Amen.**

Let us pray the prayer that Jesus taught us:
**Our Father...**

✠ **In the name of the Father, and of the Son, and of the Holy Spirit. Amen.**

---

Note: Today's reading is John 5:33-36.

✠ **In the name of the Father, and of the Son, and of the Holy Spirit. Amen.**

Introduction: In the liturgy of the Church, today marks the first day of intense preparation for the coming of Jesus. Today's reading tells us that the symbol of power – the sceptre – will not leave the possession of the people of Judah until it is given to the one to whom it belongs.

A reading from the book of Genesis

Then Jacob called his sons, and said:
"Assemble and hear, O sons of Jacob;
listen to Israel your father.
Judah, your brothers shall praise you;
your hand shall be
on the neck of your enemies;
your father's sons shall bow down
before you.
Judah is a lion's whelp;
from the prey, my son, you have gone up.
He crouches down,
he stretches out like a lion,
like a lioness – who dares rouse him up?
The sceptre shall not depart from Judah,
nor the ruler's staff from between his feet,
until tribute comes to him;
and the obedience of the peoples is his."

The word of the Lord.
**Thanks be to God.**

Let us pray the first of the O Antiphons,*
which the whole Church prays today:
O wisdom,
O holy Word of God,
you govern all creation
with your strong yet tender care.
Come and show your people
the way to salvation.
**Amen.**

Let us pray the prayer that Jesus taught us:
**Our Father...**

✠ **In the name of the Father, and of the Son, and of the Holy Spirit. Amen.**

---

Note: Today's reading is Genesis 49:1a, 2, 8-10.

\* The O Antiphons are taken from the Liturgy of the Hours, and are the antiphons from December 17 to 23 for the Gospel Canticle of Evening Prayer, which is the Magnificat. In abbreviated form, they are also the gospel acclamations for the same days. Each of these antiphons begin with "O," hence the name "O Antiphons." These beautiful prayers sum up the longing the people of God had for the coming of the Messiah. Each one begins with a title from the Old Testament that refers to the Messiah.

✠ **In the name of the Father, and of the Son, and of the Holy Spirit. Amen.**

Introduction: In our reading today, God talks about choosing a king, a descendant of King David, who will be called "The Lord is our righteousness." Although this biblical reading was written long before Jesus lived on earth, it is describing him!

Jesus is sometimes called "Son of David" to show that he descended from this great king.

A reading from the book of the prophet Jeremiah

The days are surely coming, says the Lord,
when I will raise up for David
a righteous Branch,
and he shall reign as king and deal wisely,
and shall execute justice and righteousness
in the land.
In his days Judah will be saved
and Israel will live in safety.
And this is the name
by which he will be called:
"The Lord is our righteousness."

The word of the Lord.
**Thanks be to God.**

Let us pray the prayer the whole Church*
prays today:
O sacred Lord of ancient Israel,
who showed yourself to Moses
in the burning bush,
who gave him the holy law
on Sinai mountain:
come, stretch out your mighty hand
to set us free.
**Amen.**

Let us pray the prayer that Jesus taught us:
**Our Father…**

✠ **In the name of the Father, and of the Son, and of the Holy Spirit. Amen.**

Note: Today's reading is Jeremiah 23:5-6.

* See note on December 17.

✠ **In the name of the Father, and of the Son, and of the Holy Spirit. Amen.**

Introduction: Today we hear the story of the angel who appeared to Zechariah, telling him that his wife Elizabeth, who had no children and was getting on in age, would soon have a son. This son, to be named John, became known as John the Baptist.

As we discover in this reading, nothing is impossible with God!

A reading from the holy gospel according to Luke
**Glory to you, Lord.**

In the days of King Herod of Judea,
there was a priest named Zechariah,
who belonged to the priestly order of
Abijah.
His wife was a descendant of Aaron,
and her name was Elizabeth.
Both of them were righteous before God,
living blamelessly according to all the
commandments and regulations of the Lord.
But they had no children,
because Elizabeth was barren,
and both were getting on in years.
Once when he was serving as priest
before God, then there appeared to him
an angel of the Lord.
When Zechariah saw him, he was terrified;
and fear overwhelmed him.
But the angel said to him,
"Do not be afraid, Zechariah,
for your prayer has been heard.
Your wife Elizabeth will bear you a son,
and you will name him John.
You will have joy and gladness,
and many will rejoice at his birth,
for he will be great in the sight of the Lord.

He must never drink wine or strong drink;
even before his birth
he will be filled with the Holy Spirit.
He will turn many of the people of Israel
to the Lord their God.
With the spirit and power of Elijah
he will go before him."

The gospel of the Lord.
**Praise to you, Lord Jesus Christ.**

Let us pray the prayer the whole Church*
prays today:
O Flower of Jesse's stem,
you have been raised up as a sign
for all peoples;
kings stand silent in your presence;
the nations bow down in worship
before you.
Come, let nothing keep you
from coming to our aid.
**Amen.**

Let us pray the prayer that Jesus taught us:
**Our Father...**

✠ **In the name of the Father, and of the Son, and of the Holy Spirit. Amen.**

Note: Today's reading is Luke 1:5-7, 8a, 11a, 12-17a.

* See note on December 17.

✠ **In the name of the Father, and of the Son, and of the Holy Spirit. Amen.**

Introduction: In our reading today, God sends the prophet Isaiah to King Ahaz, who is to ask God for a sign. The king refuses to obey God's message. So God tells Ahaz the sign, which will reveal who is to be the redeemer of Israel. Listen carefully to hear what this sign is, for it is what we are waiting for during Advent.

A reading from the book of the prophet Isaiah

Again the Lord spoke to Ahaz, saying,
Ask a sign of the Lord your God;
let it be deep as Sheol or high as heaven.
But Ahaz said, I will not ask,
and I will not put the Lord to the test.
Then Isaiah said:
"Hear then, O house of David!
Is it too little for you to weary mortals,
that you weary my God also?
Therefore the Lord himself
will give you a sign.
Look, the young woman is with child
and shall bear a son,
and shall name him Immanuel."

The word of the Lord.
**Thanks be to God.**

Let us pray the prayer the whole Church*
prays today:
O Key of David,
O royal power of Israel
controlling at your will the gate of heaven:
come, break down the prison walls of death
for those who dwell in darkness
and the shadow of death;
and lead your captive people into freedom.
**Amen.**

Let us pray the prayer that Jesus taught us:
**Our Father…**

✠ **In the name of the Father, and of the Son, and of the Holy Spirit. Amen.**

---

Note: Today's reading is Isaiah 7:10-14.

* See note on December 17.

✠ **In the name of the Father, and of the Son, and of the Holy Spirit. Amen.**

Introduction: In our reading today, we hear the story of the Visitation of Mary to her cousin Elizabeth, who was also going to have a baby. Her baby would grow up to be John the Baptist. Elizabeth greets Mary with the words that later became part of the "Hail Mary" prayer.

A reading from the holy gospel according to Luke
**Glory to you, Lord.**

In those days Mary set out
and went with haste to a Judean town
in the hill country,
where she entered the house of Zechariah
and greeted Elizabeth.
When Elizabeth heard Mary's greeting,
the child leaped in her womb.
And Elizabeth was filled with
the Holy Spirit
and exclaimed with a loud cry,
"Blessed are you among women,
and blessed is the fruit of your womb.
And why has this happened to me,
that the mother of my Lord comes to me?
For as soon as I heard the sound
of your greeting,
the child in my womb leaped for joy.
And blessed is she who believed
that there would be a fulfillment
of what was spoken to her by the Lord."

The gospel of the Lord.
**Praise to you, Lord Jesus Christ.**

Let us pray the prayer the whole Church*
prays today:
O radiant dawn,
splendour of eternal light,
sun of justice:
come,
shine on those who dwell in darkness
and the shadow of death.
**Amen.**

In honour of the Visitation, we pray:
**Hail Mary...**

✠ **In the name of the Father, and of the Son, and of the Holy Spirit. Amen.**

Note: Today's reading is Luke 1:39-45.

* See note on December 17.

✠ In the name of the Father, and of the Son, and of the Holy Spirit. Amen.

Introduction: Today's reading is Mary's song of praise, known as the Magnificat. In this beautiful hymn, Mary praises God for all the wonderful things he has done for her and for her people. Listen carefully to Mary's words, and pray them along with her.

A reading from the holy gospel according to Luke
**Glory to you, Lord.**

Mary said, "My soul magnifies the Lord,
and my spirit rejoices in God my Saviour,
for he has looked with favour
on the lowliness of his servant.
Surely, from now on all generations
will call me blessed; for the Mighty One
has done great things for me,
and holy is his name.
His mercy is for those who fear him
from generation to generation.
He has shown strength with his arm;
he has scattered the proud
in the thoughts of their hearts.
He has brought down the powerful
from their thrones, and lifted up the lowly;
he has filled the hungry with good things,
and sent the rich away empty.
He has helped his servant Israel,
in remembrance of his mercy,
according to the promise he made
to our ancestors,
to Abraham and to his descendants forever."
And Mary remained with Elizabeth
about three months
and then returned to her home.

The gospel of the Lord.
**Praise to you, Lord Jesus Christ.**

Let us pray the prayer the whole Church*
prays today:
O king of all the nations,
the only joy of every human heart;
O Keystone of the mighty arch of man,
come and save the creature
you have fashioned from the dust.
**Amen.**

In honour of Mary, we pray:
**Hail Mary...**

✠ In the name of the Father, and of the Son, and of the Holy Spirit. Amen.

---

Note: Today's reading is Luke 1:46-56.

* See note on December 17.

✠ **In the name of the Father, and of the Son, and of the Holy Spirit. Amen.**

Introduction: Our reading today is about the birth of John the Baptist. John's father, Zechariah, had not been able to speak from the time the angel told him that his wife would have a baby, and that the baby was to be called John. He did not believe the angel's message. After the baby was born and Zechariah insisted he be called John, his speech returned.

Do we believe in the messages that God gives us, and the messengers God sends us?

A reading from the holy gospel according to Luke
**Glory to you, Lord.**

Now the time came for Elizabeth
to give birth,
and she bore a son.
Her neighbours and relatives heard
that the Lord had shown his great mercy
to her, and they rejoiced with her.
On the eighth day
they came to circumcise the child,
and they were going to name him Zechariah
after his father.
But his mother said, "No;
he is to be called John."
They said to her,
"None of your relatives has this name."
Then they began motioning to his father
to find out what name
he wanted to give him.
He asked for a writing tablet and wrote,
"His name is John."
And all of them were amazed.
Immediately his mouth was opened
and his tongue freed,
and he began to speak, praising God.
Fear came over all their neighbours,
and all these things were talked about
throughout the entire hill country of Judea.

All who heard them pondered them and
said, "What then will this child become?"
For, indeed, the hand of the Lord
was with him.

The gospel of the Lord.
**Praise to you, Lord Jesus Christ.**

Let us pray the prayer the whole Church*
prays today:
O Emmanuel,
king and lawgiver,
desire of the nations,
Saviour of all people,
come and set us free,
Lord our God.
**Amen.**

Let us pray the prayer that Jesus taught us:
**Our Father…**

✠ **In the name of the Father, and of the Son, and of the Holy Spirit. Amen.**

---

Note: Today's reading is Luke 1:57-66.

* See note on December 17.

# MONDAY AFTER EPIPHANY*

✠ **In the name of the Father, and of the Son, and of the Holy Spirit. Amen.**

Introduction: Yesterday we celebrated the feast of the Epiphany, when the Magi visited Jesus and brought him gifts. The Christmas season does not end until the feast of the Baptism of our Lord, which we will celebrate this coming Sunday.

In the gospel readings of this week, we see the beginnings of Jesus' mission – preaching the Good News and healing the sick.

A reading from the holy gospel according to Matthew
**Glory to you, Lord.**

Now when Jesus heard
that John had been arrested,
he withdrew to Galilee.
He left Nazareth
and made his home in Capernaum
by the sea,
in the territory of Zebulun and Naphtali.
From that time Jesus began to proclaim,
"Repent, for the kingdom of heaven
has come near."
Jesus went throughout Galilee,
teaching in their synagogues
and proclaiming the good news
of the kingdom
and curing every disease and every sickness
among the people.

The gospel of the Lord.
**Praise to you, Lord Jesus Christ.**

Let us pray:
Most holy and gracious God,
in your deep and unending love for us
you sent your beloved Son, Jesus,
to preach the Good News.
Grant that we may open our hearts
to hear what Jesus has to say,
and put it into practice every day.
We ask this through Christ our Lord.
**Amen.**

Let us pray the prayer that Jesus taught us:
**Our Father…**

✠ **In the name of the Father, and of the Son, and of the Holy Spirit. Amen.**

---

Note: Today's reading is Matthew 4:12-13, 17, 23.

*Check Appendix 4: In 2006, for example, the Monday after Epiphany is celebrated as the Feast of the Baptism of the Lord (January 9).

# TUESDAY AFTER EPIPHANY

✠ In the name of the Father, and of the Son, and of the Holy Spirit. Amen.

Introduction: In our reading today, we hear that love comes from God, and love is the mark of a child of God. God is love!

A reading from the first letter of John

Beloved, let us love one another,
because love is from God;
everyone who loves
is born of God and knows God.
Whoever does not love does not know God,
for God is love.
God's love was revealed among us
in this way:
God sent his only Son into the world
so that we might live through him.
In this is love,
not that we loved God but that he loved us
and sent his Son
to be the atoning sacrifice for our sins.

The word of the Lord.
**Thanks be to God.**

Let us pray:
Loving God,
you are the source of all love,
and your love marks us
as your sons and daughters.
Help us to be loving and kind to everyone,
especially when this is hard to do.
We ask this through Christ our Lord.
**Amen.**

Let us pray the prayer that Jesus taught us:
**Our Father…**

✠ In the name of the Father, and of the Son, and of the Holy Spirit. Amen.

Note: Today's reading is 1 John 4:7-10.

# WEDNESDAY AFTER EPIPHANY

✠ **In the name of the Father, and of the Son, and of the Holy Spirit. Amen.**

Introduction: In today's reading, St. John tells us why we should love one another: because God loves us so much! Through our faith in Jesus, we live in God's love.

A reading from the first letter of John

Beloved, since God loved us so much,
we also ought to love one another.
No one has ever seen God;
if we love one another, God lives in us,
and his love is perfected in us.
By this we know that we abide in him
and he in us,
because he has given us of his Spirit.
God abides in those who confess
that Jesus is the Son of God,
and they abide in God.
So we have known and believe
the love that God has for us.
God is love, and those who abide in love
abide in God, and God abides in them.
There is no fear in love,
but perfect love casts out fear.

The word of the Lord.
**Thanks be to God.**

Let us pray:
Dear God,
we know that you are love,
and that love unites us to you.
Through the gift of your Holy Spirit,
help us to grow in love
and in imitation of your Son, Jesus.
We ask this through Christ our Lord.
**Amen.**

Let us pray the prayer that Jesus taught us:
**Our Father…**

✠ **In the name of the Father, and of the Son, and of the Holy Spirit. Amen.**

---

Note: Today's reading is 1 John 4:11-13, 15-16, 18a.

✠ **In the name of the Father, and of the Son, and of the Holy Spirit. Amen.**

Introduction: In our reading today, St. John tells us that we cannot say we love God unless we also love one another. We show our love for God by following God's ways.

How do we show our love for others?

A reading from the first letter of John

We love because he first loved us.
Those who say, "I love God,"
and hate their brothers or sisters, are liars;
for those who do not love a brother or sister
whom they have seen,
cannot love God whom they have not seen.
The commandment we have from him
is this: those who love God
must love their brothers and sisters also.
Everyone who believes
that Jesus is the Christ
has been born of God,
and everyone who loves the parent
loves the child.
By this we know
that we love the children of God,
when we love God
and obey his commandments.
For the love of God is this,
that we obey his commandments.
And his commandments
are not burdensome.

The word of the Lord.
**Thanks be to God.**

Let us pray:
Most holy God,
you love us
with a deep and everlasting love.
Help us to show our love for you
by following your ways,
because they lead to holiness and goodness.
Help us to love one another,
and show kindness and respect to everyone.
We ask this through Christ our Lord.
**Amen.**

Let us pray the prayer that Jesus taught us:
**Our Father…**

✠ **In the name of the Father, and of the Son, and of the Holy Spirit. Amen.**

Note: Today's reading is 1 John 4:19–5:3.

✠ **In the name of the Father, and of the Son, and of the Holy Spirit. Amen.**

Introduction: In today's reading Jesus heals a person who has leprosy. Notice what Jesus does after he teaches and heals – he goes to a quiet place and prays. Through prayer he receives strength and listens to what God asks him to do. Here Jesus teaches us by example; we, too, are to pray – for strength, for the ability to know God's will, and for others.

Do we take time to pray each day? Do we do what God wants of us?

A reading from the holy gospel according to Luke
**Glory to you, Lord.**

Once, when Jesus was in one of the cities,
there was a man covered with leprosy.
When he saw Jesus,
he bowed with his face to the ground
and begged him, "Lord, if you choose,
you can make me clean."
Then Jesus stretched out his hand,
touched him, and said,
"I do choose. Be made clean."
Immediately the leprosy left him.
And he ordered him to tell no one.
"Go," he said,
"and show yourself to the priest,
and, as Moses commanded,
make an offering for your cleansing,
for a testimony to them."
But now more than ever
the word about Jesus spread abroad;
many crowds would gather to hear him
and to be cured of their diseases.
But he would withdraw to deserted places
and pray.

The gospel of the Lord.
**Praise to you, Lord Jesus Christ.**

Let us pray:
Father in heaven,
your beloved Son, Jesus,
spent time in prayer,
deepening and strengthening
his bond with you.
Grant that we may be children of prayer,
spending time with you,
getting to know you better,
and allowing our love for you to grow.
We ask this through Christ our Lord.
**Amen.**

Let us pray the prayer that Jesus taught us:
**Our Father...**

✠ **In the name of the Father, and of the Son, and of the Holy Spirit. Amen.**

Note: Today's reading is Luke 5:12-16.

## MONDAY

✠ **In the name of the Father, and of the Son, and of the Holy Spirit. Amen.**

Introduction: Today is the first day of Ordinary Time. Ordinary Time begins after the Feast of the Baptism of Our Lord, which the Church celebrated yesterday.

Jesus begins his work after his cousin, John the Baptist, is arrested by King Herod. Today we hear about the calling of the first disciples.

A reading from the holy gospel according to Mark
**Glory to you, Lord.**

Now after John was arrested,
Jesus came to Galilee,
proclaiming the good news of God,
and saying, "The time is fulfilled,
and the kingdom of God has come near;
repent, and believe in the good news."
As Jesus passed along the Sea of Galilee,
he saw Simon and his brother Andrew
casting a net into the sea —
for they were fishermen.
And Jesus said to them,
"Follow me and I will make you
fish for people."
And immediately they left their nets
and followed him.
As he went a little farther,
he saw James son of Zebedee
and his brother John,
who were in their boat mending the nets.
Immediately he called them;
and they left their father Zebedee
in the boat with the hired men,
and followed him.

The gospel of the Lord.
**Praise to you, Lord Jesus Christ.**

Let us pray:
Jesus,
when you called
Simon, Andrew, James and John,
they immediately left everything they had
and followed you.
Grant that we may always choose
to follow you, too.
**Amen.**

Let us pray the prayer that Jesus taught us:
**Our Father...**

✠ **In the name of the Father, and of the Son, and of the Holy Spirit. Amen.**

Note: Today's reading is Mark 1:14-20.

*Check Appendix 4 for where this week falls in a particular calendar year.

## TUESDAY

✠ **In the name of the Father, and of the Son, and of the Holy Spirit. Amen.**

Introduction: In our reading today, Jesus visits the town of Capernaum, where he goes to the synagogue and begins to teach the people. Jesus does something surprising there. The people are amazed, and start to spread the word about him.

How do we spread the word about the amazing things Jesus has done for us?

A reading from the holy gospel according to Mark
**Glory to you, Lord.**

Jesus and his disciples went to Capernaum;
and when the sabbath came,
he entered the synagogue and taught.
They were astounded at his teaching,
for he taught them as one having authority,
and not as the scribes.
Just then there was in their synagogue
a man with an unclean spirit,
and he cried out,
"What have you to do with us,
Jesus of Nazareth?
Have you come to destroy us?
I know who you are, the Holy One of God."
But Jesus rebuked him, saying,
"Be silent, and come out of him!"
And the unclean spirit, convulsing him and
crying with a loud voice,
came out of him.

They were all amazed,
and they kept on asking one another,
"What is this?
A new teaching – with authority!
He commands even the unclean spirits,
and they obey him."
At once his fame began to spread
throughout the surrounding region
of Galilee.

The gospel of the Lord.
**Praise to you, Lord Jesus Christ.**

Let us pray:
Most loving God,
your Son, Jesus,
amazed the people of Capernaum
by teaching with authority,
an authority that came from you.
Help us to listen carefully, with open hearts,
to all Jesus has to say to us,
and to spread the Good News
to those we meet.
We ask this through Christ our Lord.
**Amen.**

Let us pray the prayer that Jesus taught us:
**Our Father…**

✠ **In the name of the Father, and of the Son, and of the Holy Spirit. Amen.**

---

Note: Today's reading is Mark 1:21-28.

## WEDNESDAY

✠ **In the name of the Father, and of the Son, and of the Holy Spirit. Amen.**

Introduction: In today's reading, we hear the story of the call of Samuel. Samuel was young, and he needed the advice of someone more experienced in God's ways to know who was calling him. Sometimes, like Samuel, we need the help and advice of those who are more experienced than us. And sometimes, as in Samuel's case, it takes a few times before we get the message straight.

A reading from the book of Samuel

Now the boy Samuel was ministering
to the Lord under Eli.
The word of the Lord
was rare in those days;
visions were not widespread.
At that time Eli,
whose eyesight had begun to grow dim
so that he could not see,
was lying down in his room;
the lamp of God had not yet gone out,
and Samuel was lying down
in the temple of the Lord,
where the ark of God was.
Then the Lord called, "Samuel! Samuel!"
and he said, "Here I am!" and ran to Eli,
and said, "Here I am, for you called me."
But he said, "I did not call; lie down again."
So he went and lay down.
The Lord called again, "Samuel!"
Samuel got up and went to Eli,
and said, "Here I am, for you called me."
But he said,
"I did not call, my son; lie down again."
Now Samuel did not yet know the Lord,
and the word of the Lord
had not yet been revealed to him.
The Lord called Samuel again,
a third time.
And he got up and went to Eli, and said,
"Here I am, for you called me."
Then Eli perceived that the Lord
was calling the boy.
Therefore Eli said to Samuel,
"Go, lie down; and if he calls you,
you shall say, 'Speak, Lord,
for your servant is listening.'"
So Samuel went and lay down in his place.
Now the Lord came and stood there,
calling as before, "Samuel! Samuel!"
And Samuel said,
"Speak, for your servant is listening."
As Samuel grew up, the Lord was with him
and let none of his words fall to the ground.
And all Israel from Dan to Beer-sheba
knew that Samuel was a trustworthy
prophet of the Lord.

The word of the Lord.
**Thanks be to God.**

Let us pray:
God in heaven,
Samuel listened to your call
and was faithful to you.
Help us to listen for your voice,
recognize your call,
and be ready to do what you ask.
We ask this through Christ our Lord.
**Amen.**

Let us pray the prayer that Jesus taught us:
**Our Father…**

✠ **In the name of the Father, and of the Son, and of the Holy Spirit. Amen.**

Note: Today's reading is 1 Samuel 3:1-10, 19-20.

## THURSDAY

✠ **In the name of the Father, and of the Son, and of the Holy Spirit. Amen.**

Introduction: In our reading today, Jesus heals a man who has leprosy, a very contagious disease. Lepers were not only sick – they had to leave their families and friends and live far away from healthy people to keep the disease from spreading. They were poor and lonely.

For Jesus to heal someone with leprosy was big news: once he was healed, the man could return home to his family and rejoin the community.

The man was so happy, he told everyone he met what Jesus had done!

A reading from the holy gospel according to Mark
**Glory to you, Lord.**

A leper came to Jesus begging him,
and kneeling he said to him,
"If you choose, you can make me clean."
Moved with pity,
Jesus stretched out his hand
and touched him,
and said to him,
"I do choose. Be made clean!"
Immediately the leprosy left him, and he
was made clean.
After sternly warning him
he sent him away at once, saying to him,
"See that you say nothing to anyone;
but go, show yourself to the priest,
and offer for your cleansing
what Moses commanded,
as a testimony to them."

But he went out
and began to proclaim it freely,
and to spread the word,
so that Jesus could no longer
go into a town openly,
but stayed out in the country;
and people came to him from every quarter.

The gospel of the Lord.
**Praise to you, Lord Jesus Christ.**

Let us pray:
All-powerful God,
the man who was healed
was so excited
he told everyone what had happened,
even though Jesus told him not to.
Send us your Holy Spirit
to guide us and heal us, too.
We ask this through Christ our Lord.
**Amen.**

Let us pray the prayer that Jesus taught us:
**Our Father…**

✠ **In the name of the Father, and of the Son, and of the Holy Spirit. Amen.**

---

Note: Today's reading is Mark 1:40-45.

## FRIDAY

✠ **In the name of the Father, and of the Son, and of the Holy Spirit. Amen.**

Introduction: In our reading today, Jesus heals a man who is paralyzed, who cannot move. The man and his friends find a creative way to approach Jesus: they have faith that Jesus can heal people.

Do we have faith like that of the paralyzed man and his friends, who believed so strongly in Jesus that they overcame all obstacles to reach Jesus, knowing that Jesus could help them?

A reading from the holy gospel according to Mark
**Glory to you, Lord.**

When Jesus returned to Capernaum
after some days,
it was reported that he was at home.
So many gathered around
that there was no longer room for them,
not even in front of the door;
and he was speaking the word to them.
Then some people came,
bringing to him a paralyzed man,
carried by four of them.
And when they could not bring him to Jesus
because of the crowd,
they removed the roof above him;
and after having dug through it,
they let down the mat
on which the paralytic lay.
When Jesus saw their faith,
he said to the paralytic,
"Son, your sins are forgiven."
Now some of the scribes were sitting there,
questioning in their hearts,
"Why does this fellow speak in this way?
It is blasphemy!
Who can forgive sins but God alone?"

At once Jesus perceived in his spirit
that they were discussing these questions
among themselves; and he said to them,
"Why do you raise such questions
in your hearts?
Which is easier, to say to the paralytic,
'Your sins are forgiven,' or to say,
'Stand up and take your mat and walk'?
But so that you may know
that the Son of Man
has authority on earth to forgive sins" –
he said to the paralytic –
"I say to you, stand up,
take your mat and go to your home."
And he stood up,
and immediately took the mat
and went out before all of them.

The gospel of the Lord.
**Praise to you, Lord Jesus Christ.**

Let us pray:
Most loving God,
the paralyzed man and his friends
believed so strongly in Jesus
that they went to great lengths
to get to him.
Help us remember that all we need to do
is ask for your help, and it will be given.
We ask this through Christ our Lord.
**Amen.**

Let us pray the prayer that Jesus taught us:
**Our Father…**

✠ **In the name of the Father, and of the Son, and of the Holy Spirit. Amen.**

Note: Today's reading is Mark 2:1-12.

# SECOND WEEK OF ORDINARY TIME

## MONDAY

✠ In the name of the Father, and of the Son, and of the Holy Spirit. Amen.

Introduction: In our reading today, some people ask Jesus why his disciples are not fasting (going without food), when the followers of John the Baptist and the Pharisees are fasting. Jesus compares himself to a bridegroom and God's covenant with us to a marriage. The prophets who lived long before Jesus saw God's covenant in the same way. Who fasts at a wedding party? No one – it is not the right place or time to do so. A wedding is time for feasting and celebrating!

A reading from the holy gospel according to Mark
**Glory to you, Lord.**

Now John's disciples and the Pharisees
were fasting;
and people came and said to Jesus,
"Why do John's disciples
and the disciples of the Pharisees fast,
but your disciples do not fast?"
Jesus said to them,
"The wedding guests cannot fast
while the bridegroom is with them,
can they?
As long as they have the bridegroom with
them, they cannot fast.
The days will come when the bridegroom
is taken away from them,
and then they will fast on that day.
No one sews a piece of unshrunk cloth
on an old cloak;
otherwise, the patch pulls away from it,
the new from the old,
and a worse tear is made.

And no one puts new wine
into old wineskins;
otherwise, the wine will burst the skins,
and the wine is lost, and so are the skins;
but one puts new wine into fresh wineskins."

The gospel of the Lord.
**Praise to you, Lord Jesus Christ.**

Let us pray:
Most holy and loving God,
help us to constantly grow in your ways,
become new again,
and be filled with the new life of your grace.
We ask this through Christ our Lord.
**Amen.**

Let us pray the prayer that Jesus taught us:
**Our Father…**

✠ In the name of the Father, and of the Son, and of the Holy Spirit. Amen.

---

Note: Today's reading is Mark 2:18-22.

## TUESDAY

✠ **In the name of the Father, and of the Son, and of the Holy Spirit. Amen.**

Introduction: In our reading today, God has decided to choose a new king of Israel. God tells Samuel to go to Bethlehem, to Jesse, because he has chosen a king among Jesse's sons. Samuel does as the Lord asks; God tells him that he will be given further instructions when he gets there. As Jesse's sons are presented, God reminds Samuel that he looks at the heart, not at appearances; it is the heart that is important.

What kind of heart does God see in us?

A reading from the first book of Samuel

When they came, he looked on Eliab
and thought,
"Surely the Lord's anointed
is now before the Lord."
But the Lord said to Samuel,
"Do not look on his appearance
or on the height of his stature,
because I have rejected him;
for the Lord does not see as mortals see;
they look on the outward appearance,
but the Lord looks on the heart."
Jesse made seven of his sons
pass before Samuel,
and Samuel said to Jesse,
"The Lord has not chosen any of these."
Samuel said to Jesse,
"Are all your sons here?" And he said,
"There remains yet the youngest,
but he is keeping the sheep."
And Samuel said to Jesse,
"Send and bring him;
for we will not sit down
until he comes here."
He sent and brought him in.
Now he was ruddy, and had beautiful eyes,
and was handsome.

The Lord said, "Rise and anoint him;
for this is the one."
Then Samuel took the horn of oil,
and anointed him
in the presence of his brothers;
and the spirit of the Lord
came mightily upon David
from that day forward.

The word of the Lord.
**Thanks be to God.**

Let us pray:
Most merciful God,
you do not see what we look like
on the outside; you look at our hearts.
Give us your help and your grace,
that we may have hearts
that are pleasing to you.
We ask this through Christ our Lord.
**Amen.**

Let us pray the prayer that Jesus taught us:
**Our Father...**

✠ **In the name of the Father, and of the Son, and of the Holy Spirit. Amen.**

---

Note: Today's reading is 1 Samuel 16:6, 7, 10-13b.

## WEDNESDAY

✠ **In the name of the Father, and of the Son, and of the Holy Spirit. Amen.**

Introduction: In today's gospel reading, Jesus cures a man with a paralyzed hand. This miracle happened on the Sabbath, a day of rest when no work (including healing) was to be done. The leaders watched closely to see what Jesus would do.

A reading from the holy gospel according to Mark
**Glory to you, Lord.**

Again Jesus entered the synagogue,
and a man was there
who had a withered hand.
They watched him to see
whether he would cure him on the sabbath,
so that they might accuse him.
And he said to the man
who had the withered hand,
"Come forward."
Then he said to them,
"Is it lawful to do good or to do harm
on the sabbath, to save life or to kill?"
But they were silent.
He looked around at them with anger;
he was grieved at their hardness of heart
and said to the man,
"Stretch out your hand."
He stretched it out,
and his hand was restored.
The Pharisees went out and immediately
conspired with the Herodians
against him, how to destroy him.

The gospel of the Lord.
**Praise to you, Lord Jesus Christ.**

Let us pray:
Most loving God,
Jesus cured a man on the Sabbath.
Although he did the right thing,
the leaders made plans to kill him.
Help us to do what is right at all times,
even if this will get us into trouble
with others.
We ask this through Christ our Lord.
**Amen.**

Let us pray the prayer that Jesus taught us:
**Our Father...**

✠ **In the name of the Father, and of the Son, and of the Holy Spirit. Amen.**

_____

Note: Today's reading is Mark 3:1-6.

# SECOND WEEK OF ORDINARY TIME

## THURSDAY

✠ In the name of the Father, and of the Son, and of the Holy Spirit. Amen.

Introduction: In our reading today, we hear that Jesus cured many people. The people approached him with faith that he could cure them.

We can ask Jesus to heal us whenever we need it – from physical illness, sadness, loneliness, or anything that stops us from living life fully. While we may not always be cured of an illness, Jesus will heal our hearts so we can find the courage and hope we need to carry on.

A reading from the holy gospel according to Mark
**Glory to you, Lord.**

Jesus departed with his disciples to the sea,
and a great multitude from Galilee
followed him;
hearing all that he was doing,
they came to him in great numbers
from Judea, Jerusalem, Idumea,
beyond the Jordan,
and the region around Tyre and Sidon.
He told his disciples to have a boat ready
for him because of the crowd,
so that they would not crush him;
for he had cured many,
so that all who had diseases
pressed upon him to touch him.

The gospel of the Lord.
**Praise to you, Lord Jesus Christ.**

Let us pray:
Jesus,
the sick of your time flocked to you
because they knew you could heal them.
We ask you to heal all those who are sick
or hurting in any way,
as you touch them with your comfort
and your love.
Help us remember to ask you for healing
whenever we need it.
**Amen.**

Let us pray the prayer that Jesus taught us:
**Our Father…**

✠ In the name of the Father, and of the Son, and of the Holy Spirit. Amen.

Note: Today's reading is Mark 3:7-10.

## FRIDAY

✠ **In the name of the Father, and of the Son, and of the Holy Spirit. Amen.**

Introduction: Jesus chose twelve people out of all his disciples to be his constant companions. They received more training and deeper explanations of what Jesus was saying and doing. He was preparing them to continue his work on earth, spreading the Good News of the kingdom of God.

A reading from the holy gospel according to Mark
**Glory to you, Lord.**

Jesus went up the mountain
and called to him
those whom he wanted,
and they came to him.
And he appointed twelve,
whom he also named apostles,
to be with him,
and to be sent out to proclaim the message,
and to have authority to cast out demons.
So he appointed the twelve:
Simon (to whom he gave the name Peter);
James son of Zebedee
and John the brother of James
(to whom he gave the name Boanerges,
that is, Sons of Thunder);
and Andrew, and Philip, and Bartholomew,
and Matthew, and Thomas,
and James son of Alphaeus,
and Thaddaeus, and Simon the Cananaean,
and Judas Iscariot, who betrayed him.

The gospel of the Lord.
**Praise to you, Lord Jesus Christ.**

Let us pray:
Creator in heaven,
you love us very much;
you call each of us by name.
By our baptism,
we are your sons and daughters.
Help us to spread the Good News
of your kingdom
by doing what is right,
and by following your laws and your ways.
We ask this through Christ our Lord.
**Amen.**

Let us pray the prayer that Jesus taught us,
for the leaders of the Church, the Pope and
all bishops, the successors of the apostles:
**Our Father…**

✠ **In the name of the Father, and of the Son, and of the Holy Spirit. Amen.**

Note: Today's reading is Mark 3:13-19.

## MONDAY

✠ In the name of the Father, and of the Son, and of the Holy Spirit. Amen.

Introduction: In our reading today, some people think Jesus can cast out demons because he is possessed by one! Jesus explains that this is impossible: when those from the same group fight each other, the group falls apart. He also explains that no one can break into a strong man's house and take his things without tying up the strong man. The strong man is Satan and Jesus is the one who breaks into his house. Jesus is telling his accusers that the hold Satan has on the world is coming to an end.

A reading from the holy gospel according to Mark
**Glory to you, Lord.**

And the scribes
who came down from Jerusalem said,
"He has Beelzebul,
and by the ruler of the demons
he casts out demons."
And Jesus called them to him,
and spoke to them in parables,
"How can Satan cast out Satan?
If a kingdom is divided against itself,
that kingdom cannot stand.
And if a house is divided against itself,
that house will not be able to stand.
And if Satan has risen up against himself
and is divided, he cannot stand,
but his end has come.
But no one can enter a strong man's house
and plunder his property
without first tying up the strong man;
then indeed the house can be plundered.
Truly I tell you,
people will be forgiven for their sins
and whatever blasphemies they utter."

The gospel of the Lord.
**Praise to you, Lord Jesus Christ.**

Let us pray:
God, the source of all goodness,
your Son, Jesus, is our help and stronghold
against the evil one.
Help us to turn to Jesus with all our needs,
especially in times of trouble
and temptation.
We ask this through Christ our Lord.
**Amen.**

Let us pray the prayer that Jesus taught us:
**Our Father…**

✠ In the name of the Father, and of the Son, and of the Holy Spirit. Amen.

---

Note: Today's reading is Mark 3:22-28.

## TUESDAY

✠ **In the name of the Father, and of the Son, and of the Holy Spirit. Amen.**

Introduction: In our reading today, Jesus' mother and relatives are looking for him. Jesus tells the people that his mother and brothers and sisters are those who do what God wants. Jesus is not saying that his mother and relatives are not important; he is reminding them that the most important thing is doing what God wants.

Are we willing to do what God wants above all other things?

A reading from the holy gospel according to Mark
**Glory to you, Lord.**

Then Jesus' mother and his brothers came;
and standing outside,
they sent to him and called him.
A crowd was sitting around him;
and they said to him,
"Your mother and your brothers and sisters
are outside, asking for you."
And he replied,
"Who are my mother and my brothers?"
And looking at those who sat around him,
he said,
"Here are my mother and my brothers!
Whoever does the will of God
is my brother and sister and mother."

The gospel of the Lord.
**Praise to you, Lord Jesus Christ.**

Let us pray:
Most gracious and merciful God,
your Son, Jesus,
tells us that the most important thing
is to do what you want.
Give us the grace and help we need
to do what you want at all times,
especially when it is difficult.
We ask this through Christ our Lord.
**Amen.**

Let us pray the prayer that Jesus taught us:
**Our Father…**

✠ **In the name of the Father, and of the Son, and of the Holy Spirit. Amen.**

Note: Today's reading is Mark 3:31-35.

# THIRD WEEK OF ORDINARY TIME

## WEDNESDAY

✠ **In the name of the Father, and of the Son, and of the Holy Spirit. Amen.**

Introduction: Our reading today is a parable. A man planted some seeds. Some fell on the path, some on rocky ground, some in thorn bushes and some in good soil. The seed is God's word. The different kinds of soil are our hearts.

What kind of soil are our hearts made of? Will God's message grow in our hearts and bear fruit?

A reading from the holy gospel according to Mark
**Glory to you, Lord.**

Again Jesus began to teach beside the sea.
Such a very large crowd gathered
around him
that he got into a boat on the sea
and sat there, while the whole crowd
was beside the sea on the land.
He began to teach them many things
in parables, and in his teaching
he said to them: "Listen!
A sower went out to sow.
And as he sowed,
some seed fell on the path,
and the birds came and ate it up.
Other seed fell on rocky ground,
where it did not have much soil,
and it sprang up quickly,
since it had no depth of soil.
And when the sun rose, it was scorched;
and since it had no root, it withered away.
Other seed fell among thorns,
and the thorns grew up and choked it,
and it yielded no grain.

Other seed fell into good soil
and brought forth grain,
growing up and increasing
and yielding thirty and sixty
and a hundredfold."
And he said,
"Let anyone with ears to hear listen!"

The gospel of the Lord.
**Praise to you, Lord Jesus Christ.**

Let us pray:
Creator God,
Jesus tells us that seed that falls in good soil
bears much fruit.
Help us to be the good soil
where the seed, your word,
may grow in our hearts
and yield a good harvest.
We ask this through Christ our Lord.
**Amen.**

Let us pray the prayer that Jesus taught us:
**Our Father…**

✠ **In the name of the Father, and of the Son, and of the Holy Spirit. Amen.**

Note: Today's reading is Mark 4:1-9.

## THURSDAY

✠ **In the name of the Father, and of the Son, and of the Holy Spirit. Amen.**

Introduction: In our reading today, Jesus reminds us that what we think we have hidden in our hearts will eventually be brought out into the light for all to see.

A reading from the holy gospel according to Mark
**Glory to you, Lord.**

Jesus said to them,
"Is a lamp brought in
to be put under the bushel basket,
or under the bed, and not on the lampstand?
For there is nothing hidden,
except to be disclosed;
nor is anything secret,
except to come to light.
Let anyone with ears to hear listen!"

The gospel of the Lord.
**Praise to you, Lord Jesus Christ.**

Let us pray:
Most merciful and holy God,
your Son, Jesus,
tells us that we cannot really hide anything
– eventually it will come to light.
Please show us your mercy and love,
for we know that you are kind and just.
Help us to do what you ask us,
and to grow in holiness and grace
as your children.
We ask this through Christ our Lord.
**Amen.**

Let us pray the prayer that Jesus taught us:
**Our Father…**

✠ **In the name of the Father, and of the Son, and of the Holy Spirit. Amen.**

Note: Today's reading is Mark 4:21-23.

## FRIDAY

✠ **In the name of the Father, and of the Son, and of the Holy Spirit. Amen.**

Introduction: In today's reading, we hear another story about sowing seeds. In this parable, the seed is the kingdom of God. The seed will produce a harvest, growing from hidden beginnings. God's kingdom, which is the harvest, will surely come, because Jesus has brought its beginnings into the world.

We also hear about the mustard seed, starting out very small, but growing to shelter many birds. The seed, again, is God's kingdom, and the birds are the people of the kingdom.

A reading from the holy gospel according to Mark
**Glory to you, Lord.**

Jesus also said, "The kingdom of God
is as if someone would scatter seed
on the ground,
and would sleep and rise night and day,
and the seed would sprout and grow,
he does not know how.
The earth produces of itself,
first the stalk,
then the head,
then the full grain in the head.
But when the grain is ripe,
at once he goes in with his sickle,
because the harvest has come."
He also said, "With what can we compare
the kingdom of God,
or what parable will we use for it?

It is like a mustard seed, which,
when sown upon the ground,
is the smallest of all the seeds on earth;
yet when it is sown it grows up
and becomes the greatest of all shrubs,
and puts forth large branches,
so that the birds of the air
can make nests in its shade."

The gospel of the Lord.
**Praise to you, Lord Jesus Christ.**

Let us pray:
Lord,
may your word grow in our hearts
like the grains of wheat
and the mustard seed,
so that we may help your kingdom grow.
**Amen.**

Let us pray the prayer that Jesus taught us:
**Our Father…**

✠ **In the name of the Father, and of the Son, and of the Holy Spirit. Amen.**

Note: Today's reading is Mark 4:26-32.

## MONDAY

✠ In the name of the Father, and of the Son, and of the Holy Spirit. Amen.

Introduction: In our reading today, we hear that the Lord is with those who fear him and trust in him. God's gifts and graces come to them. Our God is always faithful, and his love for us is unending. We need to trust God more and more each day. Faith and trust go hand in hand; as we grow in trust, we grow in faith, and as we grow in faith, we grow in trust. We need to open our hearts to God.

A reading from the book of Psalms

O how abundant is your goodness
that you have laid up
for those who fear you,
and accomplished
for those who take refuge in you,
in the sight of everyone!
In the shelter of your presence
you hide them from human plots;
you hold them safe under your shelter
from contentious tongues.
Blessed be the Lord,
for he has wondrously shown
his steadfast love to me
when I was beset as a city under siege.
I had said in my alarm,
"I am driven far from your sight."
But you heard my supplications
when I cried out to you for help.
Love the Lord, all you his saints.
The Lord preserves the faithful,
but abundantly repays
the one who acts haughtily.
Be strong, and let your heart take courage,
all you who wait for the Lord.

The word of the Lord.
**Thanks be to God.**

Let us pray:
Most loving and faithful God,
you hear and answer the prayers
of those who place their trust in you.
Grant that we may grow in faith and trust.
Help us to be open to you,
believing in your love for us.
We ask this through Christ our Lord.
**Amen.**

Let us pray the prayer that Jesus taught us:
**Our Father…**

✠ **In the name of the Father, and of the Son, and of the Holy Spirit. Amen.**

Note: Today's reading is Psalm 31:19-24.

## TUESDAY

✠ In the name of the Father, and of the Son, and of the Holy Spirit. Amen.

Introduction: In our reading today, a large crowd gathers around Jesus. A woman in the crowd who has been ill for twelve years believes that if she touches Jesus' clothes, she will be healed. Jesus is not angry; he tells her that her faith has made her well.

Do we believe that Jesus will help us if we ask? Do we have the strong faith that the woman in this story has?

A reading from the holy gospel according to Mark
**Glory to you, Lord.**

A large crowd followed him
and pressed in on Jesus.
Now there was a woman
who had been suffering from hemorrhages
for twelve years.
She had endured much
under many physicians,
and had spent all that she had;
and she was no better,
but rather grew worse.
She had heard about Jesus,
and came up behind him in the crowd
and touched his cloak, for she said,
"If I but touch his clothes,
I will be made well."
Immediately her hemorrhage stopped;
and she felt in her body
that she was healed of her disease.
Immediately aware that power
had gone forth from him,
Jesus turned about in the crowd and said,
"Who touched my clothes?"
And his disciples said to him,
"You see the crowd pressing in on you;
how can you say, 'Who touched me?'"

He looked all around
to see who had done it.
But the woman,
knowing what had happened to her,
came in fear and trembling,
fell down before him,
and told him the whole truth.
He said to her,
"Daughter, your faith has made you well;
go in peace, and be healed of your disease."

The gospel of the Lord.
**Praise to you, Lord Jesus Christ.**

Let us pray:
Most loving God,
the woman who was healed
placed all her faith in Jesus.
Help us to follow her example.
We ask this through Christ our Lord.
**Amen.**

Let us pray the prayer that Jesus taught us:
**Our Father…**

✠ In the name of the Father, and of the Son, and of the Holy Spirit. Amen.

Note: Today's reading is Mark 5:24-34.

## WEDNESDAY

✠ **In the name of the Father, and of the Son, and of the Holy Spirit. Amen.**

Introduction: In our reading today, Jesus returns to Nazareth, and preaches in the synagogue. But the people there have known Jesus all his life, and they know all of his family. They cannot accept this side of Jesus that they knew nothing about. They turn their hearts against him.

Sometimes we are like the people of Nazareth; we cannot believe that people can change, or we judge them because we think we know them. We need to be open and see with our hearts, accepting people when they change.

A reading from the holy gospel according to Mark
**Glory to you, Lord.**

Jesus left that place
and came to his hometown,
and his disciples followed him.
On the sabbath he began to teach
in the synagogue,
and many who heard him were astounded.
They said, "Where did this man get all this?
What is this wisdom
that has been given to him?
What deeds of power
are being done by his hands!
Is not this the carpenter, the son of Mary
and brother of James and Joses
and Judas and Simon,
and are not his sisters here with us?"
And they took offence at him.
Then Jesus said to them,
"Prophets are not without honour,
except in their hometown,
and among their own kin,
and in their own house."

And he could do no deed of power there,
except that he laid his hands
on a few sick people and cured them.
And he was amazed at their unbelief.
Then he went about
among the villages teaching.

The gospel of the Lord.
**Praise to you, Lord Jesus Christ.**

Let us pray:
Creator God,
your only Son, Jesus,
was not accepted in his own town
because people thought they knew
everything about him.
Help us to be open to others,
especially those about whom
we think we know everything,
using the eyes of our hearts
to see their gifts and their goodness.
We ask this through Christ our Lord.
**Amen.**

Let us pray the prayer that Jesus taught us:
**Our Father…**

✠ **In the name of the Father, and of the Son, and of the Holy Spirit. Amen.**

Note: Today's reading is Mark 6:1-6.

## THURSDAY

✠ In the name of the Father, and of the Son, and of the Holy Spirit. Amen.

Introduction: In our reading today, Jesus sends out the twelve apostles two by two to spread the Good News. They have seen how Jesus worked and have watched him teach. Now it is their turn to preach and heal.

Jesus gives them some instructions before they go: what to take with them, where to stay, and when to move on. They have an important job to do!

A reading from the holy gospel according to Mark
**Glory to you, Lord.**

Then Jesus went about
among the villages teaching.
He called the twelve
and began to send them out two by two,
and gave them authority
over the unclean spirits.
He ordered them
to take nothing for their journey
except a staff; no bread, no bag,
no money in their belts;
but to wear sandals
and not to put on two tunics.
He said to them,
"Wherever you enter a house,
stay there until you leave the place.
If any place will not welcome you
and they refuse to hear you,
as you leave,
shake off the dust that is on your feet
as a testimony against them."
So they went out
and proclaimed that all should repent.

They cast out many demons,
and anointed with oil
many who were sick and cured them.

The gospel of the Lord.
**Praise to you, Lord Jesus Christ.**

Let us pray:
Jesus,
you sent your apostles
to tell people about God
and to heal the sick.
Help us to open our hearts
to God's word and healing power
today and every day.
**Amen.**

Let us pray the prayer that Jesus taught us:
**Our Father…**

✠ In the name of the Father, and of the Son, and of the Holy Spirit. Amen.

Note: Today's reading is Mark 6:6b-13.

## FRIDAY

✠ In the name of the Father, and of the Son, and of the Holy Spirit. Amen.

Introduction: Today we hear about a shepherd boy named David who was chosen by God to be king of Israel.

David loved God and in all he did he gave thanks and praise to God. Even when he made mistakes, he loved God and asked for forgiveness.

Do we praise and thank God every day? Do we ask for God's help daily, as David did? Do we place our trust in God in all things?

A reading from the book of Sirach

In his youth did David not kill a giant,
and take away the people's disgrace,
when he whirled the stone in the sling
and struck down the boasting Goliath?
For he called on the Lord, the Most High,
and he gave strength to his right arm
to strike down a mighty warrior,
and to exalt the power of his people.
In all that he did he gave thanks
to the Holy One, the Most High,
proclaiming his glory;
he sang praise with all his heart,
and he loved his Maker.
He placed singers before the altar,
to make sweet melody with their voices.
He gave beauty to the festivals,
and arranged their times
throughout the year,
while they praised God's holy name,
and the sanctuary resounded
from early morning.

The Lord took away his sins,
and exalted his power for ever;
he gave him a covenant of kingship
and a glorious throne in Israel.

The word of the Lord.
**Thanks be to God.**

Let us pray:
Holy God, the Most High,
David loved you with all his heart.
You chose him to be king,
and he thanked you
for your kindness to him.
Help us to always ask you for help,
and to praise and thank you
for your goodness every day.
We ask this through Christ our Lord.
**Amen.**

Let us pray the prayer that Jesus taught us:
**Our Father…**

✠ In the name of the Father, and of the Son, and of the Holy Spirit. Amen.

---

Note: Today's reading is Sirach 47:4-5, 8-11.

## MONDAY

✠ In the name of the Father, and of the Son, and of the Holy Spirit. Amen.

Introduction: The people of the area around the Sea of Galilee believed in Jesus' power to heal. They believed that even if they just touched the edge of his cloak they would be cured, and it was true.

Do we believe in Jesus' power to touch our lives and change our hearts?

A reading from the holy gospel according to Mark
**Glory to you, Lord.**

When they had crossed over,
they came to land at Gennesaret
and moored the boat.
When they got out of the boat,
people at once recognized Jesus,
and rushed about that whole region
and began to bring the sick on mats
to wherever they heard he was.
And wherever he went,
into villages or cities or farms,
they laid the sick in the marketplaces,
and begged him that they might touch
even the fringe of his cloak;
and all who touched it were healed.

The gospel of the Lord.
**Praise to you, Lord Jesus Christ.**

Let us pray:
Most holy and all-powerful God,
the people recognized the compassion
and the gift of healing Jesus had;
they believed him and in him.
Grant us this deep faith
and opens our hearts to his healing power.
We ask this through Christ our Lord.
**Amen.**

Let us pray the prayer that Jesus taught us:
**Our Father...**

✠ In the name of the Father, and of the Son, and of the Holy Spirit. Amen.

Note: Today's reading is Mark 6:53-56.

## TUESDAY

✠ **In the name of the Father, and of the Son, and of the Holy Spirit. Amen.**

Introduction: Today we hear the prayer of King Solomon, King David's son. Solomon built the first Temple to God. Before this, the Ark of the Covenant, which contained the tablets that held the Ten Commandments, was housed in a tent. Solomon proclaims the greatness of God. He knows that nothing is big enough to contain God, who is beyond our understanding.

A reading from the first book of Kings

Then Solomon stood before
the altar of the Lord
in the presence of all the assembly of Israel,
and spread out his hands to heaven.
He said, "O Lord, God of Israel,
there is no God like you
in heaven above or on earth beneath,
keeping covenant and steadfast love
for your servants who walk before you
with all their heart.
But will God indeed dwell on the earth?
Even heaven and the highest heaven
cannot contain you,
much less this house that I have built!
Have regard to your servant's prayer
and his plea, O Lord my God,
heeding the cry and the prayer
that your servant prays to you today;
that your eyes may be open night and day
towards this house,
the place of which you said,
'My name shall be there',
that you may heed the prayer
that your servant prays towards this place.

Hear the plea of your servant
and of your people Israel
when they pray towards this place;
O hear in heaven your dwelling-place;
heed and forgive."

The word of the Lord.
**Thanks be to God.**

Let us pray:
Most holy God,
Solomon loved you and prayed to you.
He built a beautiful Temple in your honour.
Help us always to respect your house,
because the real presence of your son, Jesus,
dwells there,
and to honour each other,
for your presence is found
in everyone we meet.
We ask this through Christ our Lord.
**Amen.**

Let us pray the prayer that Jesus taught us:
**Our Father…**

✠ **In the name of the Father, and of the Son, and of the Holy Spirit. Amen.**

Note: Today's reading is 1 Kings 8:22-23, 27-30.

## WEDNESDAY

✠ **In the name of the Father, and of the Son, and of the Holy Spirit. Amen.**

Introduction: For centuries, many Jewish people have followed certain rules about what foods to eat. These rules are linked to the Bible and their belief in God. Jesus, who was Jewish, said something new: that nothing from the outside, such as food, can make people "unclean" according to religious rules.

It is the hurtful things that come out of our hearts – evil ideas – that lead to sin.

A reading from the holy gospel according to Mark
**Glory to you, Lord.**

Then Jesus called the crowd again
and said to them, "Listen to me,
all of you, and understand:
there is nothing outside a person
that by going in can defile,
but the things that come out
are what defile."
When he had left the crowd
and entered the house,
his disciples asked him about the parable.
He said to them,
"Then do you also fail to understand?
Do you not see
that whatever goes into a person
from outside cannot defile,
since it enters, not the heart but the stom-
ach, and goes out into the sewer?"
(Thus he declared all foods clean.)
And he said,
"It is what comes out of a person
that defiles.

For it is from within, from the human heart,
that evil intentions come: fornication,
theft, murder, adultery, avarice, wickedness,
deceit, licentiousness, envy,
slander, pride, folly.
All these evil things come from within, and
they defile a person."

The gospel of the Lord.
**Praise to you, Lord Jesus Christ.**

Let us pray:
Loving Father,
your Son, Jesus, taught us
that what comes out of our hearts
is the important thing.
Help us to have clean hearts
by following your laws and your ways.
We ask this through Christ our Lord.
**Amen.**

Let us pray the prayer that Jesus taught us:
**Our Father…**

✠ **In the name of the Father, and of the Son, and of the Holy Spirit. Amen.**

---

Note: Today's reading is Mark 7:14-23.

## THURSDAY

✠ **In the name of the Father, and of the Son, and of the Holy Spirit. Amen.**

Introduction: In today's reading, we hear the story of a woman who asked Jesus to heal her daughter, who had an evil spirit in her. In the time of Jesus, people believed sickness was caused by evil spirits or demons. The woman was a Gentile, not a Jew. Because of this, Jesus tells her that he was sent to help the Jewish people first. In this passage, when Jesus says "dogs," he means those who were not Jews. But this lady reminds him that even dogs eat the children's leftovers. And that is what she was asking – for the leftovers from the Jews whom Jesus cured, so that her daughter would be made well. Because of her belief in Jesus' power and her love for her daughter, Jesus healed the sick girl.

A reading from the holy gospel according to Mark
**Glory to you, Lord.**

From there Jesus set out and went away
to the region of Tyre. He entered a house
and did not want anyone to know
he was there.
Yet he could not escape notice,
but a woman whose little daughter
had an unclean spirit
immediately heard about him,
and she came and bowed down at his feet.
Now the woman was a Gentile,
of Syrophoenician origin.
She begged him to cast the demon
out of her daughter.
He said to her, "Let the children be fed first,
for it is not fair to take the children's food
and throw it to the dogs."
But she answered him, "Sir, even the dogs
under the table eat the children's crumbs."

Then he said to her,
"For saying that, you may go –
the demon has left your daughter."
So she went home,
found the child lying on the bed,
and the demon gone.

The gospel of the Lord.
**Praise to you, Lord Jesus Christ.**

Let us pray:
Most loving God,
the Gentile woman believed in your Son
even though she was not Jewish.
Help us to believe
in the words and actions of Jesus,
knowing that he loves us deeply.
We ask this through Christ our Lord.
**Amen.**

Let us pray the prayer that Jesus taught us:
**Our Father…**

✠ **In the name of the Father, and of the Son, and of the Holy Spirit. Amen.**

---

Note: Today's reading is Mark 7:24-30.

## FRIDAY

✠ **In the name of the Father, and of the Son, and of the Holy Spirit. Amen.**

Introduction: Today we hear about a man who could not hear or speak. People brought him to Jesus to be healed.

Sometimes we are like this man – we don't hear what others say to us. We turn a deaf ear to them.

Let us ask God today to help us listen and hear, even when we really don't want to hear it!

A reading from the holy gospel according to Mark
**Glory to you, Lord.**

Then Jesus returned
from the region of Tyre,
and went by way of Sidon
towards the Sea of Galilee,
in the region of the Decapolis.
They brought to him a deaf man
who had an impediment in his speech;
and they begged him
to lay his hand on him.
He took him aside in private,
away from the crowd,
and put his fingers into his ears,
and he spat and touched his tongue.
Then looking up to heaven,
he sighed and said to him, "Ephphatha,"
that is, "Be opened."
And immediately his ears were opened,
his tongue was released,
and he spoke plainly.

Then Jesus ordered them to tell no one;
but the more he ordered them,
the more zealously they proclaimed it.
They were astounded beyond measure.

The gospel of the Lord.
**Praise to you, Lord Jesus Christ.**

Let us pray:
Most holy God,
your Son, Jesus, healed a man
who could not speak or hear.
We thank you for the gifts
for of hearing and speech.
Help us to use them wisely,
saying kind things to others,
and listening to them carefully.
We ask this through Christ our Lord.
**Amen.**

Let us pray the prayer that Jesus taught us:
**Our Father...**

✠ **In the name of the Father, and of the Son, and of the Holy Spirit. Amen.**

Note: Today's reading is Mark 7:31-37.

## MONDAY

✠ **In the name of the Father, and of the Son, and of the Holy Spirit. Amen.**

Introduction: In today's gospel reading, the Pharisees try to trick Jesus. Instead of getting into an argument or a fight, Jesus simply leaves the situation.

This is a lesson for us. Sometimes the best thing to do is to let it go, and to leave.

A reading from the holy gospel according to Mark
**Glory to you, Lord.**

The Pharisees came
and began to argue with Jesus,
asking him for a sign from heaven,
to test him.
And he sighed deeply in his spirit and said,
"Why does this generation ask for a sign?
Truly I tell you,
no sign will be given to this generation."
And he left them,
and getting into the boat again,
he went across to the other side.

The gospel of the Lord.
**Praise to you, Lord Jesus Christ.**

Let us pray:
Most merciful and just God,
your Son saw through the Pharisees' request
for a miracle, and left the situation
rather than fight with them.
Grant that your Holy Spirit
will lead and guide us
when we are faced with a difficult situation,
and help us to make the right choice.
We ask this through Christ our Lord.
**Amen.**

Let us pray the prayer that Jesus taught us
for the peacemakers of the world:
**Our Father…**

✠ **In the name of the Father, and of the Son, and of the Holy Spirit. Amen.**

---

Note: Today's reading is Mark 8:11-13.

## TUESDAY

✠ In the name of the Father, and of the Son, and of the Holy Spirit. Amen.

Introduction: Jesus warns his disciples in today's reading to be on guard against the yeast of the Pharisees and the yeast of Herod. They do not understand what he is telling them.

Jesus wants his disciples, and us, to be aware of those things that are not of God in the world. He is warning them not to let that bad yeast grow and multiply within them.

A reading from the holy gospel according to Mark
**Glory to you, Lord.**

Now the disciples had forgotten
to bring any bread;
and they had only one loaf with them
in the boat.
And Jesus cautioned them, saying,
"Watch out –
beware of the yeast of the Pharisees
and the yeast of Herod."
They said to one another,
"It is because we have no bread."
And becoming aware of it,
Jesus said to them,
"Why are you talking about having no
bread?
Do you still not perceive or understand?
Are your hearts hardened?
Do you have eyes, and fail to see?
Do you have ears, and fail to hear?"

The gospel of the Lord.
**Praise to you, Lord Jesus Christ.**

Let us pray:
Most holy God,
your Son, Jesus, warns us
about the yeast of those in charge
who do not do your will
and tempt us with the things of this world.
Help us to keep our eyes on you,
following your commands
and letting the yeast of your kingdom
grow within us.
We ask this through Christ our Lord.
**Amen.**

Let us pray the prayer that Jesus taught us:
**Our Father…**

✠ In the name of the Father, and of the Son, and of the Holy Spirit. Amen.

Note: Today's reading is Mark 8:14-18.

## WEDNESDAY

✠ **In the name of the Father, and of the Son, and of the Holy Spirit. Amen.**

Introduction: In today's reading, some people bring a blind man to Jesus and beg him to touch the man. They know that Jesus has the power to heal.

The people in this reading are a good example for us. We can bring those we know who are sick to Jesus in prayer, asking Jesus to help and heal them.

A reading from the holy gospel according to Mark
**Glory to you, Lord.**

They came to Bethsaida.
Some people brought a blind man to Jesus
and begged him to touch him.
He took the blind man by the hand
and led him out of the village;
and when he had put saliva on his eyes
and laid his hands on him, he asked him,
"Can you see anything?"
And the man looked up and said,
"I can see people,
but they look like trees, walking."
Then Jesus laid his hands on his eyes again;
and he looked intently
and his sight was restored,
and he saw everything clearly.
Then he sent him away to his home, saying,
"Do not even go into the village."

The gospel of the Lord.
**Praise to you, Lord Jesus Christ.**

Let us pray:
Most loving and merciful God,
your Son, Jesus, healed the blind man.
Grant that he may heal the blindness in us
so that we may see what you want us to see,
and be open to your goodness and grace.
Heal those who are sick:
people in our families and in our school
and everyone who needs
your healing touch.
We ask this through Christ our Lord.
**Amen.**

Let us pray the prayer that Jesus taught us:
**Our Father…**

✠ **In the name of the Father, and of the Son, and of the Holy Spirit. Amen.**

---

Note: Today's reading is Mark 8:22-26.

## THURSDAY

✠ In the name of the Father, and of the Son, and of the Holy Spirit. Amen.

Introduction: In today's reading, Jesus asks his disciples who people say he is. Then he asks them: "Who do you say I am?" Peter replies, "You are the Messiah." ("Messiah" in Hebrew means "anointed one.") Jesus strictly orders them to tell no one.

The people of Israel had been waiting for the Messiah, the promised one, for hundreds of years. Jesus was born in a time when the Romans had conquered Israel and were the rulers. The people were hoping and praying for the Messiah to come and rescue them from oppression under the Romans. But Jesus' kingdom was not to be an earthly one.

If Jesus asked us the same question: "Who do you say I am?" – what would we answer?

A reading from the holy gospel according to Mark
**Glory to you, Lord.**

Jesus went on with his disciples
to the villages of Caesarea Philippi;
and on the way he asked his disciples,
"Who do people say that I am?"
And they answered him,
"John the Baptist; and others, Elijah;
and still others, one of the prophets."
He asked them,
"But who do you say that I am?"
Peter answered him, "You are the Messiah."
And he sternly ordered them
not to tell anyone about him.

The gospel of the Lord.
**Praise to you, Lord Jesus Christ.**

Let us pray:
Most gracious God,
Peter recognized that your Son, Jesus,
was the promised one, the Messiah.
Help us to see that Jesus is the Messiah,
who has come to help and save us.
We ask this through Christ our Lord.
**Amen.**

Let us pray the prayer that Jesus taught us:
**Our Father…**

✠ In the name of the Father, and of the Son, and of the Holy Spirit. Amen.

Note: Today's reading is Mark 8:27-30.

## FRIDAY

✠ **In the name of the Father, and of the Son, and of the Holy Spirit. Amen.**

Introduction: In our reading today, Jesus tells the crowd and his disciples that to follow him, they must forget themselves, take up their cross and lose their life for him.

This means setting aside selfish things and putting God first in our lives. By spending our lives doing good, we will gain eternal life.

How can we follow Jesus each and every day?

A reading from the holy gospel according to Mark
**Glory to you, Lord.**

Jesus called the crowd with his disciples,
and said to them,
"If any want to become my followers,
let them deny themselves
and take up their cross and follow me.
For those who want to save their life
will lose it,
and those who lose their life for my sake,
and for the sake of the gospel,
will save it.
For what will it profit them
to gain the whole world
and forfeit their life?
Indeed, what can they give
in return for their life?"

The gospel of the Lord.
**Praise to you, Lord Jesus Christ.**

Let us pray:
Most loving and merciful God,
you sent your Son, Jesus,
to teach us your ways
and the paths to follow.
Help us to take up our cross,
choose things that are selfless,
and follow Jesus,
being faithful to the gospel,
and putting you first in our lives.
We ask this through Christ our Lord.
**Amen.**

Let us pray the prayer that Jesus taught us:
**Our Father…**

✠ **In the name of the Father, and of the Son, and of the Holy Spirit. Amen.**

---

Note: Today's reading is Mark 8:34-37.

✠ **In the name of the Father, and of the Son, and of the Holy Spirit. Amen.**

Introduction: Today is Ash Wednesday, the first day of Lent. During Lent, we remember the suffering and death of Jesus and prepare our hearts to celebrate his resurrection at Easter, when we recall our baptismal promises to follow Jesus. We pray for people who will be baptized at the Easter Vigil. We are asked to turn away from sin and be faithful to the message of the gospel, and to grow in holiness. The traditional way to do this is through prayer, fasting and almsgiving (giving to the poor).

On Ash Wednesday, we receive ashes, a very old sign of repentance and sorrow for our sins, on our foreheads. The ashes also remind us that one day we will die and be with God forever.

In today's reading, God invites us to turn back to him, for he will always forgive our sins.

A reading from the book of the prophet Joel

"Even now," says the Lord,
"return to me with all your heart,
with fasting, with weeping,
and with mourning;
rend your hearts and not your clothing.
Return to the Lord, your God,
for he is gracious and merciful,
slow to anger,
and abounding in steadfast love,
and relents from punishing.
Who knows whether he will not turn
and relent, and leave a blessing behind him,
a grain offering and a drink offering
for the Lord, your God?
Blow the trumpet in Zion;
sanctify a fast; call a solemn assembly."

The word of the Lord.
**Thanks be to God.**

Let us pray:
Most gracious and merciful God,
hear our prayers for a truly fruitful Lent.
Grant that our efforts
of prayer, fasting,
almsgiving and deeds of mercy
may lead us closer to you.
Help us turn away from sin
and become more faithful followers
of your Son, Jesus.
We ask this through Christ our Lord.
**Amen.**

Let us pray the prayer that Jesus taught us:
**Our Father…**

✠ **In the name of the Father, and of the Son, and of the Holy Spirit. Amen.**

Note: Today's reading is Joel 2:12-15.

# THURSDAY AFTER ASH WEDNESDAY

✠ In the name of the Father, and of the Son, and of the Holy Spirit. Amen.

Introduction: Today, Jesus tells the apostles that he is going to suffer at the hands of the leaders of the Jewish people and be put to death. He tells them they must forget themselves, take up their crosses every day, and follow him.

We all have a cross to carry – something in our lives that is hard for us to deal with, or that has hurt us in some way. This is the type of cross Jesus is talking about. When we carry our cross with courage and hope, we are doing what Jesus did. We are being faithful disciples and following in his footsteps.

A reading from the holy gospel according to Luke
**Glory to you, Lord.**

Jesus said to his disciples,
"The Son of Man
must undergo great suffering,
and be rejected by the elders, chief priests,
and scribes, and be killed,
and on the third day be raised."
Then he said to them all,
"If any want to become my followers,
let them deny themselves
and take up their cross daily and follow me.
For those who want to save their life
will lose it, and those who lose their life
for my sake will save it.
What does it profit them
if they gain the whole world,
but lose or forfeit themselves?"

The gospel of the Lord.
**Praise to you, Lord Jesus Christ.**

Let us pray:
Creator God,
your Son, Jesus,
died willingly on the cross for us
because he loved us so much.
Give us the grace we need
to do those things we have to do
that are very hard.
Help us to carry our crosses
with courage and hope.
We ask this through Christ our Lord.
**Amen.**

Let us pray the prayer that Jesus taught us:
**Our Father…**

✠ In the name of the Father, and of the Son, and of the Holy Spirit. Amen.

---

Note: Today's reading is Luke 9:22-25.

141

# FRIDAY AFTER ASH WEDNESDAY

✠ In the name of the Father, and of the Son, and of the Holy Spirit. Amen.

Introduction: Today's reading describes the kind of fasting that pleases God, and the kind of fasting that upsets God.

God wants us to mean what we do when we fast (go without food for a certain time, or give up a favourite food or habit), not just try to look good in the eyes of others. This kind of fasting is showing off – it looks good on the outside, but the inside, the heart, is not being touched, and the real reason for fasting is being missed.

What kind of fasting are we going to do this Lent – one that looks good on the outside, or one that will make us better children of God?

A reading from the book of the prophet Isaiah

Shout out, do not hold back!
Lift up your voice like a trumpet!
Announce to my people their rebellion,
to the house of Jacob their sins.
Yet day after day they seek me
and delight to know my ways,
as if they were a nation
that practised righteousness
and did not forsake the ordinance
of their God;
they ask of me righteous judgments,
they delight to draw near to God.
"Why do we fast, but you do not see?
Why humble ourselves,
but you do not notice?"
Look, you serve your own interest
on your fast day,
and oppress all your workers.
Look, you fast only to quarrel
and to fight and to strike with a wicked fist.
Such fasting as you do today
will not make your voice heard on high.
Is such the fast that I choose,
a day to humble oneself?

Is it to bow down the head like a bulrush,
and to lie in sackcloth and ashes?
Will you call this a fast,
a day acceptable to the Lord?
Is not this the fast that I choose:
to loose the bonds of injustice,
to undo the thongs of the yoke,
to let the oppressed go free,
and to break every yoke?
Is it not to share your bread
with the hungry,
and bring the homeless poor
into your house;
when you see the naked, to cover them,
and not to hide yourself from your own kin?

The word of the Lord.
**Thanks be to God.**

Let us pray:
Father in heaven,
the fast that you choose for us
is to be just and fair,
to feed the hungry,
clothe the naked,
give shelter to the homeless,
and help the members of our own families.
Help us to fast in this way
that is so pleasing to you.
We ask this through Christ our Lord.
**Amen.**

Let us pray the prayer that Jesus taught us:
**Our Father...**

✠ **In the name of the Father, and of the Son, and of the Holy Spirit. Amen.**

Note: Today's reading is Isaiah 58:1-7.

## MONDAY

✠ **In the name of the Father, and of the Son, and of the Holy Spirit. Amen.**

Introduction: Jesus tells us in today's gospel how we should treat those who need our help. When we serve others, we are also serving Jesus.

Do we see Christ in the people around us?

A reading from the holy gospel according to Matthew
**Glory to you, Lord.**

Jesus said,
"When the Son of Man comes in his glory,
and all the angels with him,
then he will sit on the throne of his glory.
All the nations will be gathered before him,
and he will separate people
one from another
as a shepherd separates the sheep
from the goats,
and he will put the sheep at his right hand
and the goats at the left.
Then the king will say
to those at his right hand,
'Come, you that are blessed by my Father,
inherit the kingdom prepared for you
from the foundation of the world;
for I was hungry and you gave me food,
I was thirsty
and you gave me something to drink,
I was a stranger and you welcomed me,
I was naked and you gave me clothing,
I was sick and you took care of me,
I was in prison and you visited me.'
Then the righteous will answer him,
'Lord, when was it that we saw you hungry
and gave you food,
or thirsty and gave you something to drink?

And when was it that we saw you a stranger
and welcomed you,
or naked and gave you clothing?
And when was it that we saw you sick
or in prison and visited you?'
And the king will answer them,
'Truly I tell you, just as you did it
to one of the least of these
who are members of my family,
you did it to me.'"

The gospel of the Lord.
**Praise to you, Lord Jesus Christ.**

Let us pray:
Father in heaven,
help us always to reach out
to help our brothers and sisters in need.
Help us to be kind and loving
to all we meet.
We ask this through Christ our Lord.
**Amen.**

Let us pray the prayer that Jesus taught us:
**Our Father…**

✠ **In the name of the Father, and of the Son, and of the Holy Spirit. Amen.**

---

Note: Today's reading is Matthew 25:31-40.

## TUESDAY

✠ In the name of the Father, and of the Son, and of the Holy Spirit. Amen.

Introduction: In today's reading, Jesus teaches his disciples how to pray. He reminds them that they do not need to use a lot of words when they pray; God knows what they need before they even ask.

But prayer is more than asking for things: it is our conversation with God. Prayer is a time to listen and talk to God.

A reading from the holy gospel according to Matthew
**Glory to you, Lord.**

Jesus said to his disciples,
"When you are praying,
do not heap up empty phrases
as the Gentiles do;
for they think that they will be heard
because of their many words.
Do not be like them,
for your Father knows what you need
before you ask him.
Pray then in this way:
Our Father in heaven,
hallowed be your name.
Your kingdom come.
Your will be done,
on earth as it is in heaven.
Give us this day our daily bread.
And forgive us our debts,
as we also have forgiven our debtors.
And do not bring us to the time of trial,
but rescue us from the evil one.
For if you forgive others their trespasses,
your heavenly Father will also forgive you."

The gospel of the Lord.
**Praise to you, Lord Jesus Christ.**

Let us pray:
Father in heaven,
give us the grace we need
to pray well
and to forgive others who have hurt us.
We ask this through Christ our Lord.
**Amen.**

Let us pray the prayer that Jesus taught us:
**Our Father…**

✠ In the name of the Father, and of the Son, and of the Holy Spirit. Amen.

Note: Today's reading is Matthew 6:7-14.

## WEDNESDAY

✠ **In the name of the Father, and of the Son, and of the Holy Spirit. Amen.**

Introduction: In today's reading, the prophet Jonah was sent to Nineveh to tell the people that God was going to destroy their city because they were not following God's ways.

The people listened to Jonah's message and repented, and God did not destroy the city because they turned away from sin.

This is the message of the season of Lent: we are called to repent – to turn away from sin and towards God, to change our hearts and follow God's laws.

A reading from the book of the prophet Jonah

The word of the Lord came to Jonah
a second time, saying,
"Get up, go to Nineveh, that great city,
and proclaim to it the message
that I tell you."
So Jonah set out and went to Nineveh,
according to the word of the Lord.
Now Nineveh was an exceedingly large city,
a three days' walk across.
Jonah began to go into the city,
going a day's walk. And he cried out,
"Forty days more,
and Nineveh shall be overthrown!"
And the people of Nineveh believed God;
they proclaimed a fast, and everyone,
great and small, put on sackcloth.
When the news reached the king of
Nineveh, he rose from his throne,
removed his robe,
covered himself with sackcloth,
and sat in ashes.
Then he had a proclamation
made in Nineveh:

"By the decree of the king and his nobles:
No human being or animal,
no herd or flock,
shall taste anything.
They shall not feed,
nor shall they drink water.
Human beings and animals
shall be covered with sackcloth,
and they shall cry mightily to God.
All shall turn from their evil ways
and from the violence that is in their hands.
Who knows? God may relent
and change his mind;
he may turn from his fierce anger,
so that we do not perish."
When God saw what they did,
how they turned from their evil ways,
God changed his mind about the calamity
that he had said he would bring upon them;
and he did not do it.

The word of the Lord.
**Thanks be to God.**

Let us pray:
Loving Creator,
help us to turn away from doing things
that are wrong,
and to follow your ways in all that we do.
We ask this through Christ our Lord.
**Amen.**

Let us pray the prayer that Jesus taught us:
**Our Father…**

✠ **In the name of the Father, and of the Son, and of the Holy Spirit. Amen.**

Note: Today's reading is Jonah 3:1-10.

## THURSDAY

✠ In the name of the Father, and of the Son, and of the Holy Spirit. Amen.

Introduction: God loves us more than anyone, even our parents. If we truly need what we ask for in prayer, Jesus says, we will get it, because God is a loving parent who gives his children what they need.

Sometimes God's answer to our prayer may surprise us: God knows better than we do what we truly need. But God always answers us. We need to remember that "no" is also an answer.

A reading from the holy gospel according to Matthew
**Glory to you, Lord.**

Jesus said, "Ask, and it will be given you;
search, and you will find;
knock, and the door will be opened for you.
For everyone who asks receives,
and everyone who searches finds,
and for everyone who knocks,
the door will be opened.
Is there anyone among you who,
if your child asks for bread, will give a
stone?
Or if the child asks for a fish,
will give a snake?
If you then, who are evil,
know how to give good gifts to your
children,
how much more will your Father in heaven
give good things to those who ask him!
In everything do to others
as you would have them do to you;
for this is the law and the prophets."

The gospel of the Lord.
**Praise to you, Lord Jesus Christ.**

Let us pray:
Most loving God,
your love for us cannot be measured.
You are the source of all that is good;
you give us what we need
when we ask you in prayer.
Help us always to turn to you with our
needs,
confident in your saving help.
We ask this through Christ our Lord.
**Amen.**

Let us pray the prayer that Jesus taught us:
**Our Father…**

✠ In the name of the Father, and of the Son, and of the Holy Spirit. Amen.

———————————

Note: Today's reading is Matthew 7:7-12.

## FRIDAY

✠ In the name of the Father, and of the Son, and of the Holy Spirit. Amen.

Introduction: In our reading today, Jesus' teaching goes beyond the Ten Commandments. We are to do more than the commandments require. He tells us that making up with those we have hurt and those who have hurt us is so important, we should do this before we even go to church!

A reading from the holy gospel according to Matthew
**Glory to you, Lord.**

Jesus said, "You have heard that it was said
to those of ancient times,
'You shall not murder'; and 'whoever
murders shall be liable to judgment.'
But I say to you that
if you are angry with a brother or sister,
you will be liable to judgment;
and if you insult a brother or sister,
you will be liable to the council;
and if you say, 'You fool,'
you will be liable to the hell of fire.
So when you are offering your gift
at the altar,
if you remember that your brother or sister
has something against you,
leave your gift there before the altar and go;
first be reconciled to your brother or sister,
and then come and offer your gift."

The gospel of the Lord.
**Praise to you, Lord Jesus Christ.**

Let us pray:
Most loving and merciful God,
your Son, Jesus, teaches us to forgive
those who have hurt us,
and to ask forgiveness
of those we have hurt.
Please give us the grace and gifts we need
to do this.
We ask this through Christ our Lord.
**Amen.**

Let us pray the prayer that Jesus taught us:
**Our Father…**

✠ In the name of the Father, and of the Son, and of the Holy Spirit. Amen.

Note: Today's reading is Matthew 5:21-24.

## MONDAY

✠ In the name of the Father, and of the Son, and of the Holy Spirit. Amen.

Introduction: In today's reading, Jesus tells us not to judge others. Instead, we are to be kind and generous, and forgive those who hurt us. The way we treat others is the way God will treat us. If we use are forgiving and kind, God will be the same with us. In fact, God promises to fill us up with his love and forgiveness!

A reading from the holy gospel according to Luke
**Glory to you, Lord.**

Jesus said, "Do not judge,
and you will not be judged;
do not condemn,
and you will not be condemned.
Forgive, and you will be forgiven;
give, and it will be given to you.
A good measure, pressed down,
shaken together, running over,
will be put into your lap;
for the measure you give
will be the measure you get back."

The gospel of the Lord.
**Praise to you, Lord Jesus Christ.**

Let us pray:
Most loving God,
you teach us how to live as your children.
Help us treat others with kindness and love,
to forgive them and care for them,
as you care for all creation.
We ask this through Christ our Lord.
**Amen.**

Let us pray the prayer that Jesus taught us:
**Our Father...**

✠ In the name of the Father, and of the Son, and of the Holy Spirit. Amen.

Note: Today's reading is Luke 6:37-38.

## TUESDAY

✠ **In the name of the Father, and of the Son, and of the Holy Spirit. Amen.**

Introduction: In our reading today, Jesus warns the crowds and his disciples to listen to and obey the teachers of the Law and the Pharisees. But they are not to act as these teachers do, because they do not practise what they preach. Humans are imperfect, but if we follow God's way, we will be true disciples of Jesus.

A reading from the holy gospel according to Matthew
**Glory to you, Lord.**

Then Jesus said to the crowds
and to his disciples,
"The scribes and the Pharisees
sit on Moses' seat;
therefore, do whatever they teach you
and follow it; but do not do as they do,
for they do not practise what they teach.
They tie up heavy burdens, hard to bear,
and lay them on the shoulders of others;
but they themselves are unwilling
to lift a finger to move them.
They do all their deeds
to be seen by others."

The gospel of the Lord.
**Praise to you, Lord Jesus Christ.**

Let us pray:
Most loving and gracious God,
Jesus teaches us
to follow your laws and ways,
to help those in need,
and to do good.
Give us the grace
to turn away from doing wrong
and do what is right
so that we will grow closer to you.
We ask this through Christ our Lord.
**Amen.**

Let us pray the prayer that Jesus taught us:
**Our Father...**

✠ **In the name of the Father, and of the Son, and of the Holy Spirit. Amen.**

Note: Today's reading is Matthew 23:1-5a.

## WEDNESDAY

✠ **In the name of the Father, and of the Son, and of the Holy Spirit. Amen.**

Introduction: In our reading today, Jesus tells his disciples what will happen to him: he will be arrested and condemned to die at the hands of the Gentiles (non-Jewish people), and then he will rise again.

He also tells them that to be great, they have to serve others. This is the opposite of the way things usually are in the world; a ruler expects to be served, not to serve others like a servant or a slave. In God's kingdom, some ideas are turned upside-down!

A reading from the holy gospel according to Matthew
**Glory to you, Lord.**

While Jesus was going up to Jerusalem,
he took the twelve disciples aside
by themselves, and said to them on the way,
"See, we are going up to Jerusalem,
and the Son of Man will be handed over
to the chief priests and scribes,
and they will condemn him to death;
then they will hand him over
to the Gentiles
to be mocked and flogged and crucified;
and on the third day he will be raised.
Whoever wishes to be great among you
must be your servant,
and whoever wishes to be first among you
must be your slave;
just as the Son of Man came
not to be served but to serve,
and to give his life a ransom for many."

The gospel of the Lord.
**Praise to you, Lord Jesus Christ.**

Let us pray:
Most loving God,
your Son, Jesus, the Son of Man,
gave up his life
so we could have eternal life with you.
He showed us that to be great,
we must serve others.
Help us always serve others
with care and kindness
as we build God's kingdom together.
We ask this through Christ our Lord.
**Amen.**

Let us pray the prayer that Jesus taught us:
**Our Father…**

✠ **In the name of the Father, and of the Son, and of the Holy Spirit. Amen.**

Note: Today's reading is Matthew 20:17-19, 26b-28.

## THURSDAY

✠ **In the name of the Father, and of the Son, and of the Holy Spirit. Amen.**

Introduction: In our reading today, God tells us that we are to put our trust in God, and not in people. Those who put their trust in God will grow and bloom, watered by the grace of God, which is like a stream.

A reading from the book of the prophet Jeremiah

Thus says the Lord:
Cursed are those who trust in mere mortals
and make mere flesh their strength,
whose hearts turn away from the Lord.
They shall be like a shrub in the desert,
and shall not see when relief comes.
They shall live in the parched places
of the wilderness,
in an uninhabited salt land.
Blessed are those who trust in the Lord,
whose trust is the Lord.
They shall be like a tree planted by water,
sending out its roots by the stream.
It shall not fear when heat comes,
and its leaves shall stay green;
in the year of drought it is not anxious,
and it does not cease to bear fruit.
The heart is devious above all else;
it is perverse – who can understand it?
I the Lord test the mind
and search the heart,
to give to all according to their ways,
according to the fruit of their doings.

The word of the Lord.
**Thanks be to God.**

Let us pray:
Most loving and gracious God,
you are the source
of all that is good and holy.
Help us always to put our trust in you,
and live according to your ways,
growing in your grace and love,
and bearing good fruit.
We ask this through Christ our Lord.
**Amen.**

Let us pray the prayer that Jesus taught us:
**Our Father…**

✠ **In the name of the Father, and of the Son, and of the Holy Spirit. Amen.**

---

Note: Today's reading is Jeremiah 17:5-10.

## FRIDAY

✠ In the name of the Father, and of the Son, and of the Holy Spirit. Amen.

Introduction: As Jesus was teaching in the Temple, he told a parable. The tenants (people who rented and worked the land) killed the two slaves that the owner of the vineyard sent to them to collect his share of the grapes. The owner then sent his own son, but the tenants killed him too. The owner is God, his slaves are the prophets, and the son is Jesus. The tenants are the people who would not listen to the prophets or Jesus. The chief priests and Pharisees, knowing that Jesus was talking about them, tried to arrest Jesus because of this.

A reading from the holy gospel according to Matthew
**Glory to you, Lord.**

Jesus asked them, "Now when the owner of the vineyard comes,
what will he do to those tenants?"
They said to him,
"He will put those wretches
to a miserable death,
and lease the vineyard to other tenants
who will give him the produce
at the harvest time."

Jesus said to them,
"Have you never read in the scriptures:
'The stone that the builders rejected
has become the cornerstone;
this was the Lord's doing,
and it is amazing in our eyes'?
Therefore I tell you, the kingdom of God
will be taken away from you
and given to a people
that produces the fruits of the kingdom.
The one who falls on this stone
will be broken to pieces;
and it will crush anyone on whom it falls."

When the chief priests and the Pharisees
heard his parables, they realized
that he was speaking about them.
They wanted to arrest him,
but they feared the crowds,
because they regarded him as a prophet.

The gospel of the Lord.
**Praise to you, Lord Jesus Christ.**

Let us pray:
Most loving God,
your Son, Jesus, is the cornerstone
of the kingdom of heaven.
Help us to produce the good fruits
of your kingdom
and be faithful followers of Jesus.
We ask this through Christ our Lord.
**Amen.**

Let us pray the prayer that Jesus taught us:
**Our Father…**

✠ In the name of the Father, and of the Son, and of the Holy Spirit. Amen.

Note: Today's reading is Matthew 21:40-45.

## MONDAY

✠ In the name of the Father, and of the Son, and of the Holy Spirit. Amen.

Introduction: In our reading today, Jesus talks about two prophets who lived long ago: Elijah and Elisha. Both of these prophets brought God's healing word – but not to Israel, where God's chosen people lived. Instead, they brought healing to people who welcomed and listened to the prophet's words.

Do we open our hearts to God's word, even when it's something we'd rather not hear because it asks us to change our ways?

A reading from the holy gospel according to Luke
**Glory to you, Lord.**

Jesus said,
"But the truth is, there were many widows
in Israel in the time of Elijah,
when the heaven was shut up
for three years and six months,
and there was a severe famine
over all the land;
yet Elijah was sent to none of them
except to a widow at Zarephath in Sidon.
There were also many lepers in Israel
in the time of the prophet Elisha,
and none of them was cleansed
except Naaman the Syrian."
When they heard this,
all in the synagogue were filled with rage.
They got up, drove him out of the town,
and led him to the brow of the hill
on which their town was built,
so that they might hurl him off the cliff.
But he passed through the midst of them
and went on his way.

The gospel of the Lord.
**Praise to you, Lord Jesus Christ.**

Let us pray:
Merciful God,
sometimes we choose not to listen to you.
Help us open our ears and our hearts
so that we may follow your ways
and live as your faithful children.
We ask this through Christ our Lord.
**Amen.**

Let us pray the prayer that Jesus taught us:
**Our Father…**

✠ In the name of the Father, and of the Son, and of the Holy Spirit. Amen.

_____

Note: Today's reading is Luke 4:25-30.

# THIRD WEEK OF LENT

## TUESDAY

✠ In the name of the Father, and of the Son, and of the Holy Spirit. Amen.

Introduction: It's not always easy to forgive someone. And sometimes we find ourselves forgiving the same person over and over again! In today's reading, Peter asks Jesus how many times he has to forgive. The answer is such a big number, it really means we must keep forgiving, just as God keeps forgiving us.

A reading from the holy gospel according to Matthew
**Glory to you, Lord.**

Then Peter came and said to Jesus,
"Lord, if another member of the church
sins against me,
how often should I forgive?
As many as seven times?"
Jesus said to him,
"Not seven times, but, I tell you,
seventy-seven times."

The gospel of the Lord.
**Praise to you, Lord Jesus Christ.**

Let us pray:
Merciful God,
your love and compassion for us
cannot be measured.
Help us to forgive from our hearts
those who hurt us,
the way you forgive us.
We ask this through Christ our Lord.
**Amen.**

Let us pray the prayer that Jesus taught us:
**Our Father…**

✠ In the name of the Father, and of the Son, and of the Holy Spirit. Amen.

Note: Today's reading is Matthew 18:21-22.

## WEDNESDAY

✠ **In the name of the Father, and of the Son, and of the Holy Spirit. Amen.**

Introduction: Today Jesus tells us that he did not come to get rid of the laws of Moses, especially the Ten Commandments, and the teachings of the prophets. He came to bring life to these teachings.

These laws come from God, and are for all people for all time. We too are to follow these laws and obey them.

Do we follow God's ways and laws? Are we doing what God asks of us?

A reading from the holy gospel according to Matthew
**Glory to you, Lord.**

Jesus said,
"Do not think that I have come to abolish the law or the prophets;
I have come not to abolish but to fulfil.
For truly I tell you,
until heaven and earth pass away,
not one letter, not one stroke of a letter,
will pass from the law
until all is accomplished.
Therefore, whoever breaks
one of the least of these commandments,
and teaches others to do the same,
will be called least
in the kingdom of heaven;
but whoever does them and teaches them
will be called great
in the kingdom of heaven."

The gospel of the Lord.
**Praise to you, Lord Jesus Christ.**

Let us pray:
Most loving God,
you gave us your laws
to help us grow in your ways
and in grace and holiness.
Help us to obey your laws
and follow your ways
to grow closer to you
and to be better followers of Jesus,
your Son.
We ask this through Christ our Lord.
**Amen.**

Let us pray the prayer that Jesus taught us:
**Our Father…**

✠ **In the name of the Father, and of the Son, and of the Holy Spirit. Amen.**

---

Note: Today's reading is Matthew 5:17-19.

## THURSDAY

✠ **In the name of the Father, and of the Son, and of the Holy Spirit. Amen.**

Introduction: In our reading today, God tells the prophet Jeremiah that the people that he has called as his own no longer listen to him, and do not follow the commands he gave them. God sent the prophets to remind them of their promises, but they still did not listen.

As we listen to the reading, we can hear that God is upset and hurt when people break their promises to God.

A reading from the book of the prophet Jeremiah

But this command I gave them,
"Obey my voice, and I will be your God,
and you shall be my people;
and walk only in the way
that I command you,
so that it may be well with you."
Yet they did not obey or incline their ear,
but, in the stubbornness of their evil will,
they walked in their own counsels,
and looked backwards rather than forwards.
From the day that your ancestors
came out of the land of Egypt until this day,
I have persistently sent all my servants
the prophets to them, day after day;
yet they did not listen to me,
or pay attention,
but they stiffened their necks.
They did worse than their ancestors did.
So you shall speak all these words to them,
but they will not listen to you.
You shall call to them,
but they will not answer you.

You shall say to them: This is the
nation that did not obey the voice
of the Lord their God,
and did not accept discipline;
truth has perished;
it is cut off from their lips.

The word of the Lord.
**Thanks be to God.**

Let us pray:
Most loving God,
sometimes we do not do what you ask,
and do not follow your laws and ways.
Yet you always forgive us
when we turn back to you.
Help us always to listen
to the people you send to us
so that we may grow in holiness
as your children.
We ask this through Christ our Lord.
**Amen.**

Let us pray the prayer that Jesus taught us:
**Our Father…**

✠ **In the name of the Father, and of the Son, and of the Holy Spirit. Amen.**

Note: Today's reading is Jeremiah 7:23-28.

## FRIDAY

✠ **In the name of the Father, and of the Son, and of the Holy Spirit. Amen.**

Introduction: What is the greatest commandment? Jesus says that the first is to love God with our whole heart, mind, soul and strength. The second is to love others as ourselves. All of God's laws can be summed up in this answer.

Do we love God and others as we love ourselves?

A reading from the holy gospel according to Matthew
**Glory to you, Lord.**

One of the scribes came near
and heard them disputing with one another,
and seeing that Jesus answered them well,
he asked him,
"Which commandment is the first of all?"
Jesus answered, "The first is,
'Hear, O Israel: the Lord our God,
the Lord is one;
you shall love the Lord your God
with all your heart,
and with all your soul,
and with all your mind,
and with all your strength.'
The second is this,
'You shall love your neighbour as yourself.'
There is no other commandment
greater than these."
Then the scribe said to him,
"You are right, Teacher;
you have truly said that 'he is one,
and besides him there is no other';
and 'to love him with all the heart,
and with all the understanding,
and with all the strength',
and 'to love one's neighbour as oneself' —

this is much more important than all
whole burnt-offerings and sacrifices."
When Jesus saw that he answered wisely,
he said to him,
"You are not far from the kingdom of God."
After that no one dared
to ask him any question.

The gospel of the Lord.
**Praise to you, Lord Jesus Christ.**

Let us pray:
Most merciful God,
Jesus loved you with all his heart, soul,
mind and strength.
He loved us so much
that he died on the cross for us.
Help us to love you
more and more each day,
and to see Jesus in those around us.
Help us to love them as we love ourselves.
We ask this through Christ our Lord.
Amen.

Let us pray the prayer that Jesus taught us:
**Our Father…**

✠ **In the name of the Father, and of the Son, and of the Holy Spirit. Amen.**

---

Note: Today's reading is Mark 12:28-34.

## MONDAY

✠ **In the name of the Father, and of the Son, and of the Holy Spirit. Amen.**

Introduction: In our reading today, a government official comes to Jesus, asking him to heal his son who is about to die. Without hesitation, the man does what Jesus tells him to do.

This man has a lot to teach us: he does what Jesus asks without doubting or questioning him. He has faith in Jesus.

Do we believe in the promises Jesus makes? Do we do what he asks?

A reading from the holy gospel according to John
**Glory to you, Lord.**

Then Jesus came again to Cana in Galilee
where he had changed the water into wine.
Now there was a royal official
whose son lay ill in Capernaum.
When he heard that Jesus had come
from Judea to Galilee,
he went and begged him to come down
and heal his son,
for he was at the point of death.
Then Jesus said to him,
"Unless you see signs and wonders
you will not believe."
The official said to him,
"Sir, come down before my little boy dies."
Jesus said to him, "Go; your son will live."
The man believed the word
that Jesus spoke to him
and started on his way.
As he was going down,
his slaves met him and told him
that his child was alive.

So he asked them the hour
when he began to recover,
and they said to him,
"Yesterday at one in the afternoon
the fever left him."
The father realized that this was the hour
when Jesus had said to him,
"Your son will live."
So he himself believed,
along with his whole household.

The gospel of the Lord.
**Praise to you, Lord Jesus Christ.**

Let us pray:
Most holy and merciful God,
your Son showed compassion
for the government official
and healed his son.
Help us to have faith in Jesus
and to live as his disciples.
We ask this through Christ our Lord.
**Amen.**

Let us pray the prayer that Jesus taught us:
**Our Father...**

✠ **In the name of the Father, and of the Son, and of the Holy Spirit. Amen.**

Note: Today's reading is John 4:46-53.

## TUESDAY

✠ **In the name of the Father, and of the Son, and of the Holy Spirit. Amen.**

Introduction: In our reading today, Jesus meets a man who has been sick for 38 years. He has never had anyone to help him get better. Jesus looks into the man's heart and sees that he truly wants to be well again, so Jesus heals him.

Jesus will heal us, too, if we open our hearts to him.

A reading from the holy gospel according to John
**Glory to you, Lord.**

After this there was a festival of the Jews,
and Jesus went up to Jerusalem.
Now in Jerusalem by the Sheep Gate
there is a pool,
called in Hebrew Beth-zatha,
which has five porticoes.
In these lay many invalids –
blind, lame, and paralyzed.
One man was there
who had been ill for thirty-eight years.
When Jesus saw him lying there and knew
that he had been there a long time,
he said to him,
"Do you want to be made well?"
The sick man answered him,
"Sir, I have no one to put me into the pool
when the water is stirred up;
and while I am making my way,
someone else steps down ahead of me."

Jesus said to him,
"Stand up, take your mat and walk."
At once the man was made well,
and he took up his mat and began to walk.

The gospel of the Lord.
**Praise to you, Lord Jesus Christ.**

Let us pray:
God our Creator,
Jesus can see the unspoken wishes
of our hearts,
and can heal us from what separates us
from your care and love.
Give us the courage to pick up our mat
and walk when he asks us to.
We ask this through Christ our Lord.
**Amen.**

Let us pray the prayer that Jesus taught us:
**Our Father…**

✠ **In the name of the Father, and of the Son, and of the Holy Spirit. Amen.**

---

Note: Today's reading is John 5:1-9.

## WEDNESDAY

✠ In the name of the Father, and of the Son, and of the Holy Spirit. Amen.

Introduction: Today's reading is a continuation of what we heard yesterday, when Jesus healed the man who was sick for 38 years. Because he healed the man on the Sabbath, the day of rest, the Jewish leaders were angry at him for breaking the law. Jesus explains that he works on the Sabbath because his Father does.

This gets him into trouble: by calling God "Father," he is making himself equal to God. This was a very serious offence in Jewish law. In the eyes of the authorities, Jesus was doing everything that was wrong.

A reading from the holy gospel according to John
**Glory to you, Lord.**

Therefore the Jews
started persecuting Jesus,
because he was doing such things
on the sabbath.
But Jesus answered them,
"My Father is still working,
and I also am working."
For this reason the Jews were seeking
all the more to kill him,
because he was not only
breaking the sabbath,
but was also calling God his own Father,
thereby making himself equal to God.

Jesus said to them,
"Very truly, I tell you,
the Son can do nothing on his own,
but only what he sees the Father doing;
for whatever the Father does,
the Son does likewise.
The Father loves the Son
and shows him all that he himself is doing."

The gospel of the Lord.
**Praise to you, Lord Jesus Christ.**

Let us pray:
Most loving God,
Jesus followed your example,
even when this got him into trouble
with the leaders of his time.
Help us always to keep our eyes on you,
doing what you ask us
and following your laws and ways,
even when other people criticize us.
We ask this through Christ our Lord.
**Amen.**

Let us pray the prayer that Jesus taught us:
**Our Father…**

✠ In the name of the Father, and of the Son, and of the Holy Spirit. Amen.

Note: Today's reading is John 5:16-20a.

## THURSDAY

✠ **In the name of the Father, and of the Son, and of the Holy Spirit. Amen.**

Introduction: In our reading today, the Jewish authorities are giving Jesus a hard time. Jesus talks to them about the witness and truth that John the Baptist gave, then says that his own testimony is even greater.

Do we show others through our actions that we believe in Jesus' words and know that he was sent to lead us to God?

A reading from the holy gospel according to John
**Glory to you, Lord.**

Jesus said,
"If I testify about myself,
my testimony is not true.
There is another who testifies on my behalf,
and I know that his testimony to me is true.
You sent messengers to John,
and he testified to the truth.
Not that I accept such human testimony,
but I say these things
so that you may be saved.
He was a burning and shining lamp,
and you were willing to rejoice for a while
in his light.
But I have a testimony greater than John's.
The works that the Father has given me
to complete, the very works that I am doing,
testify on my behalf
that the Father has sent me.
And the Father who sent me
has himself testified on my behalf."

The gospel of the Lord.
**Praise to you, Lord Jesus Christ.**

Let us pray:
Most holy and loving God,
the work you gave Jesus, your Son,
to do here on earth
speaks of your wisdom, truth and love.
Help us to know what it is you ask of us,
and to carry out your will like Jesus did.
We ask this through Christ our Lord.
**Amen.**

Let us pray the prayer that Jesus taught us:
**Our Father…**

✠ **In the name of the Father, and of the Son, and of the Holy Spirit. Amen.**

---

Note: Today's reading is John 5:31-37a.

## FRIDAY

✠ In the name of the Father, and of the Son, and of the Holy Spirit. Amen.

Introduction: In our reading today, we hear that Jesus is travelling in Galilee where it was safer for him. Jesus was aware that the authorities were looking for him. It was becoming more and more dangerous for Jesus to be out in public. He knew where all his work was leading him – to die on the cross. But that did not stop him from doing the work that God had given him to do.

Would we continue to do what God wanted, even if it made some people angry?

A reading from the holy gospel according to John
**Glory to you, Lord.**

After this Jesus went about in Galilee.
He did not wish to go about in Judea
because the Jews were looking
for an opportunity to kill him.
Now the Jewish festival of Booths was near.
But after his brothers
had gone to the festival, then he also went,
not publicly but as it were in secret.
Now some of the people of Jerusalem
were saying,
"Is not this the man
whom they are trying to kill?
And here he is, speaking openly,
but they say nothing to him!
Can it be that the authorities really know
that this is the Messiah?
Yet we know where this man is from;
but when the Messiah comes,
no one will know where he is from."

Then Jesus cried out
as he was teaching in the temple,
"You know me,
and you know where I am from.
I have not come on my own."
Then they tried to arrest him,
but no one laid hands on him,
because his hour had not yet come.

The gospel of the Lord.
**Praise to you, Lord Jesus Christ.**

Let us pray:
Most holy and all-powerful God,
your beloved Son, Jesus,
spoke your truth and did your work
knowing that it would eventually
cost him his life.
Help us to be firm in our faith,
and do what is right,
even when it makes life difficult for us.
We ask this through Christ our Lord.
**Amen.**

Let us pray the prayer that Jesus taught us:
**Our Father...**

✠ In the name of the Father, and of the Son, and of the Holy Spirit. Amen.

Note: Today's reading is John 7:1-2, 10, 25-28a, 30.

## MONDAY

✠ **In the name of the Father, and of the Son, and of the Holy Spirit. Amen.**

Introduction: Today's reading talks about the way God cares for us: like a shepherd cares for sheep. God guides us, protects us, feeds us, welcomes us. God is always with us.

Jesus knew this psalm, and was comforted by it, too, knowing the love God his Father had for him.

A reading from the book of Psalms

The Lord is my shepherd, I shall not want.
He makes me lie down in green pastures;
he leads me beside still waters;
he restores my soul.
He leads me in right paths
for his name's sake.
Even though I walk
through the darkest valley,
I fear no evil;
for you are with me;
your rod and your staff –
they comfort me.
You prepare a table before me
in the presence of my enemies;
you anoint my head with oil;
my cup overflows.
Surely goodness and mercy shall follow me
all the days of my life,
and I shall dwell in the house of the Lord
my whole life long.

The word of the Lord.
**Thanks be to God.**

Let us pray:
Most holy and loving God,
you guide us and care for us
when times are hard,
and remind us
that rest and peace lie with you.
Help us to rely on
your guidance and strength
during difficult times,
and to remember that you are always there.
We ask this through Christ our Lord.
**Amen.**

Let us pray the prayer that Jesus taught us:
**Our Father…**

✠ **In the name of the Father, and of the Son, and of the Holy Spirit. Amen.**

Note: Today's reading is Psalm 23.

## TUESDAY

✠ In the name of the Father, and of the Son, and of the Holy Spirit. Amen.

Introduction: In our reading today, Jesus tells the Jewish authorities who he is: "I Am Who I Am." This is the title God gave when he spoke to Moses from the burning bush. In using this title, Jesus reveals that he is following God's instructions, and that God is with him.

A reading from the holy gospel according to John
**Glory to you, Lord.**

They said to him, "Who are you?"
Jesus said to them,
"Why do I speak to you at all?
I have much to say about you
and much to condemn;
but the one who sent me is true,
and I declare to the world
what I have heard from him."
They did not understand
that he was speaking to them
about the Father.
So Jesus said,
"When you have lifted up the Son of Man,
then you will realize that I am he,
and that I do nothing on my own,
but I speak these things
as the Father instructed me.
And the one who sent me is with me;
he has not left me alone,
for I always do what is pleasing to him."
As he was saying these things,
many believed in him.

The gospel of the Lord.
**Praise to you, Lord Jesus Christ.**

Let us pray:
Most loving and holy God,
you were, are and will be
until the end of time.
Help us to grow in faith and belief in you,
and in your divine Son, Jesus.
We ask this through Christ our Lord.
**Amen.**

Let us pray the prayer that Jesus taught us:
**Our Father...**

✠ In the name of the Father, and of the Son, and of the Holy Spirit. Amen.

Note: Today's reading is John 8:25-30.

## WEDNESDAY

✠ **In the name of the Father, and of the Son, and of the Holy Spirit. Amen.**

Introduction: Jesus tells those who believe in him that they are truly his followers if his words find a home in their hearts and are put into practice. He says, "The truth will set you free." If we listen to his teachings and follow them, we will be free of sin, free to live in God's light.

A reading from the holy gospel according to John
**Glory to you, Lord.**

Then Jesus said to the Jews
who had believed in him,
"If you continue in my word,
you are truly my disciples;
and you will know the truth,
and the truth will make you free."
They answered him,
"We are descendants of Abraham
and have never been slaves to anyone.
What do you mean by saying,
'You will be made free'?"
Jesus answered them,
"Very truly, I tell you,
everyone who commits sin is a slave to sin.
The slave does not have a permanent place
in the household;
the son has a place there for ever.
So if the Son makes you free,
you will be free indeed.
I know that you are
descendants of Abraham;
yet you look for an opportunity to kill me,
because there is no place in you
for my word.

I declare what I have seen
in the Father's presence;
as for you, you should do
what you have heard from the Father.
But now you are trying to kill me,
a man who has told you the truth
that I heard from God."

The gospel of the Lord.
**Praise to you, Lord Jesus Christ.**

Let us pray:
God of wisdom,
Jesus revealed your truths to us.
Grant that we may grow in faith,
believing and putting into action
all he teaches us.
We ask this through Christ our Lord.
**Amen.**

Let us pray the prayer that Jesus taught us:
**Our Father...**

✠ **In the name of the Father, and of the Son, and of the Holy Spirit. Amen.**

---

Note: Today's reading is John 8:31-38a, 40.

## THURSDAY

✠ In the name of the Father, and of the Son, and of the Holy Spirit. Amen.

Introduction: In our reading today, Jesus tells the people that whoever keeps his word will never die. The people are shocked: of course we will all die someday! But Jesus is talking about eternal life, when we will live with God forever. They do not understand, and try to attack him.

We are sometimes like the people in today's gospel. When we don't understand something, we may lash out in anger or fear. How can we open our hearts and listen in order to understand better?

A reading from the holy gospel according to John
**Glory to you, Lord.**

Jesus said,
"Very truly, I tell you,
whoever keeps my word
will never see death."
The Jews said to him,
"Now we know that you have a demon.
Abraham died, and so did the prophets;
yet you say,
'Whoever keeps my word
will never taste death.'
Are you greater than our father Abraham,
who died? The prophets also died.
Who do you claim to be?"
Jesus answered, "If I glorify myself,
my glory is nothing.
It is my Father who glorifies me,
he of whom you say, 'He is our God',
though you do not know him.
But I do know him and I keep his word.
Your ancestor Abraham
rejoiced that he would see my day;
he saw it and was glad."

Then the Jews said to him,
"You are not yet fifty years old,
and have you seen Abraham?"
Jesus said to them,
"Very truly, I tell you,
before Abraham was, I am."
So they picked up stones to throw at him,
but Jesus hid himself
and went out of the temple.

The gospel of the Lord.
**Praise to you, Lord Jesus Christ.**

Let us pray:
Loving God,
Jesus tells us that if we obey his teaching,
we will have eternal life.
Help us to listen to his words,
obey his teaching
and share the Good News of eternal life
with others.
We ask this through Christ our Lord.
**Amen.**

Let us pray the prayer that Jesus taught us:
**Our Father…**

✠ In the name of the Father, and of the Son, and of the Holy Spirit. Amen.

Note: Today's reading is John 8:51-55a, d, 56-59.

## FRIDAY

✠ In the name of the Father, and of the Son, and of the Holy Spirit. Amen.

Introduction: In today's reading, the people pick up stones to throw at Jesus. They felt that he was not showing respect for God, especially in the way he talked. This is called blasphemy. They did not believe that Jesus was the Son of God.

A reading from the holy gospel according to John
**Glory to you, Lord.**

The Jews took up stones again to stone him.
Jesus replied, "I have shown you
many good works from the Father.
For which of these
are you going to stone me?"
The Jews answered,
"It is not for a good work
that we are going to stone you,
but for blasphemy, because you,
though only a human being,
are making yourself God."
Jesus answered, "Is it not written in your law,
'I said, you are gods'?
If those to whom the word of God
came were called 'gods' –
and the scripture cannot be annulled –
can you say that the one whom the Father
has sanctified and sent into the world
is blaspheming because I said,
'I am God's Son'?"
Then they tried to arrest him again,
but he escaped from their hands.

The gospel of the Lord.
**Praise to you, Lord Jesus Christ.**

Let us pray:
Loving God,
the people of Jesus' time
did not believe that you had sent him,
that he was your Son.
Help us always to believe in Jesus
and be his faithful followers.
We ask this through Christ our Lord.
**Amen.**

Let us pray the prayer that Jesus taught us:
**Our Father…**

✠ In the name of the Father, and of the Son, and of the Holy Spirit. Amen.

---

Note: Today's reading is John 10:31-36, 39.

## MONDAY

✠ In the name of the Father, and of the Son, and of the Holy Spirit. Amen.

Introduction: Holy Week began yesterday, with Palm Sunday. Today's reading, written long before Jesus was born, describes the Messiah and the work he will do on earth. Jesus is the servant of God who brings justice to the world.

A reading from the book of the prophet Isaiah

The Lord says, "Here is my servant,
whom I uphold,
my chosen, in whom my soul delights;
I have put my spirit upon him;
he will bring forth justice to the nations.
He will not cry or lift up his voice,
or make it heard in the street;
a bruised reed he will not break,
and a dimly burning wick
he will not quench;
he will faithfully bring forth justice.
He will not grow faint or be crushed
until he has established justice in the earth;
and the coastlands wait for his teaching."
Thus says God, the Lord,
"I am the Lord,
I have called you in righteousness,
I have taken you by the hand and kept you;
I have given you as a covenant
to the people,
a light to the nations,
to open the eyes that are blind,
to bring out the prisoners
from the dungeon,
from the prison those who sit in darkness."

The word of the Lord.
**Thanks be to God.**

Let us pray:
Most holy God,
you sent your Son to us
to set us free from darkness
and to bring us into your light.
Help us to be like Jesus,
not to lose hope or courage,
and to be children of the light.
We ask this through Christ our Lord.
**Amen.**

Let us pray the prayer that Jesus taught us:
**Our Father…**

✠ In the name of the Father, and of the Son, and of the Holy Spirit. Amen.

---

Note: Today's reading is Isaiah 42:1-5a, 6-7.

## TUESDAY

✠ **In the name of the Father, and of the Son, and of the Holy Spirit. Amen.**

Introduction: In our reading today, which is found in the passage about the Last Supper, we hear about Judas' betrayal of Jesus.

How do we betray Jesus sometimes – in our thoughts, our words, our actions? How can we change our hearts when this happens?

A reading from the holy gospel according to John
**Glory to you, Lord.**

After saying this Jesus was troubled in spirit, and declared,
"Very truly, I tell you,
one of you will betray me."
The disciples looked at one another,
uncertain of whom he was speaking.
One of his disciples –
the one whom Jesus loved –
was reclining next to him;
Simon Peter therefore motioned to him
to ask Jesus of whom he was speaking.
So while reclining next to Jesus,
he asked him, "Lord, who is it?"
Jesus answered, "It is the one
to whom I give this piece of bread
when I have dipped it in the dish."
So when he had dipped the piece of bread,
he gave it to Judas son of Simon Iscariot.
After he received the piece of bread,
Satan entered into him.

Jesus said to him,
"Do quickly what you are going to do."
Now no one at the table
knew why he said this to him.
So, after receiving the piece of bread,
he immediately went out. And it was night.

The gospel of the Lord.
**Praise to you, Lord Jesus Christ.**

Let us pray:
Most holy God,
Judas chose to betray Jesus, your Son.
All of us,
when we do not follow your ways and laws,
and sometimes even deny
that we are followers of Jesus,
betray him by our words and actions.
Grant us the grace we need
to be faithful disciples of Jesus.
We ask this through Christ our Lord.
**Amen.**

Let us pray the prayer that Jesus taught us:
**Our Father…**

✠ **In the name of the Father, and of the Son, and of the Holy Spirit. Amen.**

---

Note: Today's reading is John 13:21-28, 30.

## WEDNESDAY

✠ **In the name of the Father, and of the Son, and of the Holy Spirit. Amen.**

Introduction: Jesus is God's obedient servant. He always does what God asks him to do, knowing that God will help him.

God will give us, too, the strength and courage we need to stand up for what is right, and to do what God asks, even when it is hard to do.

A reading from the book of the prophet Isaiah

The Lord God has given me
the tongue of a teacher,
that I may know how to sustain
the weary with a word.
Morning by morning he wakens –
wakens my ear
to listen as those who are taught.
The Lord God has opened my ear,
and I was not rebellious,
I did not turn backwards.
I gave my back to those who struck me,
and my cheeks
to those who pulled out the beard;
I did not hide my face
from insult and spitting.
The Lord God helps me;
therefore I have not been disgraced;
therefore I have set my face like flint,
and I know that I shall not be put to shame;
he who vindicates me is near.

Who will contend with me?
Let us stand up together.
Who are my adversaries?
Let them confront me.
It is the Lord God who helps me;
who will declare me guilty?

The word of the Lord.
**Thanks be to God.**

Let us pray:
Sovereign God,
Jesus did all that you asked
and accepted your will,
even though it led to his death on the cross.
Help us always to do what is right,
even if it is hard
and others laugh or make fun of us.
Grant us the courage
to be children of light,
the children you call us to be.
We ask this through Christ our Lord.
**Amen.**

Let us pray the prayer that Jesus taught us:
**Our Father…**

✠ **In the name of the Father, and of the Son, and of the Holy Spirit. Amen.**

---

Note: Today's reading is Isaiah 50:4-9a.

## HOLY THURSDAY

✠ **In the name of the Father, and of the Son, and of the Holy Spirit. Amen.**

Introduction: Today is the first day of the most holy three days in the church year. Lent ends this evening – we are entering into the solemn Triduum. The Triduum (a word that means three days) includes Holy Thursday, Good Friday and the great Easter Vigil, which is held on Holy Saturday night. We remember and celebrate the suffering, death and resurrection of Jesus during the Triduum.

Tonight at church we celebrate the Mass of the Lord's Supper – the Last Supper. It is during this supper that Jesus gave us the sacrament of the Eucharist, where he gives us himself in Holy Communion. He also gave us the sacrament of Holy Orders, the sacrament of priesthood or servant-leadership in the Church.

The gospel tonight is the story of the washing of the feet. By washing the apostles' feet, like a servant, Jesus shows them that leadership in the Church means serving, healing and helping one another. As followers of Jesus, we are called to serve the people we meet.

A reading from the holy gospel according to John
**Glory to you, Lord.**

The devil had already put it into the heart
of Judas son of Simon Iscariot to betray him.
And during supper Jesus,
knowing that the Father had given
all things into his hands,
and that he had come from God
and was going to God,
got up from the table,
took off his outer robe,
and tied a towel around himself.
He came to Simon Peter, who said to him,
"Lord, are you going to wash my feet?"
Jesus answered,
"You do not know now what I am doing,
but later you will understand."

Peter said to him,
"You will never wash my feet."
Jesus answered, "Unless I wash you,
you have no share with me."
After he had washed their feet,
had put on his robe,
and had returned to the table,
he said to them,
"Do you know what I have done to you?
You call me Teacher and Lord –
and you are right, for that is what I am.
So if I, your Lord and Teacher,
have washed your feet,
you also ought to wash one another's feet.
For I have set you an example,
that you also should do
as I have done to you."

The gospel of the Lord.
**Praise to you, Lord Jesus Christ.**

Let us pray:
Creator God,
help us to serve others as Jesus did.
We ask this through Christ our Lord.
**Amen.**

Let us pray the prayer that Jesus taught us:
**Our Father....**

✠ **In the name of the Father, and of the Son, and of the Holy Spirit. Amen.**

Note: Today's reading is John 13:2-4, 6-8, 12-15.

## EASTER TUESDAY

✠ **In the name of the Father, and of the Son, and of the Holy Spirit. Amen.**

Introduction: Alleluia! Jesus is risen! Today we hear the story of Jesus appearing to Mary Magdalene in the garden near the tomb. Mary was the first person Jesus appeared to after his resurrection.

A reading from the holy gospel according to John
**Glory to you, Lord.**

Mary stood weeping outside the tomb.
As she wept,
she bent over to look into the tomb;
and she saw two angels in white,
sitting where the body of Jesus
had been lying,
one at the head and the other at the feet.
They said to her,
"Woman, why are you weeping?"
She said to them,
"They have taken away my Lord,
and I do not know
where they have laid him."
When she had said this, she turned round
and saw Jesus standing there,
but she did not know that it was Jesus.
Jesus said to her,
"Woman, why are you weeping?
For whom are you looking?"
Supposing him to be the gardener,
she said to him,
"Sir, if you have carried him away,
tell me where you have laid him,
and I will take him away."
Jesus said to her, "Mary!"
She turned and said to him in Hebrew,
"Rabbouni!" (which means Teacher).

Jesus said to her, "Do not hold on to me,
because I have not yet ascended
to the Father.
But go to my brothers and say to them,
'I am ascending to my Father
and your Father,
to my God and your God.'"
Mary Magdalene went
and announced to the disciples,
"I have seen the Lord"; and she told them
that he had said these things to her.

The gospel of the Lord.
**Praise to you, Lord Jesus Christ.**

Let us pray:
Jesus, Risen Lord,
Mary was crying
because she thought you were dead.
The joy she felt when she recognized you
filled her heart to overflowing.
Help us to remember
that you are with us always,
even if we cannot see or feel your presence.
Give us the grace we need
to be children of hope.
**Amen. Alleluia!**

Let us pray the prayer that Jesus taught us:
**Our Father...**

✠ **In the name of the Father, and of the Son, and of the Holy Spirit. Amen.**

Note: Today's reading is John 20:11-18.

## EASTER WEDNESDAY

✠ **In the name of the Father, and of the Son, and of the Holy Spirit. Amen.**

Introduction: Alleluia! Jesus is risen! In today's gospel, we hear about the two disciples walking to the village of Emmaus, about 10 kilometres from Jerusalem. They are discouraged because they think Jesus is dead. As they are talking, Jesus draws near and walks with them, but they do not recognize him.

As he explains things to them, their eyes are opened!

A reading from the holy gospel according to Luke
**Glory to you, Lord.**

Then Jesus said to them,
"Oh, how foolish you are,
and how slow of heart to believe all
that the prophets have declared!
Was it not necessary that the Messiah
should suffer these things
and then enter into his glory?"
Then beginning with Moses
and all the prophets,
he interpreted to them
the things about himself in all the scriptures.
As they came near the village
to which they were going,
he walked ahead as if he were going on.
But they urged him strongly, saying,
"Stay with us, because it is almost evening
and the day is now nearly over."
So he went in to stay with them.

When he was at the table with them,
he took bread, blessed and broke it,
and gave it to them.
Then their eyes were opened,
and they recognized him;
and he vanished from their sight.

The gospel of the Lord.
**Praise to you, Lord Jesus Christ.**

Let us pray:
Jesus, Risen Lord,
the disciples on the road to Emmaus
did not recognize you
until you broke the bread with them.
Help us to recognize you
in the people around us
and in the word of God, the Bible.
Teach us to listen for your voice,
and to recognize it when you speak to us.
**Amen. Alleluia!**

Let us pray the prayer that Jesus taught us:
**Our Father…**

✠ **In the name of the Father, and of the Son, and of the Holy Spirit. Amen.**

———————————

Note: Today's reading is Luke 24:25-31.

## EASTER THURSDAY

✠ In the name of the Father, and of the Son, and of the Holy Spirit. Amen.

Introduction: After the two disciples on the road to Emmaus meet Jesus, who is alive, they rush back to Jerusalem to tell the others the exciting news. Then something surprising happens. They are all full of joy!

A reading from the holy gospel according to Luke
**Glory to you, Lord.**

While they were talking about this,
Jesus himself stood among them
and said to them, "Peace be with you."
They were startled and terrified,
and thought that they were seeing a ghost.
He said to them, "Why are you frightened,
and why do doubts arise in your hearts?
Look at my hands and my feet;
see that it is I myself.
Touch me and see;
for a ghost does not have flesh and bones
as you see that I have."
And when he had said this,
he showed them his hands and his feet.
While in their joy they were disbelieving
and still wondering, he said to them,
"Have you anything here to eat?"
They gave him a piece of broiled fish,
and he took it and ate in their presence.
Then he said to them,
"These are my words that I spoke to you
while I was still with you –
that everything written about me
in the law of Moses, the prophets,
and the psalms must be fulfilled."

Then he opened their minds
to understand the scriptures,
and he said to them, "Thus it is written,
that the Messiah is to suffer
and to rise from the dead on the third day,
and that repentance and forgiveness of sins
is to be proclaimed in his name
to all nations, beginning from Jerusalem.
You are witnesses of these things."

The gospel of the Lord.
**Praise to you, Lord Jesus Christ.**

Let us pray:
Jesus, Risen Lord,
the disciples were overjoyed
and filled with wonder
when you appeared to them.
Grant that we may experience in our lives
the joy, wonder and peace
that only you can bring.
**Amen. Alleluia!**

Let us pray the prayer that Jesus taught us:
**Our Father…**

✠ In the name of the Father, and of the Son, and of the Holy Spirit. Amen.

Note: Today's reading is Luke 24:36-48.

## EASTER FRIDAY

✠ **In the name of the Father, and of the Son, and of the Holy Spirit. Amen.**

Introduction: In today's gospel, the disciples are fishing. They haven't caught anything all night. At sunrise, Jesus watches from the shore, but they do not know it is he. Something surprising happens when they do what Jesus suggests, and one of them recognizes him. Peter gets excited and can't wait to get back to shore!

Can we be as eager as Peter, and turn to Jesus immediately with our needs, our joys and all the deepest desires of our hearts?

A reading from the holy gospel according to John
**Glory to you, Lord.**

After these things
Jesus showed himself again
to the disciples by the Sea of Tiberias;
and he showed himself in this way.
Gathered there together were Simon Peter,
Thomas called the Twin,
Nathanael of Cana in Galilee,
the sons of Zebedee,
and two others of his disciples.
Simon Peter said to them,
"I am going fishing."
They said to him, 'We will go with you."
They went out and got into the boat,
but that night they caught nothing.
Just after daybreak,
Jesus stood on the beach;
but the disciples did not know
that it was Jesus.
Jesus said to them,
"Children, you have no fish, have you?"
They answered him, "No."
He said to them, "Cast the net
to the right side of the boat,
and you will find some."

So they cast it,
and now they were not able to haul it in
because there were so many fish.
That disciple whom Jesus loved
said to Peter, "It is the Lord!"
When Simon Peter heard
that it was the Lord,
he put on some clothes,
for he was naked, and jumped into the lake.
But the other disciples came in the boat,
dragging the net full of fish.
When they had gone ashore,
they saw a charcoal fire there,
with fish on it, and bread.
Jesus said to them,
"Bring some of the fish
that you have just caught."

The gospel of the Lord.
**Praise to you, Lord Jesus Christ.**

Let us pray:
Jesus, risen Lord,
Peter jumped out of the boat
as soon as he knew
you were waiting on the shore.
Help us to recognize you
and turn to you in good times and bad.
**Amen. Alleluia!**

Let us pray the prayer that Jesus taught us:
**Our Father…**

✠ **In the name of the Father, and of the Son, and of the Holy Spirit. Amen.**

Note: Today's reading is John 21:1-8a, 9-10.

## MONDAY

✠ In the name of the Father, and of the Son, and of the Holy Spirit. Amen.

Introduction: In our reading today, Jesus tells Nicodemus how he can enter the kingdom of God.

As baptized Christians, we are born of water and the Spirit – the water of baptism make us children of God, and we receive the gifts of the Holy Spirit.

Are we doing what God asks us to do? Do we live as children of the kingdom of God, following God's laws and ways?

A reading from the holy gospel according to John
**Glory to you, Lord.**

Now there was a Pharisee named
Nicodemus, a leader of the Jews.
He came to Jesus by night and said to him,
"Rabbi, we know that you are a teacher
who has come from God;
for no one can do these signs that you do
apart from the presence of God."
Jesus answered him, "Very truly, I tell you,
no one can see the kingdom of God
without being born from above."
Nicodemus said to him,
"How can anyone be born
after having grown old?
Can one enter a second time
into the mother's womb and be born?"
Jesus answered, "Very truly, I tell you,
no one can enter the kingdom of God
without being born of water and Spirit.
What is born of the flesh is flesh,
and what is born of the Spirit is spirit.
Do not be astonished that I said to you,
'You must be born from above.'

The wind blows where it chooses,
and you hear the sound of it,
but you do not know where it comes from
or where it goes.
So it is with everyone
who is born of the Spirit."

The gospel of the Lord.
**Praise to you, Lord Jesus Christ.**

Let us pray:
Creator God,
through our baptism
we become your children,
members of your kingdom.
Help us to be faithful followers of your Son,
and to remember to call upon
the Holy Spirit to help us
with all that we do,
and with all that we need.
We ask this through Christ our Risen Lord.
**Amen.**

Let us pray the prayer that Jesus taught us:
**Our Father...**

✠ In the name of the Father, and of the Son, and of the Holy Spirit. Amen.

---

Note: Today's reading is John 3:1-8.

## TUESDAY

✠ **In the name of the Father, and of the Son, and of the Holy Spirit. Amen.**

Introduction: Jesus' conversation with Nicodemus continues today. They are talking about faith, and about accepting what Jesus teaches.

It's not always easy to believe in things we can't see, but Jesus asks us to trust him, and have faith.

A reading from the holy gospel according to John
**Glory to you, Lord.**

Jesus said to Nicodemus,
"Very truly, I tell you,
we speak of what we know
and testify to what we have seen;
yet you do not receive our testimony.
If I have told you about earthly things
and you do not believe,
how can you believe
if I tell you about heavenly things?
No one has ascended into heaven
except the one who descended from heaven,
the Son of Man.
And just as Moses
lifted up the serpent in the wilderness,
so must the Son of Man be lifted up,
that whoever believes in him
may have eternal life."

The gospel of the Lord.
**Praise to you, Lord Jesus Christ**

Let us pray:
Creator in heaven,
Jesus taught us
about the things of earth
and the things of heaven.
Grant that we may believe
all that he teaches
in the depths of our hearts
so that our faith in you will grow every day.
We ask this through Christ our Lord.
**Amen.**

Let us pray the prayer that Jesus taught us:
**Our Father…**

✠ **In the name of the Father, and of the Son, and of the Holy Spirit. Amen.**

---

Note: Today's reading is John 3:11-15.

## WEDNESDAY

✠ **In the name of the Father, and of the Son, and of the Holy Spirit. Amen.**

Introduction: In today's reading, Jesus is still talking to Nicodemus. Jesus has an important message to share: God loved the world so much, he gave us his only Son, the light of the world.

Do we act as children of the light, children of truth? Do we choose the light, and do what God asks of us?

A reading from the holy gospel according to John
**Glory to you, Lord.**

Jesus said to Nicodemus,
"For God so loved the world
that he gave his only Son,
so that everyone who believes in him
may not perish but may have eternal life.
Indeed, God did not send the Son
into the world to condemn the world,
but in order that the world
might be saved through him.
Those who believe in him
are not condemned;
but those who do not believe
are condemned already,
because they have not believed
in the name of the only Son of God.
And this is the judgment,
that the light has come into the world,
and people loved darkness rather than light
because their deeds were evil.
For all who do evil hate the light
and do not come to the light,
so that their deeds may not be exposed.

But those who do what is true
come to the light,
so that it may be clearly seen
that their deeds have been done in God."

The gospel of the Lord.
**Praise to you, Lord Jesus Christ.**

Let us pray:
Father of all,
your Son came into the world
to be our saviour and our light.
Grant that our belief in Jesus may be strong,
and that we always do your will.
Help us to be children of light and truth.
We ask this through Christ our Risen Lord.
**Amen.**

Let us pray the prayer that Jesus taught us:
**Our Father…**

✠ **In the name of the Father, and of the Son, and of the Holy Spirit. Amen.**

Note: Today's reading is John 3:16-21.

## THURSDAY

✠ In the name of the Father, and of the Son, and of the Holy Spirit. Amen.

Introduction: Today we conclude Jesus' conversation with Nicodemus. Jesus reminds Nicodemus that he speaks for God, and that those who believe will have eternal life with God.

Do we believe that Jesus came from heaven? Do we believe in his message? Do we practise the truths he teaches?

A reading from the holy gospel according to John
**Glory to you, Lord.**

Jesus said to Nicodemus,
"The one who comes from above
is above all;
the one who is of the earth
belongs to the earth
and speaks about earthly things.
The one who comes from heaven
is above all.
He testifies to what he has seen and heard,
yet no one accepts his testimony.
Whoever has accepted his testimony
has certified this, that God is true.
He whom God has sent
speaks the words of God,
for he gives the Spirit without measure.
The Father loves the Son
and has placed all things in his hands.
Whoever believes in the Son
has eternal life;
whoever disobeys the Son will not see life,
but must endure God's wrath."

The gospel of the Lord.
**Praise to you, Lord Jesus Christ.**

Let us pray:
All-powerful God,
you sent your Son, Jesus,
to speak your words to us.
Help us to listen carefully
and believe what Jesus tells us,
so that it finds a home in our hearts.
Fill us with your life,
which comes to us through belief in Jesus.
We ask this through Christ our Lord.
**Amen.**

Let us pray the prayer that Jesus taught us:
**Our Father…**

✠ In the name of the Father, and of the Son, and of the Holy Spirit. Amen.

---

Note: Today's reading is John 3:31-36.

## FRIDAY

✠ **In the name of the Father, and of the Son, and of the Holy Spirit. Amen.**

Introduction: In today's reading, Jesus takes five loaves of bread and two fish and feeds five thousand people! Seeing this miracle, the people think he is the prophet they have been waiting for, the one who will free them from the rule of the Romans. They want to make him king. But Jesus didn't come to set up an earthly kingdom – he came to teach us about God's kingdom, which is better than anything we can imagine!

A reading from the holy gospel according to John
**Glory to you, Lord.**

Jesus said to Philip,
"Where are we to buy bread
for these people to eat?"
He said this to test him, for he himself
knew what he was going to do.
Philip answered him,
"Six months' wages would not buy
enough bread for each of them
to get a little."
One of his disciples, Andrew,
Simon Peter's brother, said to him,
"There is a boy here
who has five barley loaves and two fish.
But what are they among so many people?"
Jesus said, "Make the people sit down."
Then Jesus took the loaves,
and when he had given thanks,
he distributed them
to those who were seated;
so also the fish, as much as they wanted.
When they were satisfied,
he told his disciples,
"Gather up the fragments left over,
so that nothing may be lost."
So they gathered them up,
and from the fragments
of the five barley loaves,
left by those who had eaten,
they filled twelve baskets.
When the people saw the sign
that he had done, they began to say,
"This is indeed the prophet
who is to come into the world."
When Jesus realized
that they were about to come
and take him by force to make him king,
he withdrew again to the mountain
by himself.

The gospel of the Lord.
**Praise to you, Lord Jesus Christ.**

Let us pray:
Most loving God,
after Jesus fed the crowd,
they wanted to force him to be their king.
Help us to build up your kingdom
by following your laws and ways.
We ask this through Christ our Lord.
**Amen.**

Let us pray the prayer that Jesus taught us:
**Our Father…**

✠ **In the name of the Father, and of the Son, and of the Holy Spirit. Amen.**

Note: Today's reading is John 6:5b-10a, 11-15.

## MONDAY

✠ In the name of the Father, and of the Son, and of the Holy Spirit. Amen.

Introduction: Today's reading continues Friday's gospel. Jesus has left the crowd of five thousand, and later his disciples follow him. The crowd went to Capernaum, looking for Jesus. Jesus tells them to look beyond the miracle: to do what God wants, they must believe in him, the one God sent.

A reading from the holy gospel according to John
**Glory to you, Lord.**

The next day
the crowd that had stayed
on the other side of the lake
saw that there had been
only one boat there.
They also saw that Jesus had not got into
the boat with his disciples,
but that his disciples had gone away alone.
Then some boats from Tiberias
came near the place
where they had eaten the bread
after the Lord had given thanks.
So when the crowd saw that neither Jesus
nor his disciples were there,
they themselves got into the boats
and went to Capernaum looking for Jesus.
When they found him
on the other side of the lake,
they said to him,
"Rabbi, when did you come here?"
Jesus answered them, "Very truly, I tell you,
you are looking for me,
not because you saw signs,
but because you ate your fill of the loaves.
Do not work for the food that perishes,
but for the food that endures for eternal life,
which the Son of Man will give you.
For it is on him
that God the Father has set his seal."
Then they said to him, "What must we do
to perform the works of God?"
Jesus answered them,
"This is the work of God,
that you believe in him whom he has sent."

The gospel of the Lord.
**Praise to you, Lord Jesus Christ.**

Let us pray:
Creator God,
you sent your Son, Jesus,
to be the bread of life.
Grant that we may always receive him
in the Eucharist
with reverence, love and a grateful heart.
We ask this through Christ our Lord.
**Amen.**

Let us pray the prayer that Jesus taught us:
**Our Father…**

✠ In the name of the Father, and of the Son, and of the Holy Spirit. Amen.

Note: Today's reading is John 6:22-29.

## TUESDAY

✠ In the name of the Father, and of the Son, and of the Holy Spirit. Amen.

Introduction: Today we hear more from the gospel about the bread of life. The people are confused, so Jesus explains that he is the bread from heaven, broken and shared with the whole world.

A reading from the holy gospel according to John
**Glory to you, Lord.**

So they said to Jesus,
"What sign are you going to give us then,
so that we may see it and believe you?
What work are you performing?
Our ancestors ate the manna
in the wilderness; as it is written,
'He gave them bread from heaven to eat.'"
Then Jesus said to them,
"Very truly, I tell you, it was not Moses
who gave you the bread from heaven,
but it is my Father
who gives you the true bread from heaven.
For the bread of God
is that which comes down from heaven
and gives life to the world."
They said to him,
"Sir, give us this bread always."
Jesus said to them,
"I am the bread of life.
Whoever comes to me will never be hungry,
and whoever believes in me
will never be thirsty."

The gospel of the Lord.
**Praise to you, Lord Jesus Christ.**

Let us pray:
Father in heaven,
your Son, Jesus, is the bread of life.
Help us to turn to him with all our needs,
knowing that he will always give us
food for our journey to you.
We ask this through Christ our Lord.
**Amen.**

Let us pray the prayer that Jesus taught us,
for all those who are preparing for
First Communion:
**Our Father…**

✠ In the name of the Father, and of the Son, and of the Holy Spirit. Amen.

---

Note: Today's reading is John 6:30-35.

## WEDNESDAY

✠ **In the name of the Father, and of the Son, and of the Holy Spirit. Amen.**

Introduction: Today Jesus tells his followers that he is the bread of life. When we turn to Jesus, he will give us what we need to grow and live as children of God.

As Christians, we are bread for those around us, too, giving them comfort, nourishment and strength on their journey to God.

A reading from the holy gospel according to John
**Glory to you, Lord.**

Jesus said to them,
"I am the bread of life.
Whoever comes to me will never be hungry,
and whoever believes in me
will never be thirsty.
But I said to you that you have seen me
and yet do not believe.
Everything that the Father gives me
will come to me,
and anyone who comes to me
I will never drive away;
for I have come down from heaven,
not to do my own will,
but the will of him who sent me.
And this is the will of him who sent me,
that I should lose nothing
of all that he has given me,
but raise it up on the last day.
This is indeed the will of my Father,
that all who see the Son and believe in him
may have eternal life;
and I will raise them up on the last day."

The gospel of the Lord.
**Praise to you, Lord Jesus Christ.**

Let us pray:
Most loving and merciful God,
you sent your Son, Jesus,
to be our saviour.
He is the bread of life, given for us.
Help us to be bread for the people we meet.
We ask this through Christ our Lord.
**Amen.**

Let us pray the prayer that Jesus taught us:
**Our Father…**

✠ **In the name of the Father, and of the Son, and of the Holy Spirit. Amen.**

---

Note: Today's reading is John 6:35-40.

## THURSDAY

✠ In the name of the Father, and of the Son, and of the Holy Spirit. Amen.

Introduction: In today's gospel, people were having trouble understanding Jesus' message. Jesus makes his message simpler: I am the living bread. If you eat this bread, you will live forever!

A reading from the holy gospel according to John
**Glory to you, Lord.**

Jesus answered them,
"Do not complain among yourselves.
No one can come to me
unless drawn by the Father who sent me;
and I will raise that person up
on the last day.
It is written in the prophets,
'And they shall all be taught by God.'
Everyone who has heard
and learned from the Father comes to me.
Very truly, I tell you,
whoever believes has eternal life.
I am the bread of life.
Your ancestors ate the manna
in the wilderness, and they died.
This is the bread
that comes down from heaven,
so that one may eat of it and not die.
I am the living bread
that came down from heaven.
Whoever eats of this bread will live for ever;
and the bread that I will give
for the life of the world is my flesh."

The gospel of the Lord.
**Praise to you, Lord Jesus Christ.**

Let us pray:
Father in heaven,
you sent Jesus, the bread of life,
into the world so that all who believe
may have eternal life.
Help us always to welcome Jesus
into our hearts and lives
with respect, love and gratitude,
especially when we receive him
in Holy Communion.
We ask this through Christ our Lord.
**Amen.**

Let us pray the prayer that Jesus taught us:
**Our Father...**

✠ In the name of the Father, and of the Son, and of the Holy Spirit. Amen.

Note: Today's reading is John 6:43-45, 47-51.

## FRIDAY

✠ **In the name of the Father, and of the Son, and of the Holy Spirit. Amen.**

Introduction: The people of Jesus' time wondered how Jesus could give them himself as food and drink.

On the cross, Jesus' body was broken for us, and his blood was poured out for us, to end death forever. In the Eucharist we remember and give thanks for Jesus' gift of himself in the bread and wine we share.

A reading from the holy gospel according to John
**Glory to you, Lord.**

The Jews then disputed among themselves,
saying, "How can this man
give us his flesh to eat?"
So Jesus said to them,
"Very truly, I tell you,
unless you eat the flesh of the Son of Man
and drink his blood,
you have no life in you.
Those who eat my flesh and drink my blood
have eternal life,
and I will raise them up on the last day;
for my flesh is true food
and my blood is true drink.
Those who eat my flesh and drink my blood
abide in me, and I in them.
Just as the living Father sent me,
and I live because of the Father,
so whoever eats me will live because of me.
This is the bread
that came down from heaven,
not like that which your ancestors ate,
and they died.
But the one who eats this bread
will live for ever."

He said these things while he was teaching in the synagogue at Capernaum.

The gospel of the Lord.
**Praise to you, Lord Jesus Christ.**

Let us pray:
Holy One,
Jesus gives himself to us in the Eucharist.
In sharing his body and blood
we live in him and he lives in us.
Grant that we may always receive him
with reverence, joy and a grateful heart.
**Amen.**

Let us pray the prayer that Jesus taught us:
**Our Father…**

✠ **In the name of the Father, and of the Son, and of the Holy Spirit. Amen.**

---

Note: Today's reading is John 6:52-59.

## MONDAY

✠ **In the name of the Father, and of the Son, and of the Holy Spirit. Amen.**

Introduction: Today Jesus describes himself as the Good Shepherd. A good shepherd cares for his sheep, and is willing to die for them in order to protect them from harm. The sheep know the voice of the shepherd; they will not go to another shepherd whose voice they do not recognize.

Jesus cares for us, his flock, very much. We recognize his voice and follow only him, for Jesus is the way to God.

A reading from the holy gospel according to John
**Glory to you, Lord.**

Jesus said, "I am the good shepherd.
The good shepherd lays down his life
for the sheep.
The hired hand, who is not the shepherd
and does not own the sheep,
sees the wolf coming
and leaves the sheep and runs away —
and the wolf snatches them
and scatters them.
The hired hand runs away
because a hired hand
does not care for the sheep.
I am the good shepherd.
I know my own and my own know me,
just as the Father knows me
and I know the Father.
And I lay down my life for the sheep.
I have other sheep
that do not belong to this fold.
I must bring them also,
and they will listen to my voice.
So there will be one flock, one shepherd."

The gospel of the Lord.
**Praise to you, Lord Jesus Christ.**

Let us pray:
Loving God,
Jesus, the Good Shepherd,
calls each of us by name.
Help us to recognize his voice
in our daily lives
and to follow him faithfully.
**Amen.**

Let us pray the prayer that Jesus taught us:
**Our Father…**

✠ **In the name of the Father, and of the Son, and of the Holy Spirit. Amen.**

Note: Today's reading is John 10:11-16.

## TUESDAY

✠ **In the name of the Father, and of the Son, and of the Holy Spirit. Amen.**

Introduction: In our reading today, Jesus is in the Temple in Jerusalem. The Jews, who have been waiting for a messiah to free them from Roman rule, are getting impatient. They ask Jesus, "Are you the Messiah?"

Jesus is the Messiah, but not the one that they are expecting. He will not have his kingdom on earth, but in heaven.

A reading from the holy gospel according to John
**Glory to you, Lord.**

At that time the festival of the Dedication took place in Jerusalem. It was winter, and Jesus was walking in the temple, in the portico of Solomon. So the Jews gathered around him and said to him, "How long will you keep us in suspense? If you are the Messiah, tell us plainly." Jesus answered, "I have told you, and you do not believe. The works that I do in my Father's name testify to me; but you do not believe, because you do not belong to my sheep. My sheep hear my voice. I know them, and they follow me. I give them eternal life, and they will never perish. No one will snatch them out of my hand. What my Father has given me is greater than all else, and no one can snatch it out of the Father's hand. The Father and I are one."

The gospel of the Lord.
**Praise to you, Lord Jesus Christ.**

Let us pray:
Father in heaven,
you sent your Son, Jesus,
the Good Shepherd,
to lead us to eternal life.
Help us always to listen
and respond to his voice,
and to find strength and peace
as we follow where he leads us.
We ask this through Christ our Lord.
**Amen.**

Let us pray the prayer that Jesus taught us:
**Our Father...**

✠ **In the name of the Father, and of the Son, and of the Holy Spirit. Amen.**

Note: Today's reading is John 10:22-30.

## WEDNESDAY

✠ In the name of the Father, and of the Son, and of the Holy Spirit. Amen.

Introduction: In today's reading, Jesus reminds us that he is the light of the world. He leads us out of darkness, into the light of God's love and eternal life!

A reading from the holy gospel according to John
**Glory to you, Lord.**

Then Jesus cried aloud:
"Whoever believes in me
believes not in me
but in him who sent me.
And whoever sees me
sees him who sent me.
I have come as light into the world,
so that everyone who believes in me
should not remain in the darkness.
I do not judge anyone who hears my words
and does not keep them,
for I came not to judge the world,
but to save the world.
The one who rejects me
and does not receive my word has a judge;
on the last day the word that I have spoken
will serve as judge,
for I have not spoken on my own,
but the Father who sent me
has himself given me a commandment
about what to say and what to speak.
And I know that his commandment
is eternal life.
What I speak, therefore,
I speak just as the Father has told me."

The gospel of the Lord.
**Praise to you, Lord Jesus Christ.**

Let us pray:
Father in heaven,
Jesus is the light of the world!
Grant us the grace we need
to listen to his words
and put them into practice,
knowing that through him
we will have eternal life.
We ask this through Christ our Lord.
**Amen.**

Let us pray the prayer that Jesus taught us:
**Our Father…**

✠ In the name of the Father, and of the Son, and of the Holy Spirit. Amen.

Note: Today's reading is John 12:44-50.

## THURSDAY

✠ In the name of the Father, and of the Son, and of the Holy Spirit. Amen.

Introduction: In today's reading, Jesus speaks to his disciples after he washes their feet at the Last Supper, on the night before he died. He reminds them that when we welcome others, we welcome him – and when we welcome him, we welcome God.

A reading from the holy gospel according to John
**Glory to you, Lord.**

Jesus said,
"Very truly, I tell you,
servants are not greater than their master,
nor are messengers greater
than the one who sent them.
If you know these things,
you are blessed if you do them.
I am not speaking of all of you;
I know whom I have chosen.
But it is to fulfil the scripture,
"The one who ate my bread
has lifted his heel against me."
I tell you this now, before it occurs,
so that when it does occur,
you may believe that I am he.
Very truly, I tell you,
whoever receives one whom I send
receives me;
and whoever receives me
receives him who sent me."

The gospel of the Lord.
**Praise to you, Lord Jesus Christ.**

Let us pray:
Most loving God,
you sent your Son, Jesus, into the world
to show us the way to you.
Remind us always to welcome
those you send to us to help us,
and to follow Jesus' example.
We ask this through Christ our Lord.
**Amen.**

Let us pray the prayer that Jesus taught us:
**Our Father…**

✠ In the name of the Father, and of the Son, and of the Holy Spirit. Amen.

---

Note: Today's reading is John 13:16-20.

## FRIDAY

✠ **In the name of the Father, and of the Son, and of the Holy Spirit. Amen.**

Introduction: In today's reading, Jesus reminds us that he is preparing a place for all of us in God's house. How do we get there? Through Jesus: he is the way.

These words comfort the disciples, who know Jesus will die soon. They comfort us, too, because they remind us that if we follow Jesus, we will find our way to God.

A reading from the holy gospel according to John
**Glory to you, Lord.**

Jesus said,
"Do not let your hearts be troubled.
Believe in God, believe also in me.
In my Father's house
there are many dwelling-places.
If it were not so,
would I have told you that I go
to prepare a place for you?
And if I go and prepare a place for you,
I will come again
and will take you to myself,
so that where I am, there you may be also.
And you know the way to the place
where I am going."
Thomas said to him,
"Lord, we do not know
where you are going.
How can we know the way?"
Jesus said to him,
"I am the way, and the truth, and the life.
No one comes to the Father
except through me."

The gospel of the Lord.
**Praise to you, Lord Jesus Christ.**

Let us pray:
Father in heaven,
you sent Jesus to show us the way to you.
Help us to listen to him and wait in hope,
knowing that our happiness
and eternal life rest with you.
We ask this through Christ our Lord.
**Amen.**

Let us pray the prayer that Jesus taught us:
**Our Father…**

✠ **In the name of the Father, and of the Son, and of the Holy Spirit. Amen.**

---

Note: Today's reading is John 14:1-6.

# FIFTH WEEK OF EASTER

## MONDAY

✠ In the name of the Father, and of the Son, and of the Holy Spirit. Amen.

Introduction: In today's reading, Jesus tells his disciples that those who accept his commandments and obey his teachings are the ones who love him.

Love is more than a feeling: real love leads to action that shows how much we love someone.

Do our actions show that we love Jesus?

A reading from the holy gospel according to John
**Glory to you, Lord.**

Jesus said,
"They who have my commandments
and keep them
are those who love me;
and those who love me
will be loved by my Father,
and I will love them
and reveal myself to them."
Judas (not Iscariot) said to him,
"Lord, how is it that you will reveal yourself
to us, and not to the world?"
Jesus answered him,
"Those who love me will keep my word,
and my Father will love them,
and we will come to them
and make our home with them.
Whoever does not love me
does not keep my words;
and the word that you hear is not mine,
but is from the Father who sent me."

The gospel of the Lord.
**Praise to you, Lord Jesus Christ.**

Let us pray:
God our Creator,
you sent Jesus to teach us your ways.
Help us to show that we love him and you
by accepting your commandments
and obeying them.
We ask this through Christ our Lord.
**Amen.**

Let us pray the prayer that Jesus taught us:
**Our Father…**

✠ In the name of the Father, and of the Son, and of the Holy Spirit. Amen.

---

Note: Today's reading is John 14:21-24.

191

## TUESDAY

✠ **In the name of the Father, and of the Son, and of the Holy Spirit. Amen.**

Introduction: In today's reading, Jesus gives his disciples an important gift before he leaves them: peace. They are not to worry, for he will return to them.

He gives us the gift of peace, too. We can share it with the whole world!

A reading from the holy gospel according to John
**Glory to you, Lord.**

Jesus said, "Peace I leave with you;
my peace I give to you.
I do not give to you as the world gives.
Do not let your hearts be troubled,
and do not let them be afraid.
You heard me say to you,
'I am going away, and I am coming to you.'
If you loved me, you would rejoice
that I am going to the Father,
because the Father is greater than I.
And now I have told you this
before it occurs,
so that when it does occur,
you may believe.
I will no longer talk much with you,
for the ruler of this world is coming.
He has no power over me;
but I do as the Father has commanded me,
so that the world may know
that I love the Father."

The gospel of the Lord.
**Praise to you, Lord Jesus Christ.**

Let us pray:
Creator God,
Jesus gives us the gift of peace.
Help us to share it with those we meet –
a sign of hope in our world.
We ask this this through Christ our Lord.
**Amen.**

Let us pray the prayer that Jesus taught us:
**Our Father…**

✠ **In the name of the Father, and of the Son, and of the Holy Spirit. Amen.**

Note: Today's reading is John 14:27-31.

## WEDNESDAY

✠ In the name of the Father, and of the Son, and of the Holy Spirit. Amen.

Introduction: In today's gospel, Jesus tells us that he is the true vine and that we are the branches attached to him. God trims the branches, cutting away those that do not bear fruit and pruning those that do so that they can produce more fruit.Cut off from Jesus, we can do nothing.

How can we be one with Jesus, growing and sharing our gifts with those around us?

A reading from the holy gospel according to John
**Glory to you, Lord.**

Jesus said to the disciples,
"I am the true vine,
and my Father is the vine-grower.
He removes every branch in me
that bears no fruit.
Every branch that bears fruit he prunes
to make it bear more fruit.
You have already been cleansed
by the word that I have spoken to you.
Abide in me as I abide in you.
Just as the branch cannot bear fruit by itself
unless it abides in the vine,
neither can you unless you abide in me.
I am the vine, you are the branches.
Those who abide in me and I in them
bear much fruit,
because apart from me you can do nothing.
Whoever does not abide in me
is thrown away like a branch and withers;
such branches are gathered,
thrown into the fire, and burned.

If you abide in me,
and my words abide in you,
ask for whatever you wish,
and it will be done for you.
My Father is glorified by this,
that you bear much fruit
and become my disciples."

The gospel of the Lord.
**Praise to you, Lord Jesus Christ.**

Let us pray:
Creator God,
your beloved Son is the vine
and we are the branches.
Help us to remain attached to him always,
bearing much fruit,
and being faithful disciples.
We ask this through Christ our Lord.
**Amen.**

Let us pray the prayer that Jesus taught us:
**Our Father…**

✠ In the name of the Father, and of the Son, and of the Holy Spirit. Amen.

Note: Today's reading is John 15:1-8.

## THURSDAY

✠ In the name of the Father, and of the Son, and of the Holy Spirit. Amen.

Introduction: In today's reading, Jesus tells us that he loves us as much as God loves him. He invites us to remain in his love and obey his commands just as he has done with God.

A reading from the holy gospel according to John
**Glory to you, Lord.**

Jesus said to his disciples,
"As the Father has loved me,
so I have loved you; abide in my love.
If you keep my commandments,
you will abide in my love, just as I
have kept my Father's commandments
and abide in his love.
I have said these things to you
so that my joy may be in you,
and that your joy may be complete."

The gospel of the Lord.
**Praise to you, Lord Jesus Christ.**

Let us pray:
Most Holy God,
Jesus loved you so much,
he did all you asked him to do.
Help us to obey you
and follow the commands Jesus has given us
so that we may live in his love forever.
We ask this through Christ our Lord.
**Amen.**

Let us pray the prayer that Jesus taught us:
**Our Father…**

✠ In the name of the Father, and of the Son, and of the Holy Spirit. Amen.

Note: Today's reading is John 15:9-11.

## FRIDAY

✠ In the name of the Father, and of the Son, and of the Holy Spirit. Amen.

Introduction: In today's reading, Jesus has a simple but important message for all his friends: Love one another. It may be a simple message, but it's not always easy to love.

What stops us from showing love and care for our families, our neighbours, our world? How can we do what Jesus asks and truly love one another?

A reading from the holy gospel according to John
**Glory to you, Lord.**

Jesus said, "'This is my commandment,
that you love one another
as I have loved you.
No one has greater love than this,
to lay down one's life for one's friends.
You are my friends
if you do what I command you.
I do not call you servants any longer,
because the servant does not know
what the master is doing;
but I have called you friends,
because I have made known to you
everything that I have heard
from my Father.
You did not choose me but I chose you.
And I appointed you to go and bear fruit,
fruit that will last,
so that the Father will give you
whatever you ask him in my name.
I am giving you these commands
so that you may love one another."

The gospel of the Lord.
**Praise to you, Lord Jesus Christ.**

Let us pray:
Creator God,
source of all love and holiness,
Jesus commands us to love one another.
Help us to open our hearts
to the people around us,
and to treat them with kindness and care.
Help us to bear this fruit that will last.
We ask this through Christ our Lord.
**Amen.**

Let us pray the prayer that Jesus taught us:
**Our Father…**

✠ In the name of the Father, and of the Son, and of the Holy Spirit. Amen.

Note: Today's reading is John 15:12-17.

# SIXTH WEEK OF EASTER

## MONDAY

✠ In the name of the Father, and of the Son, and of the Holy Spirit. Amen.

Introduction: In today's reading, Jesus reminds us that it's not always easy to be his disciples. To help us be strong in our faith, Jesus sends us the Holy Spirit.

A reading from the holy gospel according to John
**Glory to you, Lord.**

Jesus said to his disciples:
"When the Advocate comes,
whom I will send to you from the Father,
the Spirit of truth
who comes from the Father,
he will testify on my behalf.
You also are to testify
because you have been with me
from the beginning.
I have said these things to you
to keep you from stumbling.
They will put you out of the synagogues.
Indeed, an hour is coming
when those who kill you
will think that by doing so
they are offering worship to God.
And they will do this because
they have not known the Father or me.
But I have said these things to you
so that when their hour comes
you may remember
that I told you about them."

The gospel of the Lord.
**Praise to you, Lord Jesus Christ.**

Let us pray:
Creator God,
your Son, Jesus, warned the disciples
about the hard times that lay ahead of them.
Help us to be faithful to you
and to Jesus
when things are hard for us, too.
Send us your Spirit to keep us strong.
We ask this through Christ our Lord.
**Amen.**

Let us pray the prayer that Jesus taught us:
**Our Father…**

✠ In the name of the Father, and of the Son, and of the Holy Spirit. Amen.

Note: Today's reading is John 15:26–16:4.

## TUESDAY

✠ **In the name of the Father, and of the Son, and of the Holy Spirit. Amen.**

Introduction: In our reading today, Jesus tells the disciples more about the Advocate, the Holy Spirit. Even after Jesus is gone, they will not be alone: the Spirit will keep showing them the way to God.

A reading from the holy gospel according to John
**Glory to you, Lord.**

Jesus said,
"Now I am going to him who sent me;
yet none of you asks me,
'Where are you going?'
But because I have said these things to you,
sorrow has filled your hearts.
Nevertheless, I tell you the truth:
it is to your advantage that I go away,
for if I do not go away,
the Advocate will not come to you;
but if I go, I will send him to you.
And when he comes,
he will prove the world wrong about sin
and righteousness and judgment:
about sin,
because they do not believe in me;
about righteousness, because I am going to
the Father and you will see me no longer;
about judgment, because the ruler of this
world has been condemned."

The gospel of the Lord.
**Praise to you, Lord Jesus Christ.**

Let us pray:
Most merciful God,
the Holy Spirit is always with us,
reminding us what Jesus taught us.
Help us remember that we may always
call on the Spirit for help
when we don't know what to do.
We ask this through Christ our Lord.
**Amen.**

Let us pray the prayer that Jesus taught us:
**Our Father…**

✠ **In the name of the Father, and of the Son, and of the Holy Spirit. Amen.**

—————————

Note: Today's reading is John 16:5-11.

## WEDNESDAY

✠ In the name of the Father, and of the Son, and of the Holy Spirit. Amen.

Introduction: Today, Jesus says that the Holy Spirit will lead the disciples to the truth. But what about us?

The Holy Spirit is also given to us, in the sacraments of Baptism and Confirmation. The Spirit is with us, and will help us whenever we call.

A reading from the holy gospel according to John
**Glory to you, Lord.**

Jesus said to his disciples:
"I still have many things to say to you,
but you cannot bear them now.
When the Spirit of truth comes,
he will guide you into all the truth;
for he will not speak on his own,
but will speak whatever he hears,
and he will declare to you
the things that are to come.
He will glorify me,
because he will take what is mine
and declare it to you.
All that the Father has is mine.
For this reason I said that he will take
what is mine and declare it to you."

The gospel of the Lord.
**Praise to you, Lord Jesus Christ.**

Let us pray:
Loving God,
Jesus promised to send the Holy Spirit
to be our helper and guide.
Help us to remember
that this help is always there for us,
and all we need to do is ask.
We ask this through Christ our Lord.
**Amen.**

Let us pray the prayer that Jesus taught us:
**Our Father…**

✠ In the name of the Father, and of the Son, and of the Holy Spirit. Amen.

---

Note: Today's reading is John 16:12-15.

## THURSDAY

✠ In the name of the Father, and of the Son, and of the Holy Spirit. Amen.

Introduction: In today's reading, Jesus tells the apostles that he will not be seen by them for a short time, and then they will see him again. Jesus is referring to his death and resurrection. He warns them that they will be sad, and that the world will rejoice. But he comforts them by saying their sorrow will turn to joy.

We need to remember that even if we cannot see Jesus, or feel his presence, Jesus is always with us to guide, help, comfort and support us.

A reading from the holy gospel according to John
**Glory to you, Lord.**

Jesus said to his disciples,
"A little while,
and you will no longer see me,
and again a little while,
and you will see me."
Then some of his disciples
said to one another,
"What does he mean by saying to us,
'A little while,
and you will no longer see me,
and again a little while, and you will see me';
and 'Because I am going to the Father'?"
They said, "What does he mean by this
'a little while'?
We do not know what he is talking about."
Jesus knew that they wanted to ask him,
so he said to them,
"Are you discussing among yourselves
what I meant when I said,
'A little while,
and you will no longer see me,
and again a little while,
and you will see me'?

Very truly, I tell you,
you will weep and mourn,
but the world will rejoice;
you will have pain,
but your pain will turn into joy."

The gospel of the Lord.
**Praise to you, Lord Jesus Christ.**

Let us pray:
Creator God,
you sent your Son, Jesus,
to be the redeemer of the world.
Grant that we may always know
the comfort of his love for us,
and rejoice always that he is with us,
until the end of time.
We ask this through Christ our Lord.
**Amen.**

Let us pray the prayer that Jesus taught us:
**Our Father…**

✠ In the name of the Father, and of the Son, and of the Holy Spirit. Amen.

Note: Today's reading is John 16:16-20.

## FRIDAY

✠ In the name of the Father, and of the Son, and of the Holy Spirit. Amen.

Introduction: In our reading today, Jesus tells the disciples that although they will be sad when he leaves them, their sadness will turn to gladness when he rises from the dead.

Jesus is always with us, ready to help us when we ask. Jesus turns our sorrow to joy.

A reading from the holy gospel according to John
**Glory to you, Lord.**

Jesus said, "Very truly, I tell you,
you will weep and mourn,
but the world will rejoice;
you will have pain,
but your pain will turn into joy.
When a woman is in labour,
she has pain, because her hour has come.
But when her child is born,
she no longer remembers the anguish
because of the joy of having brought
a human being into the world.
So you have pain now;
but I will see you again,
and your hearts will rejoice,
and no one will take your joy from you."

The gospel of the Lord.
**Praise to you, Lord Jesus Christ.**

Let us pray:
Most loving God,
in our moments of sadness,
send us your Spirit
of peace and consolation,
and help us remember
that gladness in you
can never be taken away.
We ask this through Christ our Lord.
**Amen.**

Let us pray the prayer that Jesus taught us:
**Our Father…**

✠ In the name of the Father, and of the Son, and of the Holy Spirit. Amen.

---

Note: Today's reading is John 16:20-22.

## MONDAY

✠ In the name of the Father, and of the Son, and of the Holy Spirit. Amen.

Introduction: We have heard in the readings these past few weeks that Jesus would send a helper, the Holy Spirit, to his followers.

Our reading today is from the Acts of the Apostles, the book in the Bible that tells us about the early days of the Church. St. Paul visits cities around the Mediterranean Sea, sharing the Good News and baptizing in the name of Jesus.

A reading from the Acts of the Apostles

While Apollos was in Corinth,
Paul passed through the inland regions
and came to Ephesus,
where he found some disciples.
He said to them,
"Did you receive the Holy Spirit
when you became believers?"
They replied, "No, we have not even heard
that there is a Holy Spirit."
Then he said,
"Into what then were you baptized?"
They answered, "Into John's baptism."
Paul said, "John baptized
with the baptism of repentance,
telling the people to believe in the one
who was to come after him, that is, in Jesus."
On hearing this, they were baptized
in the name of the Lord Jesus.
When Paul had laid his hands on them,
the Holy Spirit came upon them,
and they spoke in tongues and prophesied.

The word of the Lord.
**Thanks be to God.**

Let us pray:
Creator God,
your Son, Jesus,
gives all who are baptized
the gift of the Holy Spirit.
Help us to prepare to celebrate with joy
the Feast of Pentecost,
when the Holy Spirit
came upon the apostles.
We ask this through Christ our Lord.
**Amen.**

Let us pray the prayer that Jesus taught us:
**Our Father…**

✠ In the name of the Father, and of the Son, and of the Holy Spirit. Amen.

Note: Today's reading is Acts 19:1-6.

201

## TUESDAY

✠ **In the name of the Father, and of the Son, and of the Holy Spirit. Amen.**

Introduction: In today's reading, we hear a prayer that Jesus prayed the night before he died. Although he knew he was to die, his prayer is filled with faith, hope and praise.

A reading from the holy gospel according to John
**Glory to you, Lord.**

Jesus looked up to heaven and said,
"Father, the hour has come;
glorify your Son
so that the Son may glorify you,
since you have given him authority
over all people, to give eternal life
to all whom you have given him.
And this is eternal life,
that they may know you, the only true God,
and Jesus Christ whom you have sent.
I glorified you on earth
by finishing the work
that you gave me to do.
So now, Father,
glorify me in your own presence
with the glory that I had in your presence
before the world existed.

I have made your name known
to those whom you gave me from the world.
They were yours, and you gave them to me,
and they have kept your word.

Now they know that everything
you have given me is from you;
for the words that you gave to me
I have given to them,
and they have received them
and know in truth that I came from you;
and they have believed that you sent me.
I am asking on their behalf."

The gospel of the Lord.
**Praise to you, Lord Jesus Christ.**

Let us pray:
Father in heaven,
Jesus taught us that all that we have
comes from you.
Grant that we may follow Jesus' example,
asking you for all we need,
praising you for all you have done
and will do,
and thanking you for all your gifts.
We ask this through Christ our Lord.
**Amen.**

Let us pray the prayer that Jesus taught us:
**Our Father…**

✠ **In the name of the Father, and of the Son, and of the Holy Spirit. Amen.**

---

Note: Today's reading is John 17:1-9a.

## WEDNESDAY

✠ **In the name of the Father, and of the Son, and of the Holy Spirit. Amen.**

Introduction: In today's reading, Jesus prays for the apostles. He asks God to watch over them and protect them.

Jesus prays for all his followers, including us, and asks God to keep us safe, too.

A reading from the holy gospel according to John
**Glory to you, Lord.**

Jesus looked up to heaven and said,
"Holy Father, protect them in your name
that you have given me,
so that they may be one, as we are one.
While I was with them,
I protected them in your name
that you have given me.
I guarded them,
and not one of them was lost
except the one destined to be lost,
so that the scripture might be fulfilled.
But now I am coming to you,
and I speak these things in the world
so that they may have my joy
made complete in themselves.
I have given them your word,
and the world has hated them
because they do not belong to the world,
just as I do not belong to the world.
I am not asking you to
take them out of the world,
but I ask you to protect them
from the evil one.
They do not belong to the world,
just as I do not belong to the world.

Sanctify them in the truth;
your word is truth.
As you have sent me into the world,
so I have sent them into the world.
And for their sakes I sanctify myself,
so that they also may be sanctified in truth."

The gospel of the Lord.
**Praise to you, Lord Jesus Christ.**

Let us pray:
Creator God,
your beloved Son prayed for his apostles,
that you would protect them
and consecrate them to yourself.
We ask, as your children,
for your protection,
love and help every day.
We ask this through Christ our Lord.
**Amen.**

Let us pray the prayer that Jesus taught us:
**Our Father…**

✠ **In the name of the Father, and of the Son, and of the Holy Spirit. Amen.**

---

Note: Today's reading is John 17:11b-19.

## THURSDAY

✠ **In the name of the Father, and of the Son, and of the Holy Spirit. Amen.**

Introduction: In today's reading, we conclude Jesus' prayer at the Last Supper. We hear that Jesus is also praying for all those who believe in Jesus because of the message the apostles preached, including us, two thousand years later. Jesus prays that they may be one, as he and God are one.

A reading from the holy gospel according to John
**Glory to you, Lord.**

Jesus looked up to heaven and said,
"I ask not only on behalf of these,
but also on behalf of those
who will believe in me through their word,
that they may all be one.
As you, Father, are in me and I am in you,
may they also be in us,
so that the world may believe
that you have sent me.
The glory that you have given me
I have given them,
so that they may be one, as we are one,
I in them and you in me,
that they may become completely one,
so that the world may know
that you have sent me and have loved them
even as you have loved me.
Father, I desire that those also,
whom you have given me,
may be with me where I am,
to see my glory, which you have given me
because you loved me
before the foundation of the world.

Righteous Father,
the world does not know you,
but I know you;
and these know that you have sent me.
I made your name known to them,
and I will make it known,
so that the love with which
you have loved me may be in them,
and I in them."

The gospel of the Lord.
**Praise to you, Lord Jesus Christ.**

Let us pray:
Most holy and loving God,
Jesus prayed that we will be one,
united to you by our belief in him
and by your love for us.
Help us to love you with all our hearts,
and follow Jesus faithfully.
We ask this through Christ our Lord.
**Amen.**

Let us pray the prayer that Jesus taught us:
**Our Father…**

✠ **In the name of the Father, and of the Son, and of the Holy Spirit. Amen.**

---

Note: Today's reading is John 17:20-26.

## FRIDAY

✠ **In the name of the Father, and of the Son, and of the Holy Spirit. Amen.**

Introduction: Our reading today is set after Jesus has risen from the dead. Jesus asks Peter three times if he loves him. This reminds us of the three times Peter denied Jesus on the day Jesus died. Jesus gives Peter the task of taking care of his lambs and sheep – today we would call this the Church. Jesus chose Peter to be the first leader of the Church. The pope and the bishops of the world are the leaders of the Church today, and are considered to be descendants of the apostles.

A reading from the holy gospel according to John
**Glory to you, Lord.**

When they had finished breakfast,
Jesus said to Simon Peter,
"Simon son of John,
do you love me more than these?"
He said to him,
"Yes, Lord; you know that I love you."
Jesus said to him, "Feed my lambs."
A second time he said to him,
"Simon son of John, do you love me?"
He said to him,
"Yes, Lord; you know that I love you."
Jesus said to him, "Tend my sheep."
He said to him the third time,
"Simon son of John, do you love me?"
Peter felt hurt because he said to him
the third time, "Do you love me?"
And he said to him,
"Lord, you know everything;
you know that I love you."
Jesus said to him, "Feed my sheep.
Very truly, I tell you,
when you were younger,
you used to fasten your own belt
and to go wherever you wished.

But when you grow old,
you will stretch out your hands,
and someone else
will fasten a belt around you
and take you where you do not wish to go."
(He said this to indicate the kind of death
by which he would glorify God.)
After this he said to him, "Follow me."

The gospel of the Lord.
**Praise to you, Lord Jesus Christ.**

Let us pray:
Creator God,
you gave Simon Peter the task
of being the first leader of the Church.
Guide the Church's leaders,
and help them lead us to you.
We ask this through Christ our Lord.
**Amen.**

Let us pray the prayer that Jesus taught us,
for our Holy Father and all church leaders:
**Our Father…**

✠ **In the name of the Father, and of the Son, and of the Holy Spirit. Amen.**

---

Note: Today's reading is John 21:15-19.

## MONDAY

✠ In the name of the Father, and of the Son, and of the Holy Spirit. Amen.

Introduction: In our reading today, James helps us recognize good wisdom and understanding, which come from God, and the gifts that good wisdom brings.

What kind of wisdom and understanding do we use? How do we show that we follow the wisdom and advice that come from God?

A reading from the letter of James

Who is wise and understanding among you?
Show by your good life
that your works are done with gentleness
born of wisdom.
But if you have bitter envy
and selfish ambition in your hearts,
do not be boastful and false to the truth.
Such wisdom does not come down
from above, but is earthly,
unspiritual, devilish.
For where there is envy
and selfish ambition, there will also be
disorder and wickedness of every kind.
But the wisdom from above is first pure,
then peaceable, gentle, willing to yield,
full of mercy and good fruits,
without a trace of partiality or hypocrisy.
And a harvest of righteousness
is sown in peace for those who make peace.

The word of the Lord.
**Thanks be to God.**

Let us pray:
Most compassionate and all-knowing God,
wisdom and understanding
that come from you
bring the gifts of peace, gentleness,
friendliness and compassion.
Help us always to seek your wisdom
and put into practice
the gifts that it brings.
We ask this through Christ our Lord.
**Amen.**

Let us pray the prayer that Jesus taught us:
**Our Father…**

✠ In the name of the Father, and of the Son, and of the Holy Spirit. Amen.

---

Note: Today's reading is James 3:13-18.

## TUESDAY

✠ **In the name of the Father, and of the Son, and of the Holy Spirit. Amen.**

Introduction: In today's reading, the disciples were arguing about who was the greatest of their group. Jesus tells them that to be first they must put themselves last and be a servant of all. Then he takes a child into his arms and tells the apostles that whoever welcomes a child welcomes not only Jesus, but also God.

Children are very precious to Jesus and to God. Jesus is telling his disciples how they should treat others – as one would welcome a little child, with love.

A reading from the holy gospel according to Mark
**Glory to you, Lord.**

Then they came to Capernaum;
and when he was in the house
he asked them,
"What were you arguing about on the way?"
But they were silent,
for on the way they had argued
with one another who was the greatest.
He sat down, called the twelve,
and said to them,
"Whoever wants to be first
must be last of all and servant of all."
Then he took a little child
and put it among them;
and taking it in his arms, he said to them,
"Whoever welcomes one such child
in my name welcomes me,
and whoever welcomes me
welcomes not me but the one who sent me."

The gospel of the Lord.
**Praise to you, Lord Jesus Christ.**

Let us pray:
Most holy and loving God,
Jesus told his disciples
that whoever welcomes a child
welcomes him, and you also.
Help us to remember
that we are to treat others with love,
welcoming others
as we would welcome you.
We ask this through Christ our Lord.
**Amen.**

Let us pray the prayer that Jesus taught us:
**Our Father…**

✠ **In the name of the Father, and of the Son, and of the Holy Spirit. Amen.**

Note: Today's reading is Mark 9:33-37.

## WEDNESDAY

✠ In the name of the Father, and of the Son, and of the Holy Spirit. Amen.

Introduction: At the time of Jesus, a person's name stood for the person; to speak in someone's name was like having that person present.

Jesus allows someone who is not part of his group of disciples to do miracles in his name, because he knows this can only cause good things to happen.

Do we look beyond our group to see the good that can happen? How can we include new people in our group?

A reading from the holy gospel according to Mark
**Glory to you, Lord.**

John said to him,
"Teacher, we saw someone
casting out demons in your name,
and we tried to stop him,
because he was not following us."
But Jesus said, "Do not stop him;
for no one who does a deed of power
in my name will be able soon afterward
to speak evil of me.
Whoever is not against us is for us."

The gospel of the Lord.
**Praise to you, Lord Jesus Christ.**

Let us pray:
Most loving God,
your Son, Jesus,
accepted and welcomed others
who were doing good in his name.
Help us to follow his example
and show tolerance to others.
We ask this through Christ our Lord.
**Amen.**

Let us pray the prayer that Jesus taught us:
**Our Father…**

✠ In the name of the Father, and of the Son, and of the Holy Spirit. Amen.

_____

Note: Today's reading is Mark 9:38-40.

## THURSDAY

✠ In the name of the Father, and of the Son, and of the Holy Spirit. Amen.

Introduction: In our reading today, Jesus asks us to do simple, ordinary things to build God's kingdom: things like giving someone a glass of water, or helping someone up who has fallen down.

Are we willing to do simple things for others in Jesus' name? What can we do today to help build God's kingdom?

A reading from the holy gospel according to Mark
**Glory to you, Lord.**

Jesus said to them,
"Truly I tell you,
whoever gives you a cup of water to drink
because you bear the name of Christ
will by no means lose the reward.
If any of you put a stumbling block
before one of these little ones
who believe in me,
it would be better for you
if a great millstone
were hung around your neck
and you were thrown into the sea."

The gospel of the Lord.
**Praise to you, Lord Jesus Christ.**

Let us pray:
Most merciful and just God,
your Son, Jesus,
teaches us that we are to do what we can,
ordinary things,
to help our brothers and sisters in need.
Help us to be kind and generous
in our words and actions.
We ask this through Christ our Lord.
**Amen.**

Let us pray the prayer that Jesus taught us:
**Our Father…**

✠ In the name of the Father, and of the Son, and of the Holy Spirit. Amen.

---

Note: Today's reading is Mark 9:41-42.

## FRIDAY

✠ In the name of the Father, and of the Son,
and of the Holy Spirit. Amen.

Introduction: In our reading today, James tells us not to grumble against one another, and have patience, for God is full of mercy and compassion.

When do we complain against our classmates, our friends, our families? How can we become more patient?

A reading from the letter of James

Beloved, do not grumble
against one another,
so that you may not be judged.
See, the Judge is standing at the doors!
As an example of suffering and patience,
beloved, take the prophets
who spoke in the name of the Lord.
Indeed we call blessed
those who showed endurance.
You have heard of the endurance of Job,
and you have seen the purpose of the Lord,
how the Lord is compassionate
and merciful.

The word of the Lord.
**Thanks be to God.**

Let us pray:
Most merciful God,
your Son, Jesus,
was compassionate and loving.
Help us not to grumble against one another,
but to have patience, compassion
and understanding for one another.
We ask this through Christ our Lord.
**Amen.**

Let us pray the prayer that Jesus taught us:
**Our Father…**

✠ In the name of the Father, and of the Son,
and of the Holy Spirit. Amen.

Note: Today's reading is James 5:9-11.

# EIGHTH WEEK OF ORDINARY TIME

## MONDAY

✠ In the name of the Father, and of the Son, and of the Holy Spirit. Amen.

Introduction: In our reading today, we hear the story of a rich man who wants to be sure he will have eternal life with God after he dies. Jesus asks him to give up something that is important to him, for nothing on earth is worth more than following God.

Can he do it? Can we?

A reading from the holy gospel according to Mark
**Glory to you, Lord.**

As Jesus was setting out on a journey,
a man ran up and knelt before him,
and asked him, "Good Teacher,
what must I do to inherit eternal life?"
Jesus said to him,
"Why do you call me good?
No one is good but God alone.
You know the commandments:
'You shall not murder;
You shall not commit adultery;
You shall not steal;
You shall not bear false witness;
You shall not defraud;
Honour your father and mother.'"
He said to him, "Teacher,
I have kept all these since my youth."
Jesus, looking at him, loved him and said,
"You lack one thing; go, sell what you own,
and give the money to the poor,
and you will have treasure in heaven;
then come, follow me."

When he heard this, he was shocked
and went away grieving,
for he had many possessions.

The gospel of the Lord.
**Praise to you, Lord Jesus Christ.**

Let us pray:
Most holy and gracious God,
the rich man went away sad,
because he could not give up
his possessions:
they meant too much to him.
Help us to focus on the things of heaven,
and treasure them more
than the things of earth.
We ask this through Christ our Lord.
**Amen.**

Let us pray the prayer that Jesus taught us:
**Our Father…**

✠ In the name of the Father, and of the Son, and of the Holy Spirit. Amen.

---

Note: Today's reading is Mark 10:17-22.

# EIGHTH WEEK OF ORDINARY TIME

## TUESDAY

✠ **In the name of the Father, and of the Son, and of the Holy Spirit. Amen.**

Introduction: Jesus tells the apostles (and us) that those who leave everything to follow him will be greatly rewarded.

It was not easy for the apostles to leave their families and homes to follow Jesus, but that is what they did.

Would we be willing to leave everything to follow Jesus? To stand up for our faith when others make fun of us?

A reading from the holy gospel according to Mark
**Glory to you, Lord.**

Peter began to say to him,
"Look, we have left everything
and followed you."
Jesus said, "Truly I tell you,
there is no one who has left house
or brothers or sisters
or mother or father
or children or fields, for my sake
and for the sake of the good news,
who will not receive a hundredfold now
in this age – houses, brothers and sisters,
mothers and children,
and fields with persecutions –
and in the age to come eternal life.
But many who are first will be last,
and the last will be first."

The gospel of th Lord.
**Praise to you, Lord Jesus Christ.**

Let us pray:
Creator God,
Jesus has promised that all those who
leave everything to follow him
and spread the Good News
will be given a hundred times more
than what they gave up.
Bless all those in our world today
who have left everything
to help you build up your kingdom.
Help us all to be faithful followers of Jesus.
We ask this through Christ our Lord.
**Amen.**

Let us pray the prayer that Jesus taught us:
**Our Father…**

✠ **In the name of the Father, and of the Son, and of the Holy Spirit. Amen.**

Note: Today's reading is Mark 10:28-31.

# EIGHTH WEEK OF ORDINARY TIME

## WEDNESDAY

✠ In the name of the Father, and of the Son, and of the Holy Spirit. Amen.

Introduction: In our reading today, Jesus is on his way to Jerusalem. He takes the twelve apostles aside to tell them what is going to happen to him. James and John ask Jesus if they can sit on either side of him in his glory. Jesus reminds them that to be great, you must be a servant of all, and to be first, you have to be a slave of all.

Jesus completely turns around the idea of what leaders should do: they are not to be served, but to serve.

Are we willing to serve to become great in the eyes of Jesus?

A reading from the holy gospel according to Mark
**Glory to you, Lord.**

So Jesus called them and said to them,
"You know that among the Gentiles
those whom they recognize as their rulers
lord it over them, and their great ones
are tyrants over them.
But it is not so among you;
but whoever wishes to become great
among you must be your servant,
and whoever wishes to be first among you
must be slave of all.
For the Son of Man came not to be served
but to serve,
and to give his life a ransom for many."

The gospel of the Lord.
**Praise to you, Lord Jesus Christ.**

Let us pray:
Most holy God,
you sent your Son, Jesus, into the world
to teach us that we are to serve,
not to be served.
Help us to serve others,
because when we serve them,
we serve your divine Son.
We ask this through Christ our Lord.
**Amen.**

Let us pray the prayer that Jesus taught us:
**Our Father…**

✠ In the name of the Father, and of the Son, and of the Holy Spirit. Amen.

Note: Today's reading is Mark 10:42-45.

# EIGHTH WEEK OF ORDINARY TIME

## THURSDAY

✠ In the name of the Father, and of the Son, and of the Holy Spirit. Amen.

Introduction: Today we hear the story of a blind man, Bartimaeus. Bartimaeus knew that Jesus was passing by; he called out to Jesus because he believed that Jesus could heal him. The people told him to be quiet, but Bartimaeus did not do that. He called out even louder!

Bartimaeus was cured of his blindness because he had faith that Jesus could, and would, heal him.

Do we believe, as strongly as Bartimaeus did, that Jesus can and will help us if we ask him?

A reading from the holy gospel according to Mark
**Glory to you, Lord.**

They came to Jericho.
As Jesus and his disciples and a large crowd were leaving Jericho,
Bartimaeus son of Timaeus, a blind beggar, was sitting by the roadside.
When he heard that it was Jesus of Nazareth,
he began to shout out and say,
"Jesus, Son of David, have mercy on me!"
Many sternly ordered him to be quiet,
but he cried out even more loudly,
"Son of David, have mercy on me!"
Jesus stood still and said, "Call him here."
And they called the blind man,
saying to him,
"Take heart; get up, he is calling you."
So throwing off his cloak,
he sprang up and came to Jesus.
Then Jesus said to him,
"What do you want me to do for you?"
The blind man said to him,
"My teacher, let me see again."

Jesus said to him,
"Go; your faith has made you well."
Immediately he regained his sight
and followed him on the way.

The gospel of the Lord.
**Praise to you, Lord Jesus Christ.**

Let us pray:
Most loving God,
Jesus cured Bartimaeus of his blindness
because he had the courage to ask
and the faith that Jesus could heal him.
Give us the courage to ask Jesus for help
when we need it,
and the faith that Jesus will give it to us.
We ask this through Christ our Lord.
**Amen.**

Let us pray the prayer that Jesus taught us:
**Our Father…**

✠ In the name of the Father, and of the Son, and of the Holy Spirit. Amen.

Note: Today's reading is Mark 10:46-52.

214

## FRIDAY

✠ **In the name of the Father, and of the Son, and of the Holy Spirit. Amen.**

Introduction: On the way to Jerusalem, Jesus and his disciples pass a fig tree that has no fruit on it; Jesus tells it that no one will eat fruit from it again. On the way back, they see that it is dead, all the way to its roots. Jesus uses this fig tree to teach that we need to believe in what we ask for in prayer, and to have the faith that we will receive it. He also reminds us to forgive others.

Do we have faith that God will answer our prayers, even if the answer is not what we expect? Do we forgive those who have hurt us?

A reading from the holy gospel according to Mark
**Glory to you, Lord.**

In the morning as they passed by, they saw
the fig tree withered away to its roots.
Then Peter remembered and said to him,
"Rabbi, look! The fig tree that you cursed
has withered." Jesus answered them,
"Have faith in God. Truly I tell you,
if you say to this mountain,
'Be taken up and thrown into the sea,'
and if you do not doubt in your heart,
but believe that what you say
will come to pass,
it will be done for you.
So I tell you, whatever you ask for in prayer,
believe that you have received it,
and it will be yours.
Whenever you stand praying, forgive,
if you have anything against anyone;
so that your Father in heaven
may also forgive you your trespasses."

The gospel of the Lord.
**Praise to you, Lord Jesus Christ.**

Let us pray:
Most holy God,
Jesus teaches us to believe in you
and to have faith that you always
answer our prayers.
Help us always to have faith in you,
the faith that moves mountains,
and to forgive those who have hurt us.
We ask this through Christ our Lord.
**Amen.**

Let us pray the prayer that Jesus taught us:
**Our Father…**

✠ **In the name of the Father, and of the Son, and of the Holy Spirit. Amen.**

_____

Note: Today's reading is Mark 11:20-25.

## MONDAY

✠ In the name of the Father, and of the Son, and of the Holy Spirit. Amen.

Introduction: In today's reading, Peter tells us what we need to do to live as followers of Jesus. He also reminds us that faith is a precious gift from God.

A reading from the second letter of Peter

May grace and peace be yours in abundance
in the knowledge of God
and of Jesus our Lord.
His divine power has given us everything
needed for life and godliness,
through the knowledge of him who called
us by his own glory and goodness.
Thus he has given us, through these things,
his precious and very great promises.
For this very reason, you must make
every effort to support your faith
with goodness,
and goodness with knowledge,
and knowledge with self-control,
and self-control with endurance,
and endurance with godliness,
and godliness with mutual affection,
and mutual affection with love.

The word of the Lord.
**Thanks be to God.**

Let us pray:
Loving God,
Peter tells us to add goodness to faith,
knowledge to goodness,
self-control to knowledge,
endurance to self-control,
godliness to endurance,
mutual affection to godliness,
and love to mutual affection.
Help us to grow in these gifts and virtues,
following the example of Jesus.
We ask this through Christ our Lord.
**Amen.**

Let us pray the prayer that Jesus taught us:
**Our Father…**

✠ In the name of the Father, and of the Son, and of the Holy Spirit. Amen.

Note: Today's reading is 2 Peter 1:2-4a, 5-7.

## TUESDAY

✠ **In the name of the Father, and of the Son, and of the Holy Spirit. Amen.**

Introduction: In our reading today, some of the Jewish leaders are trying to trap Jesus with the question about whether Jews should pay taxes to Rome, which ruled the land. If Jesus said it was lawful, the Jewish people would think he was a traitor, giving in to the Romans, whom they hated. If he said it wasn't lawful, then the Romans could consider him a threat to the state.

Jesus sees through the trap, and gives them a surprising answer.

A reading from the holy gospel according to Mark
**Glory to you, Lord.**

Then they sent to Jesus some Pharisees
and some Herodians
to trap him in what he said.
And they came and said to him,
"Teacher, we know that you are sincere,
and show deference to no one;
for you do not regard people with partiality,
but teach the way of God
in accordance with truth.
Is it lawful to pay taxes to the emperor,
or not?
Should we pay them, or should we not?"
But knowing their hypocrisy,
he said to them,
"Why are you putting me to the test?
Bring me a denarius and let me see it."
And they brought one.
Then he said to them,
"Whose head is this, and whose title?"
They answered, "The emperor's."

Jesus said to them, "Give to the emperor
the things that are the emperor's,
and to God the things that are God's."
And they were utterly amazed at him.

The gospel of the Lord.
**Praise to you, Lord Jesus Christ.**

Let us pray:
Creator God,
Jesus tells us to give you
what belongs to you.
Help us to do what you ask,
to show others that our hearts
belong to you.
We ask this through Christ our Lord.
**Amen.**

Let us pray the prayer that Jesus taught us:
**Our Father...**

✠ **In the name of the Father, and of the Son, and of the Holy Spirit. Amen.**

---

Note: Today's reading is Mark 12:13-17.

## WEDNESDAY

✠ **In the name of the Father, and of the Son, and of the Holy Spirit. Amen.**

Introduction: In our reading today, St. Paul reminds his friend Timothy to keep alive the gift God gave him, and not to be afraid of giving witness to the Good News and to Jesus.

How do we keep alive the gift that God has given each of us? How do we kindle the flame of grace in our hearts? Loving others, praying, celebrating the sacraments, and following God's laws are some of the ways we can do this.

A reading from the second letter of Paul to Timothy

I am grateful to God – whom I worship
with a clear conscience,
as my ancestors did – when I remember you
constantly in my prayers night and day.
For this reason I remind you
to rekindle the gift of God
that is within you
through the laying on of my hands;
for God did not give us
a spirit of cowardice,
but rather a spirit of power and of love
and of self-discipline.
Do not be ashamed, then,
of the testimony about our Lord
or of me his prisoner,
but join with me in suffering for the gospel,
relying on the power of God,
who saved us
and called us with a holy calling,
not according to our works
but according to his own purpose and grace.

The word of the Lord.
**Thanks be to God.**

Let us pray:
Most loving God,
you give each of us the gift of your Spirit.
Help us to keep alive
the gift of faith that you have given us,
by praying, celebrating the sacraments,
loving others, and doing what is right.
We ask this through Christ our Lord.
**Amen.**

Let us pray the prayer that Jesus taught us:
**Our Father…**

✠ **In the name of the Father, and of the Son, and of the Holy Spirit. Amen.**

Note: Today's reading is 2 Timothy 1:3, 6-9.

## THURSDAY

✠ **In the name of the Father, and of the Son, and of the Holy Spirit. Amen.**

Introduction: In our reading today, Jesus is asked what is the most important commandment. Jesus replies that it is to say that there is only one God, and to love God with all that you have – heart, soul, mind and strength. This commandment was recited every day during morning prayer by the Jews before the coming of Jesus, by Jesus himself, and it is recited by Jews today. Jesus adds that the second most important commandment is to love your neighbour as yourself. These two commandments summarize the ten commandments that God gave Moses on Mount Sinai.

Do we say that the Lord our God is our God alone? Do we love God with all our heart, all our soul, all our mind and all our strength? Do we love our neighbours as ourselves?

A reading from the holy gospel according to Mark
**Glory to you, Lord.**

One of the scribes came near
and heard them disputing with one another,
and seeing that Jesus answered them well,
he asked him,
"Which commandment is the first of all?"
Jesus answered, "The first is, 'Hear, O Israel:
the Lord our God, the Lord is one;
you shall love the Lord your God
with all your heart,
and with all your soul,
and with all your mind,
and with all your strength.'
The second is this,
'You shall love your neighbour as yourself.'
There is no other commandment
greater than these."

Then the scribe said to him,
"You are right, Teacher;
you have truly said that 'he is one,
and besides him there is no other';
and 'to love him with all the heart,
and with all the understanding,
and with all the strength,'
and 'to love one's neighbour as oneself,' –
this is much more important than all
whole burnt offerings and sacrifices."
When Jesus saw that he answered wisely,
he said to him,
"You are not far from the kingdom of God."

The gospel of the Lord.
**Praise to you, Lord Jesus Christ.**

Let us pray:
Most holy and merciful God,
there is no other God but you.
Grant that we may always recognize
that you are God,
and that we may always love you
with all our heart, soul, mind and strength.
Help us to love our neighbours,
especially when this is hard to do.
We ask this through Christ our Lord.
**Amen.**

Let us pray the prayer that Jesus taught us:
**Our Father...**

✠ **In the name of the Father, and of the Son, and of the Holy Spirit. Amen.**

---

Note: Today's reading is Mark 12:28-34.

## NINTH WEEK OF ORDINARY TIME

## FRIDAY

✠ **In the name of the Father, and of the Son, and of the Holy Spirit. Amen.**

Introduction: In our reading today, St. Paul reminds Timothy that he knows what Paul has taught and all the things that have happened to him. He warns Timothy that in following Jesus, he, too, will be persecuted. He tells Timothy to continue to be faithful to what he had been taught and what he believes. The word of God, found in Scripture, is wisdom and a guide.

This is good advice for us, too. We are to be faithful to what we have been taught about Jesus, and use the Bible as a source of wisdom and a guide.

A reading from the second letter of Paul to Timothy

Now you have observed my teaching,
my conduct, my aim in life, my faith,
my patience, my love, my steadfastness,
my persecutions and suffering
the things that happened to me
in Antioch, Iconium, and Lystra.
What persecutions I endured!
Yet the Lord rescued me from all of them.
Indeed, all who want to live a godly life
in Christ Jesus will be persecuted.
But as for you, continue in what you have
learned and firmly believed,
knowing from whom you learned it,
and how from childhood you have known
the sacred writings that are able to
instruct you for salvation through faith
in Christ Jesus.

All scripture is inspired by God
and is useful for teaching,
for reproof, for correction,
and for training in righteousness,
so that everyone who belongs to God
may be proficient,
equipped for every good work.

The word of the Lord.
**Thanks be to God.**

Let us pray:
Most holy God,
your word is wisdom, light and life.
Help us to be faithful to Jesus,
and turn to your word, found in the Bible,
for guidance and help.
We ask this through Christ our Lord.
**Amen.**

Let us pray the prayer that Jesus taught us:
**Our Father…**

✠ In the name of the Father, and of the Son, and of the Holy Spirit. Amen.

Note: Today's reading is 2 Timothy 3:10-12, 14-17.

## MONDAY

✠ **In the name of the Father, and of the Son, and of the Holy Spirit. Amen.**

Introduction: Our reading today is the famous passage known as the Beatitudes. Some people play with this word and make it Be-attitudes; in other words, these are the attitudes we should have, the way we should be.

Jesus tells us that those who have these attitudes are happy, and are close to God.

Are these our attitudes? Do we act this way?

A reading from the holy gospel according to Matthew
**Glory to you, Lord.**

When Jesus saw the crowds,
he went up the mountain;
and after he sat down,
his disciples came to him.
Then he began to speak,
and taught them, saying:
"Blessed are the poor in spirit,
for theirs is the kingdom of heaven.
Blessed are those who mourn,
for they will be comforted.
Blessed are the meek,
for they will inherit the earth.
Blessed are those who hunger and thirst
for righteousness,
for they will be filled.
Blessed are the merciful,
for they will receive mercy.
Blessed are the pure in heart,
for they will see God.
Blessed are the peacemakers,
for they will be called children of God.
Blessed are those who are persecuted
for righteousness' sake,
for theirs is the kingdom of heaven.

Blessed are you when people revile you
and persecute you
and utter all kinds of evil against you
falsely on my account.
Rejoice and be glad,
for your reward is great in heaven,
for in the same way they persecuted
the prophets who were before you."

The gospel of the Lord.
**Praise to you, Lord Jesus Christ.**

Let us pray:
Most loving and merciful God,
your Son, Jesus, taught us the Beatitudes
to help us follow you
and find true happiness.
Help us to grow in these attitudes
and to walk in your ways.
We ask this through Christ our Lord.
Amen.

Let us pray the prayer that Jesus taught us:
**Our Father…**

✠ **In the name of the Father, and of the Son, and of the Holy Spirit. Amen.**

Note: Today's reading is Matthew 5:1-12.

## TUESDAY

✠ **In the name of the Father, and of the Son, and of the Holy Spirit. Amen.**

Introduction: Our reading today talks about salt and light: two very important things. We are like salt for the whole human race; we enhance the flavour of the world by being faithful to the Good News. When we are not faithful witnesses to the Good News, we are like salt that has lost its flavour. In the same way, our faithful actions and love are light to the world.

Are we faithful to the Good News of Jesus? Do we hide our light, or let it shine for all to see?

A reading from the holy gospel according to Matthew
**Glory to you, Lord.**

Jesus said, "You are the salt of the earth;
but if salt has lost its taste,
how can its saltiness be restored?
It is no longer good for anything,
but is thrown out and trampled under foot.
You are the light of the world.
A city built on a hill cannot be hid.
No one after lighting a lamp
puts it under the bushel basket,
but on the lamp stand,
and it gives light to all in the house.
In the same way,
let your light shine before others,
so that they may see your good works
and give glory to your Father in heaven."

The gospel of the Lord.
**Praise to you, Lord Jesus Christ.**

Let us pray:
Most gracious God,
Jesus taught us
that we are to be the salt of the earth
and the light for the world.
Give us the grace we need
to be faithful to the Good News of Jesus.
We ask this through Christ our Lord.
**Amen.**

Let us pray the prayer that Jesus taught us:
**Our Father…**

✠ **In the name of the Father, and of the Son, and of the Holy Spirit. Amen.**

---

Note: Today's reading is Matthew 5:13-16.

## WEDNESDAY

✠ In the name of the Father, and of the Son, and of the Holy Spirit. Amen.

Introduction: The prophets, who lived long before Jesus, brought the people important messages from God about how to follow God's ways. In today's reading, Jesus tells his apostles that he did not come to get rid of the Law (the Ten Commandments and the other laws), or what the prophets taught. He came to complete them.

As Christians, we are to obey God's laws and listen to the messages of the prophets, because in their messages we find truth, and discover the way to act.

A reading from the holy gospel according to Matthew
**Glory to you, Lord.**

Jesus said to his disciples,
"Do not think that I have come to abolish the law or the prophets;
I have come not to abolish but to fulfill.
For truly I tell you,
until heaven and earth pass away,
not one letter, not one stroke of a letter,
will pass from the law
until all is accomplished.
Therefore, whoever breaks one of the least of these commandments,
and teaches others to do the same,
will be called least
in the kingdom of heaven;
but whoever does them and teaches them
will be called great
in the kingdom of heaven."

The gospel of the Lord.
**Praise to you, Lord Jesus Christ.**

Let us pray:
Most holy and loving God,
your laws, the teachings of the prophets,
and the Good News of Jesus
are the ways to everlasting life.
Help us to obey them,
so that we may grow
in wisdom and holiness.
We ask this through Christ our Lord.
**Amen.**

Let us pray the prayer that Jesus taught us:
**Our Father…**

✠ In the name of the Father, and of the Son, and of the Holy Spirit. Amen.

---

Note: Today's reading is Matthew 5:17-19.

## THURSDAY

✠ **In the name of the Father, and of the Son, and of the Holy Spirit. Amen.**

Introduction: In today's reading, Jesus talks about anger and about calling other people names. We know this hurts others, but Jesus reminds us that it also hurts God. He tells us to make peace with others, because there are serious consequences if we don't.

This passage may make us uncomfortable, but if we forgive and make peace with others, we will be at peace with God, too.

Are we willing to make peace with those we have hurt, or who have hurt us?

A reading from the holy gospel according to Matthew
**Glory to you, Lord.**

Jesus said to his disciples,
"For I tell you, unless your righteousness
exceeds that of the scribes and Pharisees,
you will never enter the kingdom of heaven.
You have heard that it was said
to those of ancient times,
'You shall not murder'; and
'whoever murders shall be
liable to judgment.'
But I say to you that if you are angry
with a brother or sister,
you will be liable to judgment;
and if you insult a brother or sister,
you will be liable to the council;
and if you say, 'You fool,'
you will be liable to the hell of fire.

So when you are offering your gift
at the altar,
if you remember that your brother or sister
has something against you,
leave your gift there before the altar
and go; first be reconciled
to your brother or sister,
and then come and offer your gift."

The gospel of the Lord.
**Praise to you, Lord Jesus Christ.**

Let us pray:
Most holy and merciful God,
you love us with an everlasting love
and call us back to you when we sin.
Help us to be loving and forgiving
to those who hurt us,
and give us the courage
to ask for forgiveness when we are wrong.
We ask this through Christ our Lord.
**Amen.**

Let us pray the prayer that Jesus taught us:
**Our Father…**

✠ **In the name of the Father, and of the Son, and of the Holy Spirit. Amen.**

Note: Today's reading is Matthew 5:21-24.

# TENTH WEEK OF ORDINARY TIME

## FRIDAY

✠ **In the name of the Father, and of the Son, and of the Holy Spirit. Amen.**

Introduction: In our reading today, St. Paul speaks about the troubles that we all face, reminding us not to feel too burdened by them. Although we are clay pots that are easily broken or chipped, we hold within us a treasure greater than all the gold, money and diamonds in the world: our faith in God and our trust in God's love. We hold God's greatest gift to us within us: Jesus.

A reading from the second letter of Paul to the Corinthians

But we have this treasure in clay jars,
so that it may be made clear
that this extraordinary power
belongs to God
and does not come from us.
We are afflicted in every way,
but not crushed;
perplexed, but not driven to despair;
persecuted, but not forsaken;
struck down, but not destroyed;
always carrying in the body
the death of Jesus, so that the life of Jesus
may also be made visible in our bodies.

The word of the Lord.
**Thanks be to God.**

Let us pray:
Creator God,
you moulded and fashioned us
from the dust of the earth,
making us vessels of clay.
Grant that we may always cherish
the gift we hold within us,
your Son, Jesus.
Help us to see your hand
at work in our lives.
We ask this through Christ our Lord.
**Amen.**

Let us pray the prayer that Jesus taught us:
**Our Father…**

✠ **In the name of the Father, and of the Son, and of the Holy Spirit. Amen.**

Note: Today's reading is 2 Corinthians 4:7-10.

# ELEVENTH WEEK OF ORDINARY TIME

## MONDAY

✠ In the name of the Father, and of the Son, and of the Holy Spirit. Amen.

Introduction: In our reading today, Jesus tells us not to take revenge on those who hurt us. Instead, we are to give them much more than they want. In this way, the real power is with us. Because we are willing to do more, we are in charge. Our anger subsides, and peace is restored.

A reading from the holy gospel according to Matthew
**Glory to you, Lord.**

Jesus said to his disciples:
"You have heard that it was said,
'An eye for an eye and a tooth for a tooth.'
But I say to you, Do not resist an evildoer.
But if anyone strikes you on the right cheek,
turn the other also;
and if anyone wants to sue you
and take your coat, give your cloak as well;
and if anyone forces you to go one mile,
go also the second mile.
Give to everyone who begs from you,
and do not refuse anyone
who wants to borrow from you."

The gospel of the Lord.
**Praise to you, Lord Jesus Christ.**

Let us pray:
Most merciful God,
Jesus teaches us not to take revenge
on those who hurt us.
Help us to keep our focus on you
and your ways and follow them,
even though they are so different
from what the world tells us to do.
We ask this through Christ our Lord.
**Amen.**

Let us pray the prayer that Jesus taught us:
**Our Father…**

✠ In the name of the Father, and of the Son, and of the Holy Spirit. Amen.

Note: Today's reading is Matthew 5:38-42.

## TUESDAY

✠ **In the name of the Father, and of the Son, and of the Holy Spirit. Amen.**

Introduction: In our reading today, Jesus tells us to love our enemies and to pray for them, because this is what makes us children of God. It's easy to love the people who love us, but Jesus calls us to love everyone! This is not easy to do, but that is what God wants us to do.

A reading from the holy gospel according to Matthew
**Glory to you, Lord.**

Jesus said to his disciples:
"You have heard that it was said,
'You shall love your neighbour
and hate your enemy.'
But I say to you,
Love your enemies
and pray for those who persecute you,
so that you may be children
of your Father in heaven;
for he makes his sun rise on the evil
and on the good,
and sends rain on the righteous
and on the unrighteous.
For if you love those who love you,
what reward do you have?
Do not even the tax collectors do the same?
And if you greet only your brothers
and sisters,
what more are you doing than others?
Do not even the Gentiles do the same?
Be perfect, therefore,
as your heavenly Father is perfect."

The gospel of the Lord.
**Praise to you, Lord Jesus Christ.**

Let us pray:
Most holy and gracious God,
Jesus taught us to love our enemies
and to pray for those who persecute us.
Jesus did this as he died on the cross.
Help us to be like Jesus,
loving everyone and praying for them.
We ask this through Christ our Lord.
**Amen.**

Let us pray the prayer that Jesus taught us:
**Our Father…**

✠ **In the name of the Father, and of the Son, and of the Holy Spirit. Amen.**

---

Note: Today's reading is Matthew 5:43-48.

## WEDNESDAY

✠ **In the name of the Father, and of the Son, and of the Holy Spirit. Amen.**

Introduction: In our reading today, Jesus is telling us not to be show-offs when it comes to prayer and living out our faith. We are to remember why we act the way we do: to praise and honour God.

A reading from the holy gospel according to Matthew
**Glory to you, Lord.**

Jesus said to his disciples:
"Beware of practicing your piety
before others in order to be seen by them;
for then you have no reward
from your Father in heaven.
So whenever you give alms,
do not sound a trumpet before you,
as the hypocrites do in the synagogues
and in the streets,
so that they may be praised by others.
But when you give alms,
do not let your left hand know
what your right hand is doing,
so that your alms may be done in secret;
and your Father who sees in secret
will reward you.
And whenever you pray,
do not be like the hypocrites;
for they love to stand and pray
in the synagogues and at the street corners,
so that they may be seen by others.
Truly I tell you,
they have received their reward.

But whenever you pray,
go into your room and shut the door
and pray to your Father who is in secret;
and your Father who sees in secret
will reward you."

The gospel of the Lord.
**Praise to you, Lord Jesus Christ.**

Let us pray:
Most holy and loving God,
Jesus teaches us by his word and example
not to show off,
but to do things for the right reason.
Help us to be like Jesus,
praying and helping others
because we know
that this is what you want us to do.
We ask this through Christ our Lord.
**Amen.**

Let us pray the prayer that Jesus taught us:
**Our Father…**

✠ **In the name of the Father, and of the Son, and of the Holy Spirit. Amen.**

Note: Today's reading is Matthew 6:1-2a, 3-6.

## THURSDAY

✠ In the name of the Father, and of the Son, and of the Holy Spirit. Amen.

Introduction: In our reading today, Jesus teaches the disciples about prayer, and tells them (and us) how to pray. The prayer he teaches them is what we call the Our Father. He also says that if we forgive others, God will forgive us.

We pray the Our Father so often, we may not think about the words and what they mean. As we listen to this reading, let us pay close attention to the words.

A reading from the holy gospel according to Matthew
**Glory to you, Lord.**

Jesus said to his disciples:
"When you are praying,
do not heap up empty phrases
as the Gentiles do; for they think
that they will be heard
because of their many words.
Do not be like them,
for your Father knows what you need
before you ask him.
Pray then in this way:
Our Father in heaven,
hallowed be your name.
Your kingdom come.
Your will be done,
on earth as it is in heaven.
Give us this day our daily bread.
And forgive us our debts,
as we also have forgiven our debtors.
And do not bring us to the time of trial,
but rescue us from the evil one.
For if you forgive others their trespasses,
your heavenly Father will also forgive you."

The gospel of the Lord.
**Praise to you, Lord Jesus Christ.**

Let us pray:
Father in heaven,
Jesus taught us how to pray to you,
to ask you for what we need,
and to keep our focus on you
in our prayer.
Give us the grace to pray well and always.
We ask this through Christ our Lord.
**Amen.**

Let us pray the prayer that Jesus taught us:
**Our Father…**

✠ In the name of the Father, and of the Son, and of the Holy Spirit. Amen.

Note: Today's reading is Matthew 6:7-14.

## FRIDAY

✠ **In the name of the Father, and of the Son, and of the Holy Spirit. Amen.**

Introduction: In our reading today, Jesus tells us to focus on building up treasure in heaven, not on earth. Material things eventually break or tear or fall apart, but the treasures in our hearts will last forever.

We store treasure in heaven by listening carefully to God's word, doing what God asks, following God's commandments and imitating Jesus.

A reading from the holy gospel according to Matthew
**Glory to you, Lord.**

Jesus said,
"Do not store up for yourselves
treasures on earth,
where moth and rust consume
and where thieves break in and steal;
but store up for yourselves
treasures in heaven,
where neither moth nor rust consumes
and where thieves do not break in and steal.
For where your treasure is,
there your heart will be also."

The gospel of the Lord.
**Praise to you, Lord Jesus Christ.**

Let us pray:
Most gracious God,
Jesus tells us to store up riches in heaven.
Help us to be faithful sons and daughters,
following your ways and commandments,
in imitation of our brother Jesus.
We ask this through Christ our Lord.
**Amen.**

Let us pray the prayer that Jesus taught us:
**Our Father…**

✠ **In the name of the Father, and of the Son, and of the Holy Spirit. Amen.**

---

Note: Today's reading is Matthew 6:19-21.

# TWELFTH WEEK OF ORDINARY TIME

## MONDAY

✠ In the name of the Father, and of the Son, and of the Holy Spirit. Amen.

Introduction: In our reading today Jesus reminds us not to judge one another. The way we look at others and judge them is the way God will judge us.

We all find it so easy to criticize the actions of others, but we don't want to admit our own faults. Starting today, can we treat others more gently, and speak about them with kind words?

A reading from the holy gospel according to Matthew
**Glory to you, Lord.**

Jesus said,
"Do not judge,
so that you may not be judged.
For with the judgment you make
you will be judged,
and the measure you give
will be the measure you get.
Why do you see the speck
in your neighbour's eye,
but do not notice the log in your own eye?
Or how can you say to your neighbour,
'Let me take the speck out of your eye,'
while the log is in your own eye?
You hypocrite,
first take the log out of your own eye,
and then you will see clearly to take
the speck out of your neighbour's eye."

The gospel of the Lord.
**Praise to you, Lord Jesus Christ.**

Let us pray:
Most loving and merciful God,
Jesus taught us not to judge one another.
Help us to think about others
with charity and kindness,
and to speak about them in the same way.
We ask this through Christ our Lord.
**Amen.**

Let us pray the prayer that Jesus taught us:
**Our Father…**

✠ In the name of the Father, and of the Son, and of the Holy Spirit. Amen.

Note: Today's reading is Matthew 7:1-5.

# TWELFTH WEEK OF ORDINARY TIME

## TUESDAY

✠ In the name of the Father, and of the Son, and of the Holy Spirit. Amen.

Introduction: In today's reading, Jesus tells us to guard our spiritual treasures, the things that bring us closer to God. He warns us that the road to heaven is hard sometimes, and the gate is narrow, but if we follow God's ways we will get there!

A reading from the holy gospel according to Matthew
**Glory to you, Lord.**

Jesus said,
"Do not give what is holy to dogs;
and do not throw your pearls before swine,
or they will trample them under foot
and turn and maul you.
In everything do to others
as you would have them do to you;
for this is the law and the prophets.
Enter through the narrow gate;
for the gate is wide and the road is easy
that leads to destruction,
and there are many who take it.
For the gate is narrow
and the road is hard that leads to life,
and there are few who find it."

The gospel of the Lord.
**Praise to you, Lord Jesus Christ.**

Let us pray:
Most holy and gracious God,
your Son teaches us
to treasure the things of heaven,
not to throw them away.
Help us to treasure the gifts you give us,
treat others as we would like to be treated,
and follow the path that leads to you.
We ask this through Christ our Lord.
**Amen.**

Let us pray the prayer that Jesus taught us:
**Our Father…**

✠ In the name of the Father, and of the Son, and of the Holy Spirit. Amen.

Note: Today's reading is Matthew 7:6, 12-14.

## WEDNESDAY

✠ **In the name of the Father, and of the Son, and of the Holy Spirit. Amen.**

Introduction: In our reading today, Jesus tells us that we can recognize true prophets, people who lead us to God, by their actions.

Just as a healthy tree gives us delicious fruit, a true prophet brings us closer to God through good example.

A reading from the holy gospel according to Matthew
**Glory to you, Lord.**

Jesus said,
"Beware of false prophets,
who come to you in sheep's clothing
but inwardly are ravenous wolves.
You will know them by their fruits.
Are grapes gathered from thorns,
or figs from thistles?
In the same way,
every good tree bears good fruit,
but the bad tree bears bad fruit.
A good tree cannot bear bad fruit,
nor can a bad tree bear good fruit.
Every tree that does not bear good fruit
is cut down and thrown into the fire.
Thus you will know them by their fruits."

The gospel of the Lord.
**Praise to you, Lord Jesus Christ.**

Let us pray:
Most holy and gracious God,
your Son, Jesus, teaches us
that true people of God
are known by their good actions and words.
Help us to grow in holiness
and produce good fruit through our actions
and words, too.
We ask this through Christ our Lord.
**Amen.**

Let us pray the prayer that Jesus taught us:
**Our Father…**

✠ **In the name of the Father, and of the Son, and of the Holy Spirit. Amen.**

Note: Today's reading is Matthew 7:15-20.

## THURSDAY

✠ In the name of the Father, and of the Son, and of the Holy Spirit. Amen.

Introduction: In our reading today, Jesus talks about the wise man who builds his house on rock and the foolish man who builds his house on sand. If we listen to his words and obey them, we are like the man who builds on rock. When things get difficult, and there are many problems, we are unshaken, because our foundation rests on Jesus. If we do not have our foundation on Jesus, any problems and difficulties we face can really shake us up, like the house built on sand.

Are we building our lives on the rock foundation of Jesus by listening to him and obeying his words?

A reading from the holy gospel according to Matthew
**Glory to you, Lord.**

Jesus said,
"Everyone then who hears
these words of mine and acts on them
will be like a wise man
who built his house on rock.
The rain fell, the floods came,
and the winds blew and beat on that house,
but it did not fall,
because it had been founded on rock.
And everyone who hears
these words of mine
and does not act on them
will be like a foolish man
who built his house on sand.
The rain fell, and the floods came,
and the winds blew
and beat against that house, and it fell —
and great was its fall!"

The gospel of the Lord.
**Praise to you, Lord Jesus Christ.**

Let us pray:
Loving and everlasting God,
the words of your Son, Jesus,
lead to life and light.
Help us to hear his words and obey them,
so that our lives and faith
may be built on rock.
We ask this through Christ our Lord.
**Amen.**

Let us pray the prayer that Jesus taught us:
**Our Father…**

✠ In the name of the Father, and of the Son, and of the Holy Spirit. Amen.

Note: Today's reading is Matthew 7:24-27.

## FRIDAY

✠ In the name of the Father, and of the Son, and of the Holy Spirit. Amen.

Introduction: All of us need to be healed of things that have hurt our bodies, our minds or our hearts. If we, like the man with leprosy, ask Jesus to heal us, we know that he will say, "Of course I want to!"

Do we have the courage and faith we need to ask Jesus to heal us?

A reading from the holy gospel according to Matthew
**Glory to you, Lord.**

When Jesus had come down
from the mountain,
great crowds followed him;
and there was a leper who came to him
and knelt before him, saying,
"Lord, if you choose,
you can make me clean."
He stretched out his hand and touched him,
saying, "I do choose. Be made clean!"
Immediately his leprosy was cleansed.
Then Jesus said to him,
"See that you say nothing to anyone;
but go, show yourself to the priest,
and offer the gift that Moses commanded,
as a testimony to them."

The gospel of the Lord.
**Praise to you, Lord Jesus Christ.**

Let us pray:
Jesus,
when the leper asked
if you wanted to heal him,
you said, "Of course I want to!"
Help us to remember your words
when we are in trouble, sick or sad,
knowing that we can turn to you
for comfort and support.
**Amen.**

Let us pray the prayer that Jesus taught us:
**Our Father…**

✠ In the name of the Father, and of the Son, and of the Holy Spirit. Amen.

---

Note: Today's reading is Matthew 8:1-4.

## MONDAY

✠ **In the name of the Father, and of the Son, and of the Holy Spirit. Amen.**

Introduction: Today's reading is not an easy one to hear: Jesus talks about the sacrifices that are part of being his disciple. To follow him means giving up things that stop us from living as God wants. The time to follow Jesus is now – we can't make excuses for why we're not ready!

Do we give up things we want to do in order to follow Jesus?

A reading from the holy gospel according to Matthew
**Glory to you, Lord.**

Now when Jesus saw great crowds
around him, he gave orders
to go over to the other side.
A scribe then approached and said,
"Teacher, I will follow you
wherever you go."
And Jesus said to him,
"Foxes have holes,
and birds of the air have nests;
but the Son of Man has nowhere
to lay his head."
Another of his disciples said to him,
"Lord, first let me go and bury my father."
But Jesus said to him, "Follow me,
and let the dead bury their own dead."

The gospel of the Lord.
**Praise to you, Lord Jesus Christ.**

Let us pray:
Father in heaven,
your beloved Son, Jesus,
gave up many comforts
to do what you asked of him.
Grant us the grace we need
to give up those things we need to give up
in order to follow Jesus faithfully.
We ask this through Christ our Lord.
**Amen.**

Let us pray the prayer that Jesus taught us:
**Our Father…**

✠ **In the name of the Father, and of the Son, and of the Holy Spirit. Amen.**

Note: Today's reading is Matthew 8:18-22.

## TUESDAY

✠ In the name of the Father, and of the Son, and of the Holy Spirit. Amen.

Introduction: Fierce storms can come up on the Sea of Galilee, or Lake Gennesaret, without warning – and that's what happens in today's gospel.

In life, things happen to us that are unsettling and upsetting – our own personal storms. We need to remember that Jesus has promised to be with us – he is in our boat when we feel afraid or overwhelmed. He is our anchor and our safety. We turn to him in these times, confident that he is with us and will give us the strength we need to weather the storms.

A reading from the holy gospel according to Matthew
**Glory to you, Lord.**

And when Jesus got into the boat,
his disciples followed him.
A windstorm arose on the sea, so great
that the boat was being swamped
by the waves; but he was asleep.
And they went and woke him up, saying,
"Lord, save us! We are perishing!"
And he said to them,
"Why are you afraid, you of little faith?"
Then he got up and rebuked the winds
and the sea; and there was a dead calm.
They were amazed, saying,
"What sort of man is this,
that even the winds and the sea obey him?"

The gospel of the Lord.
**Praise to you, Lord Jesus Christ.**

Let us pray:
Most holy God,
Jesus was asleep in the boat,
knowing that he was safe in your hands.
Help us to remember
that when storms come up in our lives,
we are safe in your hands.
Jesus is there with us,
giving us the graces and strength we need
to get through tough times.
We ask this through Christ our Lord.
**Amen.**

Let us pray the prayer that Jesus taught us:
**Our Father…**

✠ In the name of the Father, and of the Son, and of the Holy Spirit. Amen.

---

Note: Today's reading is Matthew 8:23-27.

# THIRTEENTH WEEK OF ORDINARY TIME

## WEDNESDAY

✠ In the name of the Father, and of the Son, and of the Holy Spirit. Amen.

Introduction: Today we hear from the prophet Amos. The people of Amos' time were not following God's laws and ways or treating poor people fairly. God chose Amos to remind the people to return to the laws and ways of God, to do what was right and just.

Amos' message is for us today, too. Do we seek what is good? Are we kind and generous? Are we doing what is right and just?

A reading from the book of the prophet Amos

Seek good and not evil, that you may live;
and so the Lord, the God of hosts,
will be with you, just as you have said.
Hate evil and love good,
and establish justice in the gate;
it may be that the Lord, the God of hosts,
will be gracious to the remnant of Joseph.
But let justice roll down like waters,
and righteousness
like an ever-flowing stream.

The word of the Lord.
**Thanks be to God.**

Let us pray:
Merciful God,
you asked the prophet Amos
to remind people to do what is right,
to follow your laws and ways,
and to act justly, with kindness,
love and generosity.
Help us to be aware of those
who are in need
and to be children of your kingdom,
faithful to your laws and ways.
We ask this through Christ our Lord.
**Amen.**

Let us pray the prayer that Jesus taught us:
**Our Father…**

✠ In the name of the Father, and of the Son, and of the Holy Spirit. Amen.

Note: Today's reading is Amos 5:14-15, 24.

# THIRTEENTH WEEK OF ORDINARY TIME

## THURSDAY

✠ In the name of the Father, and of the Son, and of the Holy Spirit. Amen.

Introduction: In today's gospel, Jesus shows that faith in him means a change of heart, a turning back to God. This is repentance. Believing in God means believing in God's saving power, including the forgiveness of sins.

The teachers of the Law didn't believe in Jesus' power. So Jesus proved he could forgive sin, something that cannot be seen, by doing something that could be seen – curing the paralyzed man.

A reading from the holy gospel according to Matthew
**Glory to you, Lord.**

And after getting into a boat
Jesus crossed the sea
and came to his own town.
And just then some people were carrying
a paralyzed man lying on a bed.
When Jesus saw their faith,
he said to the paralytic,
"Take heart, son; your sins are forgiven."
Then some of the scribes said to themselves,
"This man is blaspheming."
But Jesus, perceiving their thoughts, said,
"Why do you think evil in your hearts?
For which is easier, to say, '
Your sins are forgiven,'
or to say, 'Stand up and walk'?
But so that you may know
that the Son of Man
has authority on earth to forgive sins" –
he then said to the paralytic –
"Stand up, take your bed
and go to your home."
And he stood up and went to his home.

When the crowds saw it,
they were filled with awe,
and they glorified God,
who had given such authority
to human beings.

The gospel of the Lord.
**Praise to you, Lord Jesus Christ.**

Let us pray:
Merciful Father,
your Son, Jesus, forgave the sins
of the paralyzed man,
after recognizing the faith of his friends.
Help us to approach the sacrament
of Reconciliation with the same faith,
trusting in your mercy and love.
We ask this through Christ our Lord.
**Amen.**

Let us pray the prayer that Jesus taught us:
**Our Father …**

✠ In the name of the Father, and of the Son, and of the Holy Spirit. Amen.

Note: Today's reading is Matthew 9:1-8.

## FRIDAY

✠ **In the name of the Father, and of the Son, and of the Holy Spirit. Amen.**

Introduction: Our reading today is the call of Matthew, a tax collector. Tax collectors in Jesus' time worked for Rome, a foreign power that occupied the country. Tax collectors charged as much money as they could; their income came from what they collected over and above what Rome demanded.

Jesus broke all the social rules of the time – he ate with tax collectors and other outcasts. He looked at the person's heart, not their actions. He saw the goodness in Matthew, and knew that he would be a good disciple.

Are we as open to Jesus' call to follow him as Matthew was? What is Jesus asking us to do today?

A reading from the holy gospel according to Matthew
**Glory to you, Lord.**

As Jesus was walking along,
he saw a man called Matthew
sitting at the tax booth;
and he said to him, "Follow me."
And he got up and followed him.

The gospel of the Lord.
**Praise to you, Lord Jesus Christ.**

Let us pray:
Loving God,
your Son, Jesus, looked at Matthew
and saw what was in his heart.
Help us to see the good in others.
Help us to follow your Son faithfully.
May we be open to what you wish us to do,
and do it immediately and willingly.
We ask this through Christ our Lord.
**Amen.**

Let us pray the prayer that Jesus taught us:
**Our Father…**

✠ **In the name of the Father, and of the Son, and of the Holy Spirit. Amen.**

Note: Today's reading is Matthew 9:9.

# FOURTH LAST DAY OF SCHOOL

✠ **In the name of the Father, and of the Son, and of the Holy Spirit. Amen.**

Introduction: In today's reading, St. Paul prays for the people of Ephesus, one of the first Christian communities.

Like the people of Ephesus, we are learning about our faith and trying to grow closer to God. St. Paul's words call on God to strengthen us and fill us with God's love.

A reading from the letter of Paul to the Ephesians

For this reason
I bow my knees before the Father,
from whom every family
in heaven and on earth takes its name.
I pray that,
according to the riches of his glory,
he may grant that you may be strengthened
in your inner being
with power through his Spirit,
and that Christ may dwell in your hearts
through faith,
as you are being rooted and grounded
in love.
I pray that you may have the power
to comprehend, with all the saints,
what is the breadth and length
and height and depth,
and to know the love of Christ
that surpasses knowledge,
so that you may be filled
with all the fullness of God.

Now to him who
by the power at work within us
is able to accomplish abundantly
far more than all we can ask or imagine,
to him be glory in the church
and in Christ Jesus to all generations,
for ever and ever. Amen.

The word of the Lord.
**Thanks be to God.**

Let us pray:
Most holy and loving God,
thank you for the gift of Jesus,
who lives in our hearts,
and for the Holy Spirit,
who gives us strength.
Fill us with your love!
We ask this through Christ our Lord.
**Amen.**

Let us pray the prayer that Jesus taught us:
**Our Father…**

✠ **In the name of the Father, and of the Son, and of the Holy Spirit. Amen.**

---

Note: Today's reading is Ephesians 3:14-21.

# THIRD LAST DAY OF SCHOOL

✠ **In the name of the Father, and of the Son, and of the Holy Spirit. Amen.**

Introduction: During this school year, we have worked hard and have learned lots of new things. All of us have grown, in knowledge, wisdom, grace and love of God, like Jesus did when he was growing up. Let us carry these gifts with us, thanking God for the many blessings of this year together.

A reading from the holy gospel according to Luke
**Glory to you, Lord.**

Now every year
the parents of Jesus went to Jerusalem
for the festival of the Passover.
And when he was twelve years old,
they went up as usual for the festival.
When the festival was ended
and they started to return,
the boy Jesus stayed behind in Jerusalem,
but his parents did not know it.
Assuming that he was
in the group of travellers,
they went a day's journey.
Then they started to look for him
among their relatives and friends.
When they did not find him,
they returned to Jerusalem
to search for him.
After three days
they found him in the temple,
sitting among the teachers,
listening to them
and asking them questions.
And all who heard him
were amazed at his understanding
and his answers.

When his parents saw him
they were astonished;
and his mother said to him,
"Child, why have you treated us like this?"
Then he went down with them
and came to Nazareth,
and was obedient to them.
His mother treasured all these things
in her heart.
And Jesus increased in wisdom
and in years,
and in divine and human favour.

The gospel of the Lord.
**Praise to you, Lord Jesus Christ.**

Let us pray:
Father in heaven,
we have learned many new things
and have grown in many ways this year.
We ask your blessing upon us:
send us your Spirit to lead and guide us
so that we may continue to grow
in wisdom, grace and love.
We ask this through Christ our Lord.
**Amen.**

Let us pray the prayer that Jesus taught us:
**Our Father...**

✠ **In the name of the Father, and of the Son, and of the Holy Spirit. Amen.**

Note: Today's reading is Luke 2:41-48a, 51-52.

# SECOND LAST DAY OF SCHOOL

✠ In the name of the Father, and of the Son, and of the Holy Spirit. Amen.

Introduction: Today, St. Paul shares an important lesson with us: in the race to eternal life with God, run straight for the finish line! In this race, there is more than one winner, and the prize will last forever.

A reading from the first letter of Paul to the Corinthians

I do it all for the sake of the gospel, so that I may share in its blessings.
Do you not know that in a race
the runners all compete,
but only one receives the prize?
Run in such a way that you may win it.
Athletes exercise self-control in all things;
they do it to receive a perishable wreath,
but we an imperishable one.
So I do not run aimlessly.

The word of the Lord.
**Thanks be to God.**

Let us pray:
Loving Father,
Help us to run our races well –
the races that will win us
eternal life with you in heaven.
Let us always try our best in all we do,
because it through trying
that we become the people
you created us to be.
We ask this through Christ our Lord.
**Amen.**

Let us pray the prayer that Jesus taught us:
**Our Father…**

✠ In the name of the Father, and of the Son, and of the Holy Spirit. Amen.

Note: Today's reading is 1 Corinthians 9:23-26a.

243

# LAST DAY OF SCHOOL

✠ **In the name of the Father, and of the Son, and of the Holy Spirit. Amen.**

Introduction: We have had a very busy and successful school year. For these things, we thank God with all our hearts. And as St. Paul tells us today, let us be joyful, prayerful, thankful people, carrying God's love and peace wherever we go.

A reading from the first letter of Paul to the Thessalonians

Rejoice always,
pray without ceasing,
give thanks in all circumstances;
for this is the will of God in Christ Jesus
for you.
Do not quench the Spirit.
Do not despise the words of prophets,
but test everything;
hold fast to what is good;
abstain from every form of evil.
May the God of peace himself
sanctify you entirely;
and may your spirit and soul and body
be kept sound and blameless
at the coming of our Lord Jesus Christ.
The one who calls you is faithful,
and he will do this.
The grace of our Lord Jesus Christ
be with you.

The word of the Lord.
**Thanks be to God.**

Let us pray.
Response: **Lord, we praise and thank you.**

For all the good things that have happened this year…
**Lord, we praise and thank you.**

For our teachers, our families, our parish and our friends here at school…
**Lord, we praise and thank you.**

For the times we shared, both good times and hard times…
**Lord, we praise and thank you.**

For the gift of summer vacation…
**Lord, we praise and thank you.**

For all the gifts you have given us…
**Lord, we praise and thank you.**

Let us pray the prayer that Jesus taught us:
**Our Father…**

✠ **In the name of the Father, and of the Son, and of the Holy Spirit. Amen.**

Note: Today's reading is 1 Thessalonians 5:16-24, 28.

# Feast Days

## SEPTEMBER 8
## FEAST OF THE NATIVITY OF MARY

✠ **In the name of the Father, and of the Son, and of the Holy Spirit. Amen.**

Introduction: Today we celebrate the feast of the birth of Mary; in other words, we celebrate the day Mary the Mother of God was born – her birthday.

God chose Mary to be the mother of his Son, Jesus. As we listen to today's reading, we hear the story of the birth of Jesus – for Christians, the most important birth in the history of the world.

A reading from the holy gospel according to Matthew
**Glory to you, Lord.**

Now the birth of Jesus the Messiah
took place in this way.
When his mother Mary had been engaged
to Joseph, but before they lived together,
she was found to be with child
from the Holy Spirit.
Her husband Joseph, being a righteous man
and unwilling to expose her
to public disgrace,
planned to dismiss her quietly.
But just when he had resolved to do this,
an angel of the Lord
appeared to him in a dream
and said, "Joseph, son of David,
do not be afraid to take Mary as your wife,
for the child conceived in her
is from the Holy Spirit.
She will bear a son,
and you are to name him Jesus,
for he will save his people from their sins."

All this took place
to fulfill what had been spoken
by the Lord through the prophet:
"Look, the virgin shall conceive
and bear a son,
and they shall name him Emmanuel,"
which means, "God is with us."

The gospel of the Lord.
**Praise to you, Lord Jesus Christ.**

Let us pray:
Most holy and loving God,
in your goodness to us
you chose Mary
to be the mother of your Son, Jesus.
Help us to love and honour her,
and do what you ask,
following her example.
We ask this through Christ our Lord.
**Amen.**

In honour of Mary's birth, we pray:
**Hail Mary...**

✠ **In the name of the Father, and of the Son, and of the Holy Spirit. Amen.**

---

Note: Today's reading is Matthew 1:18-23.

## SEPTEMBER 12
## FEAST OF THE MOST HOLY NAME OF MARY

✠ **In the name of the Father, and of the Son, and of the Holy Spirit. Amen.**

Introduction: Today is the feast of the Most Holy Name of Mary.

The name Mary, which has been researched by modern language scholars, has been connected to the Egyptian word mara, meaning beautiful; the Egyptian word mari, meaning loved; and in the Canaanite language, mrym (meerim), from the verb that means high or lofty, in the sense of Exalted One, or Sublime One. All these terms describe the qualities of Our Lady very well!

A reading from the holy gospel according to Luke
**Glory to you, Lord.**

In the sixth month
the angel Gabriel was sent by God
to a town in Galilee called Nazareth,
to a virgin engaged to a man
whose name was Joseph,
of the house of David.
The virgin's name was Mary.
And he came to her and said,
"Greetings, favoured one!
The Lord is with you."

The gospel of the Lord.
**Praise to you, Lord Jesus Christ.**

Let us pray:
Most holy and all-knowing God,
you prepared and chose Mary
to be the mother of your beloved Son, Jesus.
Remind us to call upon her help,
as she is our heavenly mother
and loves each one of us very much.
We ask this through Christ our Lord.
**Amen.**

In honour of Mary, we pray:
**Hail Mary...**

✠ **In the name of the Father, and of the Son, and of the Holy Spirit. Amen.**

Note: Today's reading is Luke 1:26-28.

## SEPTEMBER 14
## FEAST OF THE TRIUMPH OF THE CROSS

✠ In the name of the Father, and of the Son, and of the Holy Spirit. Amen.

Introduction: Today we celebrate the Feast of the Triumph of the Cross. Jesus triumphed over death by dying on the cross. Here Jesus explains why he must die: to bring us into eternal life with God.

A reading from the holy gospel according to John
**Glory to you, Lord.**

Jesus said to Nicodemus,
"No one has ascended into heaven
except the one who descended from heaven,
the Son of Man.
And just as Moses lifted up the serpent
in the wilderness,
so must the Son of Man be lifted up,
that whoever believes in him
may have eternal life.
For God so loved the world
that he gave his only Son,
so that everyone who believes in him
may not perish but may have eternal life.
Indeed, God did not send the Son
into the world
to condemn the world,
but in order that the world
might be saved through him."

The gospel of the Lord.
**Praise to you, Lord Jesus Christ.**

Let us pray:
We adore you, O Christ, and we bless you,
because by your holy cross
you have redeemed the world.*
Amen.

Let us pray the prayer that Jesus taught us:
**Our Father...**

✠ In the name of the Father, and of the Son, and of the Holy Spirit. Amen.

Note: Today's reading is John 3:13-17.

*The prayer "We adore you, O Christ..." is an invocation that is traditionally prayed at the beginning of each station when we pray the Stations of the Cross. Its usage is not limited to the Stations.

## SEPTEMBER 15
## FEAST OF OUR LADY OF SORROWS

✠ **In the name of the Father, and of the Son, and of the Holy Spirit. Amen.**

Introduction: Today is the feast of Our Lady of Sorrows. We remember the Seven Sorrows of Mary: the prophecy of Simeon; the flight into Egypt; the loss of Jesus for three days in Jerusalem; the ascent of Jesus to Calvary; the crucifixion and death of Jesus; Jesus taken down from the cross; and Jesus laid in the tomb.

A reading from the holy gospel according to Luke
**Glory to you, Lord.**

Jesus' father and mother were amazed
at what was being said about him.
Then Simeon blessed them
and said to his mother Mary,
"This child is destined for the falling
and the rising of many in Israel,
and to be a sign that will be opposed
so that the inner thoughts of many
will be revealed –
and a sword will pierce your own soul too."

The gospel of the Lord.
**Praise to you, Lord Jesus Christ.**

Let us pray:
God our Creator,
when Jesus died on the cross,
Mary, his mother, was there,
sharing in his sufferings.
Help us to remember
that when he was dying,
Jesus gave Mary to us as our mother.
We ask this through Christ our Lord.
**Amen.**

Let us pray the Hail Mary, thanking God for the gift of Mary:
**Hail Mary...**

✠ **In the name of the Father, and of the Son, and of the Holy Spirit. Amen.**

Note: Today's reading is Luke 2:33-35.

## SEPTEMBER 21
## FEAST OF ST. MATTHEW, APOSTLE AND EVANGELIST

✠ **In the name of the Father, and of the Son, and of the Holy Spirit. Amen.**

Introduction: Today we celebrate the Feast of St. Matthew. Jesus called Matthew, who was a tax collector and therefore despised by the Jews, to be one of his special followers, an apostle. Matthew also wrote one of the four gospels. The word evangelist comes from the Greek word meaning gospel-writer. We learn what Jesus said and did in the gospels.

A reading from the holy gospel according to Matthew
**Glory to you, Lord.**

As Jesus was walking along,
he saw a man called Matthew
sitting at the tax booth;
and he said to him, "Follow me."
And he got up and followed him.

The gospel of the Lord.
**Praise to you, Lord Jesus Christ.**

Let us pray:
Most holy God,
St. Matthew left everything
and became a faithful follower of Jesus.
Through the words of his gospel,
we know what Jesus said and did.
Help us to always listen
with open minds and hearts
to the reading of your word.
We ask this through Christ our Lord.
**Amen.**

Let us pray the prayer that Jesus taught us:
**Our Father…**

✠ **In the name of the Father, and of the Son, and of the Holy Spirit. Amen.**

Note: Today's reading is Matthew 9:9.

## SEPTEMBER 26*

## FEAST OF STS. JEAN DE BRÉBEUF AND ISAAC JOGUES, PRIESTS, AND COMPANIONS, MARTYRS

✠ **In the name of the Father, and of the Son, and of the Holy Spirit. Amen.**

Introduction: Today we celebrate the feast of the Canadian martyrs: Sts. Jean de Brébeuf, Isaac Jogues, Gabriel Lalemant, René Goupil, Charles Garnier, Anthony Daniel, Noel Chabanel and Jean De Lalonde, who are the secondary patrons of Canada. (St. Joseph is the primary patron of Canada.)

These men came to Canada from France in the early 1600s. They were Jesuit priests and lay assistants, missionaries who brought the Good News to the Huron people. They were killed by the Iroquois because of their belief in Jesus.

A reading from the second letter of Paul to the Corinthians

As servants of God we have commended ourselves in every way:
through great endurance,
in afflictions, hardships, calamities, beatings,
imprisonments, riots, labours,
sleepless nights, hunger;
by purity, knowledge, patience, kindness,
holiness of spirit, genuine love,
truthful speech, and the power of God;
with the weapons of righteousness
for the right hand and for the left;
in honour and dishonour,
in ill repute and good repute.

We are treated as impostors,
and yet are true;
as unknown, and yet are well known;
as dying, and see – we are alive;
as punished, and yet not killed;
as sorrowful, yet always rejoicing;
as poor, yet making many rich;
as having nothing,
and yet possessing everything.

The word of the Lord.
**Thanks be to God.**

Let us pray:
Most loving God,
the Canadian martyrs suffered greatly
yet did not waver in their love
and in their belief in you and Jesus.
Grant that when we are having trouble,
we too will stand firm in our love and belief
in you and in Jesus.
We ask this through Christ our Lord.
**Amen.**

Let us pray the prayer that Jesus taught us:
**Our Father...**

✠ **In the name of the Father, and of the Son, and of the Holy Spirit. Amen.**

---

Note: Today's reading is 2 Corinthians 6:4-10.

*In Canada, this feast has been transferred to September 26; for the rest of the Universal Church, it is celebrated on October 19.

## SEPTEMBER 27
## FEAST OF ST. VINCENT DE PAUL

✠ In the name of the Father, and of the Son, and of the Holy Spirit. Amen.

Introduction: St. Vincent de Paul was born in France in 1580, and was ordained a priest in 1600. He was known for his preaching and his work with the poor. The order he founded, which was devoted to missionary work among the peasants, spread quickly all over France. Vincent set up parish societies to aid the poor. (In Canada, these groups are known as the St. Vincent de Paul Society.) He also founded a religious order of women, the Sisters of Charity, with St. Louise de Marillac. Vincent spent his whole life helping those who were suffering and very poor. He died in Paris on September 27, 1660. He is the patron saint of all charitable groups.

St. Vincent de Paul had great love and care for the poor of this world. How can we imitate him? What can we do to help the poor?

A reading from the book of the prophet Isaiah

The Lord says,
"Is not this the fast that I choose:
to loose the bonds of injustice,
to undo the thongs of the yoke,
to let the oppressed go free,
and to break every yoke?
Is it not to share your
bread with the hungry,
and bring the homeless poor
into your house;
when you see the naked, to cover them,
and not to hide yourself from your own kin?
Then your light shall break forth
like the dawn,
and your healing shall spring up quickly;
your vindicator shall go before you,
the glory of the Lord
shall be your rear guard.

Then you shall call,
and the Lord will answer;
you shall cry for help, and he will say,
Here I am."

The word of the Lord.
**Thanks be to God.**

Let us pray:
Most loving God,
St. Vincent de Paul
showed great love and concern for the poor.
Help us to do what we can
to help the poor among us.
We ask this through Christ our Lord.
**Amen.**

Let us pray the prayer that Jesus taught us:
**Our Father...**

✠ In the name of the Father, and of the Son, and of the Holy Spirit. Amen.

---

Note: Today's reading is Isaiah 58:6-9a.

## SEPTEMBER 29

## FEAST OF STS. MICHAEL, GABRIEL AND RAPHAEL, ARCHANGELS

✠ **In the name of the Father, and of the Son, and of the Holy Spirit. Amen.**

Introduction: Today we celebrate the feasts of the three archangels – Michael, Gabriel and Raphael.

St. Michael is known as the leader of all the angels. God sent St. Gabriel to ask Mary to be the mother of Jesus. St. Raphael was sent by God to a man named Tobit, who was blind. Disguised as a friend, Raphael led his son Tobias on a long journey, and when they returned, told Tobias how to heal his father.

Listen to Raphael's words after he told Tobit and Tobias who he really was, and why God sent him to these two good men.

A reading from the book of Tobit

He said to them,
"Do not be afraid; peace be with you.
Bless God for evermore.
As for me, when I was with you,
I was not acting on my own will,
but by the will of God.
Bless him each and every day;
sing his praises.
Although you were watching me,
I really did not eat or drink anything –
but what you saw was a vision.
So now get up from the ground,
and acknowledge God.
See, I am ascending to him who sent me.
Write down all these things
that have happened to you."
And Raphael ascended.

The word of the Lord.
**Thanks be to God.**

Let us pray:
Most holy and eternal God,
we praise you and thank you
for all the great things you have done for us.
Grant that we may always turn to you
with grateful and loving hearts,
knowing how much you love us.
We ask this through Christ our Lord.
**Amen.**

Let us pray the prayer that Jesus taught us:
**Our Father…**

✠ **In the name of the Father, and of the Son, and of the Holy Spirit. Amen.**

Note: Today's reading is Tobit 12:17-18, 20-21a.

## SEPTEMBER 30
## FEAST OF ST. JEROME

✠ **In the name of the Father, and of the Son, and of the Holy Spirit. Amen.**

Introduction: Today we celebrate the feast of St. Jerome, a priest who lived over 1700 years ago. He is also a doctor of the Church, which means he knew a lot about our faith and worked hard to explain and promote it. (There are only 33 doctors of the Church.) Jerome was the first person to study the Bible very carefully. He translated the Bible from Greek into the language spoken at the time – Latin.

To honour St. Jerome, listen to the words that St. Paul wrote to his friend Timothy about the importance of Scripture – the Word of God written down.

A reading from the second letter of Paul to Timothy

But as for you,
continue in what you have learned
and firmly believed,
knowing from whom you learned it,
and how from childhood
you have known the sacred writings
that are able to instruct you for salvation
through faith in Christ Jesus.
All scripture is inspired by God
and is useful for teaching, for reproof,
for correction, and for training
in righteousness,
so that everyone who belongs to God
may be proficient,
equipped for every good work.

The word of the Lord.
**Thanks be to God.**

Let us pray:
All-knowing God,
You gave us your word in the Bible
to help us become
wise, holy and strong in your ways.
Help us to love your word
with all our hearts,
and put into practice what you teach.
We ask this through Christ our Lord.
**Amen.**

Let us pray the prayer that Jesus taught us, for all those who study God's word and teach it to others:
**Our Father…**

✠ **In the name of the Father, and of the Son, and of the Holy Spirit. Amen.**

---

Note: Today's reading is 2 Timothy 3:14-17.

## OCTOBER 1
## FEAST OF ST. THERESA OF THE CHILD JESUS

✠ In the name of the Father, and of the Son, and of the Holy Spirit. Amen.

Introduction: Today we celebrate the feast of St. Theresa of the Child Jesus, or St. Theresa of Lisieux, as she is also known. St. Theresa was born in France in 1873. She entered the Carmelite order when she was fifteen – five years later than she would have liked! She was only 24 when she died.

St. Theresa never did great things in her lifetime – she did ordinary, little things very well. She thought of herself as a little flower in God's garden. Because of what she taught people – during her life and through her writings published after her death – she was made one of the doctors of the Church.

A reading from the holy gospel according to Matthew
**Glory to you, Lord.**

Jesus said to his disciples,
"Truly I tell you, unless you change
and become like children,
you will never enter the kingdom of heaven.
Whoever becomes humble like this child
is the greatest in the kingdom of heaven."

The gospel of the Lord.
**Praise to you, Lord Jesus Christ.**

Let us pray:
Most holy and gracious God,
even as a very young child
St. Theresa loved you,
your beloved Son, Jesus,
and Mary, his mother,
with all her heart.
Help us to follow her example
by doing the ordinary,
little things we do each day very well,
and loving you and your will for us
with all our hearts.
We ask this through Christ our Lord.
**Amen.**

Let us pray the prayer that Jesus taught us:
**Our Father…**

✠ In the name of the Father, and of the Son, and of the Holy Spirit. Amen.

———————————

Note: Today's reading is Matthew 18:3-4.

## OCTOBER 2
## FEAST OF THE GUARDIAN ANGELS

✠ **In the name of the Father, and of the Son, and of the Holy Spirit. Amen.**

Introduction: Today we celebrate the feast of the Guardian Angels, who watch over us. Jesus tells his disciples how close these angels are to God.

A reading from the holy gospel according to Matthew
**Glory to you, Lord.**

Jesus said,
"Whoever welcomes one such child
in my name
welcomes me.
Take care that you do not despise
one of these little ones;
for, I tell you, in heaven
their angels
continually see the face
of my Father in heaven."

The gospel of the Lord.
**Praise to you, Lord Jesus Christ.**

Let us pray: (Prayer to the Guardian Angel*)
Angel sent by God to guide me,
be my light and walk beside me;
be my guardian and protect me;
on the paths of life direct me.
**Amen.**

Let us pray the prayer that Jesus taught us:
**Our Father…**

✠ **In the name of the Father, and of the Son, and of the Holy Spirit. Amen.**

---

Note: Today's reading is Matthew 18:5, 10.

* This is a revised version of the traditional Angel of God prayer. The traditional version is found in Appendix 3.

## OCTOBER 4
## FEAST OF ST. FRANCIS OF ASSISI

✠ **In the name of the Father, and of the Son, and of the Holy Spirit. Amen.**

Introduction: Today is the feast of St. Francis of Assisi. Francis was born 1181 in Assisi, Italy, to a rich family. As a youth, he loved having a good time with his friends and spent money without a thought. One day he had a vision of Jesus that caused him to change his lifestyle. He devoted himself to a life of poverty and preaching. Many men chose to live like him, so he founded the religious order known as the Franciscans. Before long he had over 5,000 men in his order! St. Francis died in 1226 and was canonized as a saint two years later. He is known for his love and concern for the sick and the poor, and for his praise of God's creation.

St. Francis had a great love and a deep respect for God's works in nature. Do we respect God's works in nature? How can we show care for the gift of the earth that God has entrusted to us?

A reading from the book of Psalms

O give thanks to the Lord, for he is good,
for his steadfast love endures for ever.
Who alone does great wonders,
for his steadfast love endures for ever;
who by understanding made the heavens,
for his steadfast love endures for ever;
who spread out the earth on the waters,
for his steadfast love endures for ever;
who made the great lights,
for his steadfast love endures for ever;
the sun to rule over the day,
or his steadfast love endures for ever;
the moon and stars to rule over the night,
for his steadfast love endures for ever;
O give thanks to the God of heaven,
for his steadfast love endures for ever.

The word of the Lord.
**Thanks be to God.**

Let us pray:
Most loving and merciful Creator,
St. Francis of Assisi loved all living things,
calling them sister and brother.
Help us to respect the earth
and its creatures,
and take care of them
the way you ask us to do.
We ask this through Christ our Lord.
**Amen.**

Let us pray the prayer that Jesus taught us:
**Our Father…**

✠ **In the name of the Father, and of the Son, and of the Holy Spirit. Amen.**

_____

Note: Today's reading is Psalm 136:1, 4-9, 26.

## OCTOBER 7

## FEAST OF OUR LADY OF THE HOLY ROSARY

✠ In the name of the Father, and of the Son, and of the Holy Spirit. Amen.

Introduction: Today we celebrate the feast of Our Lady of the Rosary. This feast was instituted in 1573 by Pope Pius V, in thanksgiving for a military victory. This means that we have been honouring Mary and her rosary on a special day every year for over 400 years!

Today we thank God for this beautiful prayer, which is so important to millions of Catholics throughout the world.

A reading from the holy gospel according to Luke
**Glory to you, Lord.**

In the sixth month
the angel Gabriel was sent by God
to a town in Galilee called Nazareth,
to a virgin engaged to a man
whose name was Joseph,
of the house of David.
The virgin's name was Mary.
And he came to her and said,
"Greetings, favoured one!
The Lord is with you.
And now, you will conceive in your womb
and bear a son, and you will name him Jesus.
He will be great, and will be called
the Son of the Most High."

The gospel of the Lord.
**Praise to you, Lord Jesus Christ.**

Let us pray:*
The response is: **Pray for us.**

Holy Mary, **pray for us.**
Holy Mother of God, **pray for us.**
Mother of Christ, **pray for us.**
Mother of Good Counsel, **pray for us.**
Mother of our Saviour, **pray for us.**
Health of the sick, **pray for us.**
Comfort of the troubled, **pray for us.**
Queen of angels, **pray for us.**
Queen of all saints, **pray for us.**
Queen of the Rosary, **pray for us.**

Let us honour Mary by praying her prayer:
**Hail Mary...**

✠ In the name of the Father, and of the Son, and of the Holy Spirit. Amen.

---

Note: Today's reading is Luke 1:26-28, 31-32a.

* This prayer is a small part of the Litany of the Blessed Virgin Mary.

## OCTOBER 15
## FEAST OF ST. TERESA OF JESUS

✠ **In the name of the Father, and of the Son, and of the Holy Spirit. Amen.**

Introduction: Today is the feast of St. Teresa of Jesus, or St. Teresa of Avila, as she is better known. She was born at Avila in Spain in 1515, entered the Carmelite order and eventually reformed the way the nuns lived their lives. She is a doctor of the Church.

Even though St. Teresa did great things, she tells us: "The Lord doesn't look so much at the greatness of our works as at the love with which they are done."

A reading from the letter of James

Who is wise and understanding among you?
Show by your good life
that your works are done with gentleness
born of wisdom.
But the wisdom from above is first pure,
then peaceable, gentle, willing to yield,
full of mercy and good fruits,
without a trace of partiality or hypocrisy.

The word of the Lord.
**Thanks be to God.**

Let us pray:
Most holy God,
St. Teresa of Avila
showed us the way to perfection
under the guidance and inspiration
of your beloved Son.
Grant that we may do everything with love,
and grow in your grace and holiness.
We ask this through Christ our Lord.
**Amen.**

Let us pray the prayer that Jesus taught us:
**Our Father…**

✠ **In the name of the Father, and of the Son, and of the Holy Spirit. Amen.**

--------

Note: Today's reading is James 3:13, 17.

## OCTOBER 16
## FEAST OF ST. MARGUERITE D'YOUVILLE

✠ **In the name of the Father, and of the Son, and of the Holy Spirit. Amen.**

Introduction: St. Marguerite D'Youville is a Canadian saint who was born at Varennes, Quebec. She married François D'Youville in 1722. When he died in 1730, she worked to support herself and her three children. She spent much of her time working for the Confraternity of the Holy Family in charitable activities.

In 1737, with three companions, Marguerite founded a community known as the Grey Nuns. Her community has set up schools, hospitals and orphanages throughout Canada, the United States, Africa and South America. They are known for their work among the Inuit. Marguerite D'Youville died in Montreal on December 23, 1771. She was canonized in 1990.

A reading from the letter of Paul to the Philippians

Rejoice in the Lord always;
again I will say, Rejoice.
Let your gentleness be known to everyone.
The Lord is near.
Do not worry about anything,
but in everything by prayer
and supplication with thanksgiving
let your requests be made known to God.
And the peace of God,
which surpasses all understanding,
will guard your hearts and your minds
in Christ Jesus.
Finally, beloved, whatever is true,
whatever is honourable,
whatever is just,
whatever is pure,
whatever is pleasing,
whatever is commendable,
if there is any excellence
and if there is anything worthy of praise,
think about these things.
Keep on doing the things
that you have learned and received
and heard and seen in me,
and the God of peace will be with you.

The word of the Lord.
**Thanks be to God.**

Let us pray:
Most loving God,
St. Marguerite D'Youville was a good wife,
mother and religious sister
who did what you asked her to do.
Help us to be helpful, kind
and faithful to whatever you ask us
to do in our lives.
Give us the grace to always listen to
and follow the Holy Spirit.
We ask this through Christ our Lord.
**Amen.**

Let us pray the prayer that Jesus taught us:
**Our Father…**

✠ **In the name of the Father, and of the Son, and of the Holy Spirit. Amen.**

---

Note: Today's reading is Philippians 4:4-9.

## OCTOBER 16 (ALTERNATE)
## FEAST OF ST. MARGARET MARY

☩ **In the name of the Father, and of the Son, and of the Holy Spirit. Amen.**

Introduction: Today is the feast of St. Margaret Mary. Margaret Mary Alacoque, born in 1647 in France, became a nun of the Visitation order. It was to St. Margaret Mary that Jesus gave the task of spreading devotion to his Sacred Heart.

She did not have an easy time doing this – some of the other sisters thought that she was crazy and that this work was of the devil, not God. St. Margaret Mary persevered, and in time won over all the sisters to love the Sacred Heart of Jesus.

A reading from the letter of Paul to the Ephesians

For this reason I bow my knees
before the Father,
from whom every family in heaven
and on earth takes its name.
I pray that,
according to the riches of his glory,
he may grant that you may be strengthened
in your inner being
with power through his Spirit,
and that Christ may dwell in your hearts
through faith, as you are being
rooted and grounded in love.
I pray that you may have
the power to comprehend, with all the
saints, what is the breadth and length
and height and depth,
and to know the love of Christ
that surpasses knowledge,
so that you may be filled
with all the fullness of God.

Now to him who by the power at work
within us is able to accomplish
abundantly far more
than all we can ask or imagine,
to him be glory in the church
and in Christ Jesus to all generations,
forever and ever. Amen.

The word of the Lord.
**Thanks be to God.**

Let us pray:
Most holy God,
your Beloved Son, Jesus,
gave St. Margaret Mary
the task of spreading love
and devotion to his Sacred Heart.
Help us to remember
the great love Jesus has for us.
Help us to grow to love and honour
his Sacred Heart more and more each day.
We ask this through Christ our Lord.
**Amen.**

Let us pray the prayer that Jesus taught us:
**Our Father…**

☩ **In the name of the Father, and of the Son, and of the Holy Spirit. Amen.**

Note: Today's reading is Ephesians 3:14-21.

## OCTOBER 18
## FEAST OF ST. LUKE, EVANGELIST

✠ **In the name of the Father, and of the Son, and of the Holy Spirit. Amen.**

Introduction: St. Luke is one of the four evangelists or gospel writers. He was not Jewish, but became a follower of Jesus through the preaching of St. Paul. He then helped St. Paul spread the Good News of Jesus. St. Luke also wrote another book found in the Bible, called the Acts of the Apostles. In Acts, we hear about the beginnings of the Church.

In our reading today, Jesus sends out his disciples to towns and places where he was about to go. Do we prepare the way of the Lord by what we say and do?

A reading from the holy gospel according to Luke
**Glory to you, Lord.**

After this the Lord appointed seventy others
and sent them on ahead of him in pairs
to every town and place
where he himself intended to go.
He said to them, "The harvest is plentiful,
but the labourers are few;
therefore ask the Lord of the harvest
to send out labourers into his harvest.
Carry no purse, no bag, no sandals;
and greet no one on the road.
Do not move about from house to house.
Whenever you enter a town
and its people welcome you,
eat what is set before you;
cure the sick who are there,
and say to them,
'The kingdom of God
has come near to you.' "

The gospel of the Lord.
**Praise to you, Lord Jesus Christ.**

Let us pray:
Most loving God,
St. Luke wrote down
the Good News of Jesus
and spread the gospel to others.
Help us to be good followers of Jesus,
by words and actions
that are pleasing to you.
We ask this through Christ our Lord.
**Amen.**

Let us pray the prayer that Jesus taught us:
**Our Father...**

✠ **In the name of the Father, and of the Son, and of the Holy Spirit. Amen.**

Note: Today's reading is Luke 10:1-2, 4, 7c-9.

## OCTOBER 28
## FEAST OF SAINT SIMON AND SAINT JUDE, APOSTLES

✠ **In the name of the Father, and of the Son, and of the Holy Spirit. Amen.**

Introduction: St. Simon and St. Jude were two of the disciples that Jesus chose to be apostles. Simon was known for strictly following Jewish law. Both of them were martyred for their belief in Jesus and for proclaiming the Good News.

In our reading today, St. Paul tells us that we are members of the family of God, built upon the foundation laid by the apostles and prophets. It is Jesus, the cornerstone, who holds the whole building together. Together we make up a place where God lives through the Spirit.

A reading from the letter of Paul to the Ephesians

So then you are no longer
strangers and aliens,
but you are citizens with the saints
and also members of the household of God,
built upon the foundation of the apostles
and prophets,
with Christ Jesus himself as the cornerstone.
In him the whole structure
is joined together
and grows into a holy temple in the Lord;
in whom you also are built together
spiritually into a dwelling-place for God.

The word of the Lord.
**Thanks be to God.**

Let us pray:
Most holy and gracious God,
your Son, Jesus, called the apostles
to become the leaders of his Church.
Grant that we may be faithful witnesses
of the Good News,
imitating the example
of St. Simon and St. Jude.
We ask this through Christ our Lord.
**Amen.**

Let us pray the prayer that Jesus taught us:
**Our Father…**

✠ **In the name of the Father, and of the Son, and of the Holy Spirit. Amen.**

---

Note: Today's reading is Ephesians 2:19-22.

## NOVEMBER 1
## SOLEMNITY OF ALL SAINTS

✠ **In the name of the Father, and of the Son, and of the Holy Spirit. Amen.**

Introduction: Today is the Feast of All Saints, the day we remember all those who have died and are in heaven with God. Some saints we know by name, like St. Francis of Assisi and St. Theresa of Lisieux. Others we do not know. The Church honours all of them on this special feast day.

Our reading today is a famous passage called the Beatitudes. The word beatitude means "blessed." These are the "attitudes" the saints had; we are to work to make these attitudes part of us.

A reading from the holy gospel according to Matthew
**Glory to you, Lord.**

When Jesus saw the crowds,
he went up the mountain;
and after he sat down,
his disciples came to him.
Then he began to speak,
and taught them, saying:
"Blessed are the poor in spirit,
for theirs is the kingdom of heaven.
Blessed are those who mourn,
for they will be comforted.
Blessed are the meek,
for they will inherit the earth.
Blessed are those
who hunger and thirst for righteousness,
for they will be filled.
Blessed are the merciful,
for they will receive mercy.
Blessed are the pure in heart,
for they will see God.
Blessed are the peacemakers,
for they will be called children of God.

Blessed are those who are persecuted
for righteousness' sake,
for theirs is the kingdom of heaven.
Blessed are you when people revile you
and persecute you
and utter all kinds of evil against you falsely
on my account.
Rejoice and be glad,
for your reward is great in heaven."

The gospel of the Lord.
**Praise to you, Lord Jesus Christ.**

Let us pray:
Most holy and loving God,
the saints in heaven rejoice and praise you.
Grant that we open our hearts
to receive the graces we need
to imitate these holy men, women
and children.
We ask this through Christ our Lord.
**Amen.**

Let us pray the prayer that Jesus taught us:
**Our Father…**

✠ **In the name of the Father, and of the Son, and of the Holy Spirit. Amen.**

Note: Today's reading is Matthew 5:3-12a.

## NOVEMBER 2
## COMMEMORATION OF ALL THE FAITHFUL DEPARTED (ALL SOULS' DAY)

✠ **In the name of the Father, and of the Son, and of the Holy Spirit. Amen.**

Introduction: The Church dedicates the month of November to the holy souls. Today, on the feast of All Souls, we remember all those who have died. We pray that they are in heaven with God. Every day this month it is good to remember and pray for people who have died.

A reading from the holy gospel according to John
**Glory to you, Lord.**

When Jesus arrived, he found that Lazarus had already been in the tomb for four days. When Martha heard that Jesus was coming, she went and met him, while Mary stayed at home. Martha said to Jesus, "Lord, if you had been here, my brother would not have died. But even now I know that God will give you whatever you ask of him." Jesus said to her, "Your brother will rise again." Martha said to him, "I know that he will rise again in the resurrection on the last day." Jesus said to her, "I am the resurrection and the life. Those who believe in me, even though they die, will live, and everyone who lives and believes in me will never die. Do you believe this?"

She said to him, "Yes, Lord, I believe that you are the Messiah, the Son of God, the one coming into the world."

The gospel of the Lord.
**Praise to you, Lord Jesus Christ.**

Let us pray:
Eternal God,
You call all people to life with you after death.
Today we remember people we know who have died,
and pray that they are with you in heaven:
Eternal rest grant unto them, O Lord,
and let perpetual light shine upon them.
May they rest in peace.
**Amen.**

Let us pray the prayer that Jesus taught us:
**Our Father…**

✠ **In the name of the Father, and of the Son, and of the Holy Spirit. Amen.**

---

Note: Today's reading is John 11:17, 20-27.

## NOVEMBER 9
## FEAST OF THE DEDICATION OF ST. JOHN LATERAN

✠ **In the name of the Father, and of the Son, and of the Holy Spirit. Amen.**

Introduction: Today we celebrate the feast of the dedication of St. John Lateran, a church in Rome that was built by the Emperor Constantine over 1700 years ago. It is called the mother church of all Christians because it is the very first church ever built!

Church buildings are very important – but the real bricks of the Church are the people who believe in Jesus.

A reading from the first letter of Paul to the Corinthians

You are God's field, God's building.
According to the grace of God given to me,
like a skilled master builder
I laid a foundation,
and someone else is building on it.
Each builder must choose with care
how to build on it.
For no one can lay any foundation
other than the one that has been laid;
that foundation is Jesus Christ.
Do you not know that you are God's temple
and that God's Spirit dwells in you?
If anyone destroys God's temple,
God will destroy that person.
For God's temple is holy, and you are that
temple.

The word of the Lord.
**Thanks be to God.**

Let us pray:
Creator God,
you made each of us in your image,
and we are your temple
because your Spirit lives in us.
Help us always to respect our bodies
and those of others,
because you have made them holy.
We ask this through Christ our Lord.
**Amen.**

Let us pray the prayer that Jesus taught us:
**Our Father…**

Let us pray for all those whose names are in our Book of Remembrance:
Eternal rest grant unto them, O Lord,
and let perpetual light shine upon them.
May they rest in peace.
**Amen.**

✠ **In the name of the Father, and of the Son, and of the Holy Spirit. Amen.**

---

Note: Today's reading is 1 Corinthians 3:9b-11, 16-17.

## NOVEMBER 11
## FEAST OF ST. MARTIN OF TOURS

✠ **In the name of the Father, and of the Son, and of the Holy Spirit. Amen.**

Introduction: St. Martin of Tours was born around 316 in Hungary and raised in Italy. He was ordained and later became a monk. He lived and worked in France for ten years; the people of Tours asked him to be their bishop. St. Martin was one of the great saints of France, and founded the first monastery there. He died in 397.

It is fitting that St. Martin's feast day is the same day as Remembrance Day, because he was forced to serve in the army at age 15. At 23 he refused to fight again because he wanted to be a soldier of Christ.

St. Martin had a great love for God, and spent a lot of time in prayer. Do we show our love for God by doing what is right in God's eyes? Do we take time to pray daily?

A reading from the letter of Paul to the Ephesians

Put on the whole armour of God,
so that you may be able to stand against
the wiles of the devil.
For our struggle is not against enemies
of blood and flesh,
but against the spiritual forces of evil
in the heavenly places.
Stand therefore, and fasten the belt of truth
around your waist,
and put on the breastplate of righteousness.
As shoes for your feet
put on whatever will make you ready to
proclaim the gospel of peace.
With all of these, take the shield of faith,
with which you will be able to quench
all the flaming arrows of the evil one.
Take the helmet of salvation,
and the sword of the Spirit,
which is the word of God.

Pray in the Spirit at all times
in every prayer and supplication.
To that end keep alert and always persevere
in supplication for all the saints.

The word of the Lord.
**Thanks be to God.**

Let us pray:
Most holy God,
St. Martin, a man devoted to prayer,
wanted to be a soldier of Christ.
Help us to put on the armour of Christ,
and be faithful followers of your Son, Jesus.
We ask this through Christ our Lord.
**Amen.**

Let us pray the prayer that Jesus taught us:
**Our Father…**

Let us pray for all those whose names are in our Book of Remembrance:
Eternal rest grant unto them, O Lord,
and let perpetual light shine upon them.
May they rest in peace.
**Amen.**

✠ **In the name of the Father, and of the Son, and of the Holy Spirit. Amen.**

Note: Today's reading is Ephesians 6:11-12a, 14-18.

## NOVEMBER 21
## FEAST OF THE PRESENTATION OF MARY

✠ **In the name of the Father, and of the Son, and of the Holy Spirit. Amen.**

Introduction: Today we celebrate the feast of the Presentation of Mary. Her parents, Anna and Joachim, offered her to God in the Temple when she was three years old.

This feast reminds us that Mary's holiness began at the very first moment of her life and continued through her early childhood and for the rest of her days.

Mary's body became a Temple, for she carried the Son of God within her. By our baptism we are made temples of God because the Holy Spirit comes to dwell within us.

A reading from the book of Judith

Then Uzziah said to her, "O daughter,
you are blessed by the Most High God
above all other women on earth;
and blessed be the Lord God,
who created the heavens and the earth.
Your praise will never depart
from the hearts of those who remember
the power of God.
May God grant this to be
a perpetual honour to you,
and may he reward you with blessings."

The word of the Lord.
**Thanks be to God.**

Let us pray:
Most holy and loving God,
from all eternity
you chose Mary to be the mother
of your divine Son, Jesus.
Help us to be children of prayer,
dedicated to Jesus,
and keep us from sin.
We ask this through Christ our Lord.
**Amen.**

Let us pray in honour of Mary:
**Hail Mary...**

Let us pray for all those whose names are in our Book of Remembrance:
Eternal rest grant unto them, O Lord,
and let perpetual light shine upon them.
May they rest in peace.
**Amen.**

✠ **In the name of the Father, and of the Son, and of the Holy Spirit. Amen.**

---

Note: Today's reading is Judith 13:18, 19-20a.

## NOVEMBER 22
## FEAST OF ST. CECILIA

✠ **In the name of the Father, and of the Son, and of the Holy Spirit. Amen.**

Introduction: Today is the feast of St. Cecilia, a young Christian of high rank who lived in the fourth century. She was engaged to a Roman named Valerian, who became a Christian because of Cecilia's influence. Along with Valerian and his brother, she became a martyr (a person who dies for the faith).

St. Cecilia most certainly sang in her heart to God, and sometimes with her voice. She is the patron saint of music. St. Augustine tells us that "to sing is to pray twice" – by words and melody. Do we sing God's praises with all our hearts during celebrations and Mass?

A reading from the book of Psalms

Praise the Lord!
Sing to the Lord a new song,
his praise in the assembly of the faithful.
Let Israel be glad in its Maker;
let the children of Zion
rejoice in their King.
Praise the Lord!
Praise God in his sanctuary;
praise him in his mighty firmament!
Praise him for his mighty deeds;
praise him according to his
surpassing greatness!
Praise him with trumpet sound;
praise him with lute and harp!
Praise him with tambourine and dance;
praise him with strings and pipe!
Praise him with clanging cymbals;
praise him with loud clashing cymbals!
Let everything that breathes praise the Lord!
Praise the Lord!

The word of the Lord.
**Thanks be to God.**

Let us pray:
Creator God,
you gave us the gift of song
and the talent to make music.
Grant that we, like St. Cecilia,
may use these gifts to praise you
and serve you and your people.
Thank you for this wondrous gift,
and for all musicians who share their talents
with us.
We ask this through Christ our Lord.
**Amen.**

Let us pray the prayer that Jesus taught us:
**Our Father…**

Let us pray for all those whose names are in our Book of Remembrance:
Eternal rest grant unto them, O Lord,
and let perpetual light shine upon them.
May they rest in peace.
**Amen.**

✠ **In the name of the Father, and of the Son, and of the Holy Spirit. Amen.**

---

Note: Today's reading is Psalm 149:1-2, Psalm 150:1-6.

## NOVEMBER 30
## FEAST OF ST. ANDREW, APOSTLE

✠ **In the name of the Father, and of the Son, and of the Holy Spirit. Amen.**

Introduction: Today is the feast of St. Andrew, one of the apostles. Andrew was a disciple of John the Baptist before he became a follower of Jesus. His brother was St. Peter. After Pentecost, Andrew preached the gospel in many lands.

A reading from the holy gospel according to Matthew
**Glory to you, Lord.**

As Jesus walked by the Sea of Galilee,
he saw two brothers,
Simon, who is called Peter,
and Andrew his brother,
casting a net into the sea –
for they were fishermen.
And he said to them,
"Follow me,
and I will make you fish for people."
Immediately they left their nets
and followed him.

The gospel of the Lord.
**Praise to you, Lord Jesus Christ.**

Let us pray:
Creator God,
St. Andrew left everything he had
to follow your Son, Jesus.
Help us to be good followers of Jesus,
doing what you ask,
and showing love and concern for others
as we bring the Good News to all we meet.
We ask this through Christ our Lord.
**Amen.**

Let us pray the prayer that Jesus taught us:
**Our Father…**

Let us pray for all those whose names are in
our Book of Remembrance:
Eternal rest grant unto them, O Lord,
and let perpetual light shine upon them.
May they rest in peace.
**Amen.**

✠ **In the name of the Father, and of the Son, and of the Holy Spirit. Amen.**

Note: Today's reading is Matthew 4:18-20.

## DECEMBER 3
## FEAST OF ST. FRANCIS XAVIER

✠ **In the name of the Father, and of the Son, and of the Holy Spirit. Amen.**

Introduction: Today we celebrate the feast of St. Francis Xavier. Born in the family castle in 1506, he later studied in Paris. There he met St. Ignatius Loyola, and in 1534 he was one of the seven people who founded the Society of Jesus, or Jesuit order of priests and brothers. He was ordained a priest in 1537, went to Rome in 1538, and went to the Far East as a missionary in 1540. He travelled thousands and thousands of kilometres to bring the Good News of Jesus to those who had never heard of him – in Mozambique, India, Japan and other faraway places. While on his way to China in 1552, he died.

Despite little money or co-operation, he won hundreds of thousands to Christianity through his great preaching, his fervour, his example, and his deep concern for the native peoples of these lands. Canonized in 1662, he is the patron of all foreign missions.

Like St. Francis, do we bring the Good News to those we meet?

A reading from the holy gospel according to Mark
**Glory to you, Lord.**

Later Jesus appeared to the eleven themselves as they were sitting at the table.
And he said to them,
"Go into all the world
and proclaim the good news
to the whole creation.
The one who believes and is baptized
will be saved;
but the one who does not believe
will be condemned."

The gospel of the Lord.
**Praise to you, Lord Jesus Christ.**

Let us pray:
Most beloved Creator,
St. Francis Xavier brought the Good News
of Jesus to thousands of people.
Help us to live our faith
with fervour and great zeal,
as St. Francis did.
We ask this through Christ our Lord.
**Amen.**

Let us pray the prayer that Jesus taught us:
**Our Father…**

✠ **In the name of the Father, and of the Son, and of the Holy Spirit. Amen.**

Note: Today's reading is Mark 16:14a, 15-16.

## DECEMBER 6
## FEAST OF ST. NICHOLAS

✠ **In the name of the Father, and of the Son, and of the Holy Spirit. Amen.**

Introduction: St. Nicholas was born in Asia Minor to wealthy parents. Later named bishop of Myra, he became known for his holiness, zeal and miracles. He was imprisoned for his faith during the persecution of Christians by the Roman Emperor Diocletian and died around the year 350. St. Nicholas is the patron saint of children, storm-beset sailors and prisoners.

St. Nicholas was known for his kindness to all, helping others when they needed help. Do we try to be kind and helpful to others, like he did? Do others see our love for God by our actions, as they did with St. Nicholas?

A reading from the holy gospel according to Matthew
**Glory to you, Lord.**

At that time the disciples came to Jesus
and asked,
"Who is the greatest
in the kingdom of heaven?"
He called a child,
whom he put among them,
and said, "Truly I tell you, unless you change
and become like children,
you will never enter the kingdom of heaven.
Whoever becomes humble like this child
is the greatest in the kingdom of heaven.
Whoever welcomes one such child
in my name welcomes me."

The gospel of the Lord.
**Praise to you, Lord Jesus Christ.**

Let us pray:
Most loving God,
St. Nicholas was a man of deep faith,
holiness, prayer and charity.
Help us to live as your children,
faithful to the teachings of Jesus,
following the example of St. Nicholas.
We ask this through Christ our Lord.
**Amen.**

Let us pray the prayer that Jesus taught us:
**Our Father…**

✠ **In the name of the Father, and of the Son, and of the Holy Spirit. Amen.**

—————————

Note: Today's reading is Matthew 18:1-5.

## DECEMBER 8
## SOLEMNITY OF THE IMMACULATE CONCEPTION

✠ **In the name of the Father, and of the Son, and of the Holy Spirit. Amen.**

Introduction: Today is the Feast of the Immaculate Conception. We celebrate and remember today that Mary was without sin from the first moment of her life.

Our reading today is the Annunciation story, when Gabriel visits Mary to tell her that she has been chosen to be Jesus' mother.

A reading from the holy gospel according to Luke
**Glory to you, Lord.**

In the sixth month the angel Gabriel
was sent by God
to a town in Galilee called Nazareth,
to a virgin engaged to a man
whose name was Joseph,
of the house of David.
The virgin's name was Mary.
And he came to her and said,
"Greetings, favoured one!
The Lord is with you."
But she was much perplexed by his words
and pondered what sort of greeting
this might be.
The angel said to her,
"Do not be afraid, Mary,
for you have found favour with God.
And now, you will conceive in your womb
and bear a son, and you will name him Jesus.
He will be great, and will be called
the Son of the Most High."
Mary said to the angel,
"How can this be, since I am a virgin?"

The angel said to her,
"The Holy Spirit will come upon you,
and the power of the Most High
will overshadow you;
therefore the child to be born will be holy;
he will be called Son of God."
Then Mary said, "Here am I,
the servant of the Lord;
let it be with me according to your word."
Then the angel departed from her.

The gospel of the Lord.
**Praise to you, Lord Jesus Christ.**

Let us pray:
All-powerful God,
for you, nothing is impossible.
Help us to imitate Mary
and always say "Yes" to what you ask of us.
We ask this through Christ our Lord.
**Amen.**

Let us pray in honour of Mary:
**Hail Mary…**

✠ **In the name of the Father, and of the Son, and of the Holy Spirit. Amen.**

---

Note: Today's reading is Luke 1:26-32a, 34-35, 38. The full reading for today is Luke 1:26-38.

## DECEMBER 12
## FEAST OF OUR LADY OF GUADALUPE

✠ **In the name of the Father, and of the Son, and of the Holy Spirit. Amen.**

Introduction: Today is the feast of Our Lady of Guadalupe. On December 9, 1531, Mary appeared on a hill called Tepeyac to Juan Diego, a poor Aboriginal Mexican, as a young Native American maiden dressed like an Aztec princess. She spoke to him in his own language. Juan was on his way to attend Mass in honour of Our Lady. She sent him to the bishop of Mexico, and asked for a chapel to be built where she appeared. The bishop told Juan Diego to ask for a sign. Juan's uncle became ill, and he tried to avoid Mary, but she found him, told him his uncle would be well, and provided roses, in winter, for Juan to carry to the bishop in his cape, called a tilma. Our Lady herself arranged the roses in Juan's tilma. When he opened it in the bishop's presence, the roses fell out, and the bishop fell to his knees, because on the tilma appeared a painting of Mary as she had appeared at the hill of Tepeyac.

When we look at the appearances of Mary, it seems that she always entrusts her most important messages to children and the poorest people. This tells us that all of us are important to her.

A reading from the holy gospel according to Luke
**Glory to you, Lord.**

At that same hour
Jesus rejoiced in the Holy Spirit and said,
"I thank you, Father,
Lord of heaven and earth,
because you have hidden these things
from the wise and the intelligent
and have revealed them to infants;
yes, Father,
for such was your gracious will."

The gospel of the Lord.
**Praise to you, Lord Jesus Christ.**

Let us pray:
Most loving God,
Mary appeared to a poor young man,
Juan Diego,
to show her motherly love for the poor
and for all of us.
Through her, you showed your love
for all of us.
Help us to remember to turn to her
with our needs,
as she in turn
will present them to her Son, Jesus.
We ask this through Christ our Lord.
**Amen.**

Let us pray in honour of Mary:
**Hail Mary...**

✠ **In the name of the Father, and of the Son, and of the Holy Spirit. Amen.**

---

Note: Today's reading is Luke 10:21.

## DECEMBER 14
## FEAST OF ST. JOHN OF THE CROSS

✠ In the name of the Father, and of the Son, and of the Holy Spirit. Amen.

Introduction: Today is the feast of St. John of the Cross, a Carmelite friar who is one of the doctors of the Church. Together with St. Teresa of Avila, he re-formed the Carmelite order, forming the branch known as the Order of Discalced Carmelites. (Discalced means barefoot.) Members of these communities either walk barefoot or wear sandals. These two orders are among the great contemplative orders of the Church. Contemplative monks and nuns spend their lives giving themselves over to God alone in solitude and silence, spending much time praying and putting God before their own desires.

A reading from the first letter of Paul to the Corinthians

When I came to you, brothers and sisters,
I did not come proclaiming the mystery
of God to you in lofty words or wisdom.
For I decided to know nothing among you
except Jesus Christ, and him crucified.
And I came to you in weakness and in fear
and in much trembling.
My speech and my proclamation
were not with plausible words of wisdom,
but with a demonstration
of the Spirit and of power.

The word of the Lord.
**Thanks be to God.**

Let us pray:
Most gracious God,
in your infinite wisdom
you gave St. John of the Cross
a spirit of self-denial,
a great love of the cross,
and the gift to write beautifully
about you.
Help us to grow in love of you daily,
recognizing that
you are the centre of our hearts.
We ask this through Christ our Lord.
**Amen.**

Let us pray the prayer that Jesus taught us:
**Our Father…**

✠ In the name of the Father, and of the Son, and of the Holy Spirit. Amen.

_____

Note: Today's reading is 1 Corinthians 2:1-4.

## JANUARY
## FEAST OF THE BAPTISM OF THE LORD*

✠ **In the name of the Father, and of the Son, and of the Holy Spirit. Amen.**

Introduction: Today we celebrate the Feast of the Baptism of the Lord. When Jesus was thirty years old, he went to the Jordan River. His cousin, John the Baptist, was there, preaching, telling people to turn back to the ways of God, for the kingdom of God was near. After the people were baptized, John baptized Jesus. This marks the beginning of Jesus' ministry.

Something special happened after his baptism that tells us who Jesus is.

A reading from the holy gospel according to Luke
**Glory to you, Lord.**

Now when all the people were baptized,
and when Jesus also had been baptized
and was praying, the heaven was opened,
and the Holy Spirit descended upon him
in bodily form like a dove.
And a voice came from heaven,
"You are my Son, the Beloved;
with you I am well pleased."

The gospel of the Lord.
**Praise to you, Lord Jesus Christ.**

Let us pray:
Most loving Father,
when Jesus was baptized
you sent the Holy Spirit upon him
and told him that you
were pleased with him.
Help us, your sons and daughters,
to do what is pleasing to you always,
and to be faithful followers of Jesus.
We ask this through Christ our Lord.
**Amen.**

Let us pray the prayer that Jesus taught us:
**Our Father…**

✠ **In the name of the Father, and of the Son, and of the Holy Spirit. Amen.**

---

Note: Today's reading is Luke 3:21-22.

*This feast is usually celebrated on the Sunday after Epiphany; however, the feast of the Baptism of the Lord is celebrated on the Monday following Epiphany when this Sunday is January 7 or later.

## JANUARY 12
## FEAST OF ST. MARGUERITE BOURGEOYS

✠ **In the name of the Father, and of the Son, and of the Holy Spirit. Amen.**

Introduction: Today is the feast of St. Marguerite Bourgeoys. Born in 1620 in France, Marguerite came to Quebec in 1653 to teach the children there. The only available building for her first school was a stone stable. She founded the first Canadian community of religious sisters – the Congregation of Notre Dame. Marguerite died on January 12, 1700, in Ville Marie, which is now known as Montreal.

In our reading today, the Lamb that St. John speaks about is the Risen Jesus.

A reading from the book of Revelation

After this I heard what seemed to be
the loud voice of a great multitude
in heaven, saying, "Hallelujah!
Salvation and glory and power to our God!"
And from the throne came a voice saying,
"Praise our God, all you his servants,
and all who fear him, small and great."
Then I heard what seemed to be
the voice of a great multitude,
like the sound of many waters
and like the sound of mighty thunder peals,
crying out, "Hallelujah!
For the Lord our God the Almighty reigns.

Let us rejoice and exult
and give him the glory,
for the marriage of the Lamb has come,
and his bride has made herself ready;
to her it has been granted
to be clothed with fine linen, bright and
pure" – for the fine linen
is the righteous deeds of the saints.

The word of the Lord.
**Thanks be to God.**

Let us pray:
Most holy God,
St. Marguerite Bourgeoys
left her country, her family, and all she knew
to come to New France,
because she believed it was your will for her.
Grant that we may always do your will,
even if it is hard or, in our eyes, impossible,
because with you all things are possible.
We ask this through Christ our Lord.
**Amen.**

Let us pray the prayer that Jesus taught us:
**Our Father...**

✠ **In the name of the Father, and of the Son, and of the Holy Spirit. Amen.**

Note: Today's reading is Revelation 19:1, 5-8.

## JANUARY 21
## FEAST OF ST. AGNES

✠ **In the name of the Father, and of the Son, and of the Holy Spirit. Amen.**

Introduction: Today is the feast of St. Agnes. Agnes was a beautiful girl from a wealthy Roman family who decided she would never marry but would consecrate herself to God. When she was about 13, in the year 304, she gave her life for her belief in Jesus. Agnes has become the great Christian symbol of purity and innocence.

A reading from the book of Revelation

After this I looked,
and there was a great multitude
that no one could count,
from every nation,
from all tribes and peoples
and languages,
standing before the throne
and before the Lamb, robed in white,
with palm branches in their hands.
Then one of the elders addressed me,
saying,
"Who are these, robed in white,
and where have they come from?"
I said to him,
"Sir, you are the one that knows."
Then he said to me, "These are they
who have come out of the great ordeal;
they have washed their robes
and made them white
in the blood of the Lamb.

For this reason
they are before the throne of God,
and worship him day and night
within his temple,
and the one who is seated on the throne
will shelter them."

The word of the Lord.
**Thanks be to God.**

Let us pray:
Gracious and holy God,
even though St. Agnes was a young girl
she was strong and brave,
dying for her belief in you
and in your divine Son.
Help us to be brave
and stand up for our faith
and for what is right,
when others are making fun of our beliefs
and encouraging us to do things
that are wrong.
We ask this through Christ our Lord.
**Amen.**

Let us pray the prayer that Jesus taught us:
**Our Father...**

✠ **In the name of the Father, and of the Son, and of the Holy Spirit. Amen.**

Note: Today's reading is Revelation 7:9, 13-15.

## JANUARY 24

## FEAST OF ST. FRANCIS DE SALES, BISHOP AND DOCTOR

✠ **In the name of the Father, and of the Son, and of the Holy Spirit. Amen.**

Introduction: Today is the feast of St. Francis de Sales, a bishop who is a doctor of the Church. St. Francis was born in 1567. He worked very hard and was known for his service to the poor and his preaching, which he did with great love and compassion, patience and understanding. He also wrote many books. St. Francis de Sales is the patron saint of writers. He died in 1622.

St. Francis is a good example of St. Paul's words in our reading today.

A reading from the second letter of Paul to Timothy

Hold to the standard of sound teaching
that you have heard from me,
in the faith and love that are in Christ Jesus.
Guard the good treasure entrusted to you,
with the help of the Holy Spirit living in us.
You, then, my child, be strong
in the grace that is in Christ Jesus;
and what you have heard from me
through many witnesses
entrust to faithful people who will
be able to teach others as well.
Share in suffering
like a good soldier of Christ Jesus.

The word of the Lord.
**Thanks be to God.**

Let us pray:
Most holy God,
St. Francis de Sales chose to become a priest
and spread the gospel
through preaching and writing.
Help us to be like him,
bringing the Good News to all we meet,
faithful to your will for us,
and treasuring the teachings of Jesus.
We ask this through Christ our Lord.
**Amen.**

Let us pray the prayer that Jesus taught us:
**Our Father…**

✠ **In the name of the Father, and of the Son, and of the Holy Spirit. Amen.**

———————

Note: Today's reading is 2 Timothy 1:13-14, 2:3-4.

## JANUARY 25
## FEAST OF THE CONVERSION OF ST. PAUL, APOSTLE

✠ **In the name of the Father, and of the Son, and of the Holy Spirit. Amen.**

Introduction: Today is the feast of the Conversion of St. Paul. Paul lived at the same time as the apostles. At first, he was one of the greatest persecutors of those who believed in Jesus. But Jesus appeared to him one day and said, "Why are you persecuting me?" Paul became a Christian, and began to bring the Good News to the known world at that time. Called the apostle to the Gentiles (non-Jewish people), he was eventually killed by the Romans for his belief in Jesus.

This week is the Week of Prayer for Christian Unity. Christians of all traditions around the world – such as Roman Catholic, Anglican, United Church, Lutheran and Orthodox – pray that we will all become one Church.

A reading from the holy gospel according to Mark
**Glory to you, Lord.**

Later Jesus appeared to the eleven themselves as they were sitting at the table. And he said to them, "Go into all the world and proclaim the good news to the whole creation. The one who believes and is baptized will be saved; but the one who does not believe will be condemned."

The gospel of the Lord.
**Praise to you, Lord Jesus Christ.**

Let us pray:
Creator God,
St. Paul had a great change of heart, and went from being one of the greatest persecutors of Christians to being one of the greatest proclaimers of the gospel.
Help us to live as your children, proclaiming the Good News of Jesus and being faithful to your ways.
We ask this through Christ our Lord.
**Amen.**

Let us pray the prayer that Jesus taught us:
**Our Father…**

✠ **In the name of the Father, and of the Son, and of the Holy Spirit. Amen.**

Note: Today's reading is Mark 16:14a, 15-16.

## JANUARY 26
## FEAST OF ST. TIMOTHY AND
## ST. TITUS, BISHOPS

✠ **In the name of the Father, and of the Son, and of the Holy Spirit. Amen.**

Introduction: Today we celebrate the feast day of St. Timothy and St. Titus, who became Christians through the work of St. Paul. They became leaders of their communities; they were bishops. Both were special to St. Paul; we still hear at Mass the letters he wrote to them or read them in the Bible. St. Paul wrote to both of them, saying he thought each of them was a "true child of mine in the faith we share."

A reading from the second letter of Paul to Timothy

Paul, an apostle of Christ Jesus
by the will of God,
for the sake of the promise of life
that is in Christ Jesus,
To Timothy, my beloved child:
Grace, mercy, and peace from
God the Father and Christ Jesus our Lord.
I am reminded of your sincere faith, a faith
that lived first in your grandmother Lois
and your mother Eunice
and now, I am sure, lives in you.
For this reason I remind you to rekindle the
gift of God that is within you
through the laying on of my hands;
for God did not give us a spirit of
cowardice, but rather a spirit of power
and of love and of self-discipline.

Do not be ashamed, then,
of the testimony about our Lord
or of me his prisoner,
but join with me in suffering for the gospel,
relying on the power of God.

The word of the Lord.
**Thanks be to God.**

Let us pray:
Creator God,
St. Timothy and St. Titus
spread the Good News
and were good leaders of their people.
Grant that all Christian leaders
may follow their example.
We ask this through Christ our Lord.
**Amen.**

Let us pray the prayer that Jesus taught us:
**Our Father…**

✠ **In the name of the Father, and of the Son, and of the Holy Spirit. Amen.**

---

Note: Today's reading is 2 Timothy 1:1-2, 5-8.

## JANUARY 28
## FEAST OF ST. THOMAS AQUINAS, PRIEST AND DOCTOR

✠ **In the name of the Father, and of the Son, and of the Holy Spirit. Amen.**

Introduction: Today is the feast of St. Thomas Aquinas. A Dominican friar who lived over 700 years ago, he is a doctor of the Church and the patron saint of schools and students. Thomas was a brilliant man, yet when he was a student, his fellow classmates made fun of him because he was big and didn't participate much in class. They nicknamed him the "dumb ox." He wrote one of the most famous books explaining things about God, and today we still pray prayers that he wrote.

Even though it was written long before he was born, today's reading tells us what St. Thomas was like.

A reading from the book of Sirach

If the great Lord is willing, he will be filled
with the spirit of understanding;
he will pour forth words of wisdom
of his own
and give thanks to the Lord in prayer.
The Lord will direct his counsel and
knowledge,
as he meditates on his mysteries.
He will show the wisdom
of what he has learned,
and will glory in the law
of the Lord's covenant.
Many will praise his understanding;
it will never be blotted out.
His memory will not disappear,
and his name will live
through all generations.
Nations will speak of his wisdom, and the
congregation will proclaim his praise.

The word of the Lord.
**Thanks be to God.**

Let us pray one of St. Thomas's prayers:
Grant me, O Lord my God,
a mind to know you,
a heart to seek you,
wisdom to find you,
conduct pleasing to you,
faithful perseverance in waiting for you,
and a hope of finally embracing you.
**Amen.**

Let us pray the prayer that Jesus taught us:
**Our Father…**

✠ **In the name of the Father, and of the Son, and of the Holy Spirit. Amen.**

Note: Today's reading is Sirach 39:6-10.

## FEBRUARY 2
## FEAST OF THE PRESENTATION OF THE LORD

✠ **In the name of the Father, and of the Son, and of the Holy Spirit. Amen.**

Introduction: Today is the Feast of the Presentation of the Lord, when we remember and celebrate the day Joseph and Mary brought Jesus to the Temple in Jerusalem and presented him to God when he was 40 days old. According to Jewish Law, all boys who were born first in their families were to be consecrated to God, and to have a sacrifice offered for them. Simeon, who was to do this sacrifice for Jesus, recognized Jesus' importance right away.

Today the Church also celebrates the World Day of Consecrated Life: those who have been consecrated for the service of God and the Church as religious priests, brothers, sisters, monks, nuns, hermits, consecrated virgins and members of secular institutes.

A reading from the holy gospel according to Luke
**Glory to you, Lord.**

Now there was a man in Jerusalem
whose name was Simeon;
this man was righteous and devout,
looking forward to the consolation of Israel,
and the Holy Spirit rested on him.
It had been revealed to him
by the Holy Spirit
that he would not see death
before he had seen the Lord's Messiah.
Guided by the Spirit,
Simeon came into the temple;
and when the parents
brought in the child Jesus, to do for him
what was customary under the law,
Simeon took him in his arms
and praised God, saying,
"Master, now you are dismissing
your servant in peace,
according to your word;
for my eyes have seen your salvation,
which you have prepared
in the presence of all peoples,
a light for revelation to the Gentiles
and for glory to your people Israel."

The gospel of the Lord.
**Praise to you, Lord Jesus Christ.**

Let us pray:
Creator of the universe,
Simeon was a man of prayer
who followed all your laws and ways.
He recognized Jesus as the Messiah
even though Jesus was still a baby.
Help us to recognize you in our lives
and be your faithful children.
We ask this through Christ our Lord.
**Amen.**

Let us pray the prayer that Jesus taught us:
**Our Father...**

✠ **In the name of the Father, and of the Son, and of the Holy Spirit. Amen.**

Note: Today's reading is Luke 2:25-32.

## FEBRUARY 11
## FEAST OF OUR LADY OF LOURDES;
## WORLD DAY OF THE SICK

✠ **In the name of the Father, and of the Son, and of the Holy Spirit. Amen.**

Introduction: Today is the feast of Our Lady of Lourdes. Mary appeared to a young girl named Bernadette in Lourdes, France, in 1858. At Our Lady's direction, Bernadette dug down in the earth with her hands and a spring of water bubbled up. This water has cured many people of their illnesses, and millions have visited the shrine at Lourdes to seek healing.

Today, as we also celebrate the World Day of the Sick, we highlight the importance of the healing ministry of the Church. The gospels contain many stories of Jesus healing people and bringing them into the light to God's love.

A reading from the letter of James

Are any among you sick?
They should call for the elders
of the church
and have them pray over them,
anointing them with oil
in the name of the Lord.
The prayer of faith will save the sick,
and the Lord will raise them up;
and anyone who has committed sins
will be forgiven.

The word of the Lord.
**Thanks be to God.**

Let us pray:
The response is:
**Hear our prayer.**

For all those who are sick:
Lord, in your mercy,
**hear our prayer.**

For all doctors, nurses, and other health care workers:
Lord, in your mercy,
**hear our prayer.**

For all hospital chaplains
and those who visit the sick:
Lord, in your mercy,
**hear our prayer.**

Let us pray the prayer that Jesus taught us:
**Our Father…**

✠ **In the name of the Father, and of the Son, and of the Holy Spirit. Amen.**

—————————————

Note: Today's reading is James 5:14-15.

## FEBRUARY 22
## FEAST OF THE CHAIR OF PETER

✠ **In the name of the Father, and of the Son, and of the Holy Spirit. Amen.**

Introduction: Today we celebrate the Feast of the Chair of Peter. Each bishop has a chair that only he uses in his own cathedral. The chair of Peter refers to the pope, who is the bishop of Rome. This day reminds us of St. Peter, and all his successors.

In our reading today, Jesus gives the authority of the Church to Simon, whom he renames Peter.

A reading from the holy gospel according to Matthew
**Glory to you, Lord.**

Now when Jesus came into the district
of Caesarea Philippi, he asked his disciples,
"Who do people say
that the Son of Man is?"
And they said, "Some say John the Baptist,
but others Elijah, and still others Jeremiah
or one of the prophets."
He said to them,
"But who do you say that I am?"
Simon Peter answered,
"You are the Messiah,
the Son of the living God."
And Jesus answered him,
"Blessed are you, Simon son of Jonah!
For flesh and blood has not revealed
this to you,
but my Father in heaven.
And I tell you, you are Peter,
and on this rock I will build my church, and
the gates of Hades will not prevail against it.

I will give you the keys
of the kingdom of heaven,
and whatever you bind on earth
will be bound in heaven,
and whatever you loose on earth
will be loosed in heaven."

The gospel of the Lord.
**Praise to you, Lord Jesus Christ.**

Let us pray:
Most holy and loving God,
your Son, Jesus, made Peter the head
of your Church on earth.
We ask you to bless our Pope
and give him every gift,
grace and blessing he needs
to guide the Church today.
We ask this through Christ our Lord.
**Amen.**

Let us pray the prayer that Jesus taught us:
**Our Father…**

✠ **In the name of the Father, and of the Son, and of the Holy Spirit. Amen.**

---

Note: Today's reading is Matthew 16:13-19.

## MARCH 17
## FEAST OF ST. PATRICK

✠ **In the name of the Father, and of the Son, and of the Holy Spirit. Amen.**

Introduction: Today is the feast of St. Patrick. Born around 389 in Britain to Roman parents, he was captured by Irish raiders when he was 16 and sold as a slave in Ireland, where he was forced to work as a shepherd. Six years later, Patrick escaped and returned to Britain. His spirituality had grown in captivity, and after his return to Britain, he studied and became a priest. He wanted to bring the Good News to the Irish. Ordained a bishop when he was 43, he was sent to do this work. He faced much danger and opposition, but through his great efforts, Ireland became a country of Christians.

St. Patrick was a humble man, and very brave, returning to the place where he had been a slave to teach the people about Jesus.

A reading from the book of the prophet Isaiah

The Lord says,
"Here is my servant, whom I uphold,
my chosen, in whom my soul delights;
I have put my spirit upon him;
he will bring forth justice to the nations.
He will not cry or lift up his voice,
or make it heard in the street;
a bruised reed he will not break,
and a dimly burning wick
he will not quench;
he will faithfully bring forth justice.
He will not grow faint or be crushed
until he has established justice in the earth;
and the coastlands wait for his teaching."

The word of the Lord.
**Thanks be to God.**

Let us pray:
Most loving God,
through prayer and suffering,
St. Patrick came to know you and love you.
He wanted to teach the people of Ireland
about your Son and your ways.
Help us to be humble and courageous,
standing up for what is right,
especially when it is hard to do.
We ask this through Christ our Lord.
**Amen.**

Let us pray the prayer that Jesus taught us:
**Our Father…**

✠ **In the name of the Father, and of the Son, and of the Holy Spirit. Amen.**

Note: Today's reading is Isaiah 42:1-4.

## MARCH 19
## SOLEMNITY OF JOSEPH, HUSBAND OF MARY

✠ **In the name of the Father, and of the Son, and of the Holy Spirit. Amen.**

Introduction: Today is the feast of St. Joseph, husband of Mary – the man God chose to take care of his Son, Jesus, while Jesus was growing up.

The gospels do not tell us much about him, but we do know that St. Joseph was a good, just, loving and holy man. Would God choose anyone without these qualities to take care of his Son? St. Joseph is the patron saint of the universal Church, and is also the principal patron saint of Canada.

A reading from the holy gospel according to Matthew
**Glory to you, Lord.**

Jacob was the father of Joseph
the husband of Mary,
of whom Jesus was born,
who is called the Messiah.
Now the birth of Jesus the Messiah
took place in this way.
When his mother Mary
had been engaged to Joseph,
but before they lived together,
she was found to be with child
from the Holy Spirit.
Her husband Joseph, being a righteous man
and unwilling to expose her
to public disgrace,
planned to dismiss her quietly.
But just when he had resolved to do this,
an angel of the Lord appeared to him
in a dream and said, "Joseph, son of David,
do not be afraid to take Mary as your wife,
for the child conceived in her
is from the Holy Spirit.

She will bear a son,
and you are to name him Jesus,
for he will save his people from their sins."
When Joseph awoke from sleep, he did as
the angel of the Lord commanded him;
he took Mary as his wife.

The gospel of the Lord.
**Praise to you, Lord Jesus Christ.**

Let us pray:
Most holy and loving God,
you chose Joseph to be Mary's husband
and the father of Jesus on earth.
Help us to turn to St. Joseph
with our needs,
and be people of prayer,
trusting always
in the mercy and love of God, as he did.
We ask this through Christ our Lord.
**Amen.**

Let us pray the prayer that Jesus taught us:
**Our Father…**

✠ **In the name of the Father, and of the Son, and of the Holy Spirit. Amen.**

---

Note: Today's reading is Matthew 1:16, 18-21, 24.

## MARCH 25

## SOLEMNITY OF THE ANNUNCIA-TION OF THE LORD

✠ **In the name of the Father, and of the Son, and of the Holy Spirit. Amen.**

Introduction: Today we celebrate and remember the Annunciation – the wonderful day when the archangel Gabriel visited Mary to ask her to be the mother of Jesus.

Today we thank God for the gift of Jesus, and for the goodness of Mary, his mother.

A reading from the holy gospel according to Luke
**Glory to you, Lord.**

In the sixth month
the angel Gabriel was sent by God
to a town in Galilee called Nazareth,
to a virgin engaged to a man
whose name was Joseph,
of the house of David.
The virgin's name was Mary.
And he came to her and said,
"Greetings, favoured one!
The Lord is with you."
But she was much perplexed by his words
and pondered what sort of greeting
this might be.
The angel said to her,
"Do not be afraid, Mary,
for you have found favour with God.
And now, you will conceive in your womb
and bear a son, and you will name him Jesus.
He will be great, and will be called
the Son of the Most High,
and the Lord God will give to him
the throne of his ancestor David."

The angel said to her,
"The Holy Spirit will come upon you,
and the power of the Most High
will overshadow you;
therefore the child to be born will be holy;
he will be called Son of God."
Then Mary said,
"Here am I, the servant of the Lord;
let it be with me according to your word."
Then the angel departed from her.

The gospel of the Lord.
**Praise to you, Lord Jesus Christ.**

Let us pray:
Most holy God,
you sent the archangel Gabriel to Mary
to ask her to be the mother
of your Son, Jesus.
Help us always to do your will
and grow in love for you and Jesus,
as Mary did.
We ask this through Christ our Lord.
**Amen.**

Let us pray that we may be open to God's call to us, and do what he asks, in imitation of Mary:*
**Hail Mary…**

✠ **In the name of the Father, and of the Son, and of the Holy Spirit. Amen.**

---

Note: Today's reading is Luke 1:26-32, 35, 38.

*If you wish, you could replace the Hail Mary with the Angelus prayer (see Appendix 3 – Traditional Prayers).

## APRIL 17
## FEAST OF BLESSED KATERI TEKAKWITHA

✠ In the name of the Father, and of the Son, and of the Holy Spirit. Amen.

Introduction: Today is the feast of Blessed Kateri. Her father was chief of the Iroquois, and her mother was a Christian. When she was very little, her whole family died of smallpox, so she went to live with her uncle and aunt. Even though they treated her unkindly, she tried to be cheerful and obedient. Kateri wanted to become a Christian, but at first her family would not let her. After a while, they agreed, and she was baptized when she was 20 years old. She received the name Kateri, the Indian name for Katherine. After her baptism, her family and friends tried to get her to abandon her faith. They made fun of her and and the children were encouraged to call her names and throw stones at her. Kateri escaped and went to a Christian Indian village, where she celebrated her first communion. Kateri died on April 17, 1680. She was only 24 years old.

Kateri was gentle, kind, brave and holy. Even when people were mean to her, she still was kind and gentle with others. We can follow her example and do the same.

A reading from the holy gospel according to Matthew
**Glory to you, Lord.**

Jesus said,
"Blessed are the pure in heart,
for they will see God.
Blessed are the peacemakers,
for they will be called children of God.
Blessed are those who are persecuted
for righteousness' sake,
for theirs is the kingdom of heaven.
Blessed are you when people revile you
and persecute you
and utter all kinds of evil against you falsely
on my account.

Rejoice and be glad,
for your reward is great in heaven."

The gospel of the Lord.
**Praise to you, Lord Jesus Christ.**

Let us pray:
Holy and gracious God,
Blessed Kateri
was kind and gentle
even to those who teased her and hurt her.
Help us to do this, also,
and to be brave,
to stand up for our faith
when we are teased or made fun of
because of our belief in Jesus.
We ask this through Christ our Lord.
**Amen.**

Let us pray the prayer that Jesus taught us:
**Our Father…**

✠ In the name of the Father, and of the Son, and of the Holy Spirit. Amen.

---

Note: Today's reading is Matthew 5:8-12a.

## APRIL 25
## FEAST OF ST. MARK, EVANGELIST

✠ **In the name of the Father, and of the Son, and of the Holy Spirit. Amen.**

Introduction: Today is the feast of St. Mark, Evangelist (gospel writer). Mark accompanied St. Paul and Barnabas on their first journey to spread the gospel message to the known world. Mark's journeys are recorded in the book of the Acts of the Apostles. Mark was a disciple of St. Peter, who affectionately called him "my son, Mark." St. Mark wrote the earliest gospel between 60 and 70 AD, based on the teaching of Peter. (Even though Matthew's gospel comes first in the Bible, Mark's was written first.) Mark died around 74. In art, he is represented by a lion.

St. Mark put down in writing the teachings of Jesus and what Jesus did while he was with us here on earth. Let us thank God today for the gift of the gospel that Mark wrote, a source of light and grace to us all.

A reading from the holy gospel according to Mark
**Glory to you, Lord.**

Later Jesus appeared to the eleven themselves
as they were sitting at the table.
And he said to them,
"Go into all the world
and proclaim the good news
to the whole creation.
The one who believes and is baptized
will be saved;
but the one who does not believe
will be condemned.
And these signs will accompany
those who believe: by using my name
they will cast out demons;
they will speak in new tongues;
they will pick up snakes in their hands,
and if they drink any deadly thing,
it will not hurt them;
they will lay their hands on the sick,
and they will recover."
And they went out
and proclaimed the good news everywhere,
while the Lord worked with them
and confirmed the message
by the signs that accompanied it.

The gospel of the Lord.
**Praise to you, Lord Jesus Christ.**

Let us pray:
All-powerful and ever-living God,
the disciples of your beloved Son, Jesus,
went out to the whole world,
inspired by the Holy Spirit,
to spread the Good News.
Help us to be faithful to Jesus like St. Mark
and spread the Good News
through our words and actions.
We ask this through Christ our Lord.
**Amen.**

Let us pray the prayer that Jesus taught us:
**Our Father...**

✠ **In the name of the Father, and of the Son, and of the Holy Spirit. Amen.**

Note: Today's reading is Mark 16:14a, 15-18, 20.

## APRIL 29
## FEAST OF ST. CATHERINE OF SIENA

✠ **In the name of the Father, and of the Son, and of the Holy Spirit. Amen.**

Introduction: Today is the feast of St. Catherine of Siena, one of the three female doctors of the Church. The youngest child of a family of 20 or more children, she devoted herself to a life of prayer and penance from a very early age. After refusing to consider marriage, she became an associate of the Dominican order. A group of disciples went with her on her journeys, where she called for reform and repentance through a renewal of total love for God. She also worked to solve a big problem the Church had at the time. Catherine died on April 29, 1380.

Our reading today describes what is needed to live like Catherine and the saints.

A reading from the letter of Paul to the Ephesians

Lead a life worthy of the calling
to which you have been called,
with all humility and gentleness,
with patience,
bearing with one another in love,
making every effort to maintain
the unity of the Spirit in the bond of peace.
There is one body and one Spirit,
just as you were called
to the one hope of your calling,
one Lord, one faith, one baptism,
one God and Father of all,
who is above all and through all and in all.
But each of us was given grace
according to the measure of Christ's gift.

The gifts he gave
were that some would be apostles,
some prophets, some evangelists,
some pastors and teachers,
to equip the saints for the work of ministry,
for building up the body of Christ.

The word of the Lord.
**Thanks be to God.**

Let us pray:
Creator God,
source of all love and holiness,
St. Catherine preached and taught
that we should be a people of prayer,
loving you with all our hearts.
Grant us the grace we need
to love you with all our hearts,
growing closer to you and Jesus
by being faithful to your ways.
We ask this through Christ our Lord.
**Amen.**

Let us pray the prayer that Jesus taught us:
**Our Father…**

✠ **In the name of the Father, and of the Son, and of the Holy Spirit. Amen.**

Note: Today's reading is Ephesians 4:1b-7, 11-12.

## MAY 1
## FEAST OF ST. JOSEPH THE WORKER

✠ **In the name of the Father, and of the Son, and of the Holy Spirit. Amen.**

Introduction: Today is the feast of St. Joseph the Worker. It reminds us that St. Joseph was a worker, a carpenter, someone who makes things out of wood. He taught Jesus the skills he needed to be a carpenter.

St. Joseph worked very hard to take care of Mary and Jesus, to give them the things they needed to live, because he loved them very much. He is the patron saint of all workers.

Our parents work hard, too, to take care of us. Children also have a job to do: to study and work hard at school, and to be helpful at home.

A reading from the letter of Paul to the Colossians

Above all, clothe yourselves with love,
which binds everything together
in perfect harmony.
And let the peace of Christ
rule in your hearts,
to which indeed you were called
in the one body.
And be thankful.
And whatever you do, in word or deed,
do everything in the name of the Lord Jesus,
giving thanks to God the Father
through him.
Whatever your task, put yourselves into it,
as done for the Lord
and not for your masters,
since you know that from the Lord
you will receive the inheritance
as your reward; you serve the Lord Christ.

The word of the Lord.
**Thanks be to God.**

Let us pray:
Creator of the universe,
St. Joseph worked hard
to take care of his family.
Help those who are without jobs
to find the work they need
to take care of their families.
Help all workers to receive fair wages
and have safe working conditions.
Give us the grace we need to do our best,
knowing that it will help
build up your kingdom.
We ask this through Christ our Lord.
**Amen.**

Let us pray the prayer that Jesus taught us:
**Our Father…**

✠ **In the name of the Father, and of the Son, and of the Holy Spirit. Amen.**

Note: Today's reading is Colossians 3:14-15, 17, 23-24.

## MAY 3

## FEAST OF ST. PHILIP AND ST. JAMES, APOSTLES

✠ **In the name of the Father, and of the Son, and of the Holy Spirit. Amen.**

Introduction: Today is the feast of St. Philip and St. James, who were apostles of Jesus. St. Philip came from Bethsaida in Galilee; his name is mentioned in the gospel of the feeding of the 5000. During the Last Supper, he asked Jesus to show him the Father. Jesus replied that to see him was to see the Father. James was sentenced to death in the year 62.

A reading from the holy gospel according to John
**Glory to you, Lord.**

Jesus said to him,
"I am the way, and the truth, and the life.
No one comes to the Father
except through me.
If you know me,
you will know my Father also.
From now on you do know him
and have seen him."
Philip said to him,
"Lord, show us the Father,
and we will be satisfied."
Jesus said to him,
"Have I been with you all this time, Philip,
and you still do not know me?
Whoever has seen me has seen the Father.
How can you say, 'Show us the Father'?
Do you not believe that I am in the Father
and the Father is in me?

The words that I say to you
I do not speak on my own;
but the Father who dwells in me
does his works.
Believe me that I am in the Father
and the Father is in me."

The gospel of the Lord.
**Praise to you, Lord Jesus Christ.**

Let us pray:
Creator God,
St. Philip and St. James gave their lives
because they believed in Jesus
and spread the Good News of Jesus
to others.
Help us to be faithful witnesses
of your beloved Son.
We ask this through Christ our Lord.
**Amen.**

Let us pray the prayer that Jesus taught us:
**Our Father…**

✠ **In the name of the Father, and of the Son, and of the Holy Spirit. Amen.**

---

Note: Today's reading is John 14:6-11a.

## MAY 14
## FEAST OF ST. MATTHIAS, APOSTLE

✠ **In the name of the Father, and of the Son, and of the Holy Spirit. Amen.**

Introduction: In today's reading, we hear how Matthias was chosen to take the place of Judas after Jesus' resurrection.

It is important to note that they prayed before they chose Matthias. This is what Jesus did before he called the twelve apostles – he spent the night in prayer. It reminds us to pray for guidance when we are facing important decisions.

A reading from the Acts of the Apostles

Peter stood up among the believers
and said, "So one of the men
who have accompanied us
throughout the time that the Lord Jesus
went in and out among us,
beginning from the baptism of John
until the day when he was taken up from us
– one of these must become
a witness with us to his resurrection."
So they proposed two,
Joseph called Barsabbas,
who was also known as Justus,
and Matthias.
Then they prayed and said,
"Lord, you know everyone's heart.
Show us which one of these two
you have chosen to take the place
in this ministry and apostleship
from which Judas turned aside
to go to his own place."

And they cast lots for them,
and the lot fell on Matthias;
and he was added to the eleven apostles.

The word of the Lord.
**Thanks be to God.**

Let us pray:
Creator God,
before every decision,
your beloved Son prayed to you
to find out your will for him,
what you wanted him to do and to say.
Help us to remember to follow his example
and pray for your help and guidance.
Help us to be faithful witnesses
of the gospel, like St. Matthias was.
We ask this through Christ our Lord.
**Amen.**

Let us pray the prayer that Jesus taught us:
**Our Father…**

✠ **In the name of the Father, and of the Son, and of the Holy Spirit. Amen.**

---

Note: Today's reading is Acts 1:15b, 21-26.

## MAY 26
## FEAST OF ST. PHILIP NERI

✠ **In the name of the Father, and of the Son, and of the Holy Spirit. Amen.**

Introduction: Today is the feast of St. Philip Neri. Born in 1515, he went to Rome when he was 18. He became a missionary to Rome itself – teaching and preaching in the streets, because at that time the people of Rome were not practising their religion very well. He was known for his good humour, which helped him in his work. Besides being a founder of a religious order, he is the patron saint of home missions.

We often think of missions as being in faraway countries, but Canada has missions, too, especially in remote areas of our big country.

A reading from the second letter of Paul to Timothy

In the presence of God and of Christ Jesus,
who is to judge the living and the dead,
and in view of his appearing
and his kingdom,
I solemnly urge you: proclaim the message;
be persistent
whether the time is favourable
or unfavourable;
convince, rebuke, and encourage,
with the utmost patience in teaching.
For the time is coming when people will not
put up with sound doctrine,
but having itching ears,
they will accumulate for themselves
teachers to suit their own desires,
and will turn away
from listening to the truth
and wander away to myths.

As for you, always be sober,
endure suffering,
do the work of an evangelist,
carry out your ministry fully.

The word of the Lord.
**Thanks be to God.**

Let us pray:
Most holy and loving God,
St. Philip Neri preached the Good News
by both word and action,
with love and with humour.
Grant that the missions in Canada
will receive the help they need,
and that many graces and blessings
will be poured upon the missionaries
and their people.
We ask this through Christ our Lord.
**Amen.**

Let us pray the prayer that Jesus taught us:
**Our Father…**

✠ **In the name of the Father, and of the Son, and of the Holy Spirit. Amen.**

---

Note: Today's reading is 2 Timothy 4:1-5.

## MAY 31
## FEAST OF THE VISITATION

✠ **In the name of the Father, and of the Son, and of the Holy Spirit. Amen.**

Introduction: Today we celebrate the Feast of the Visitation, when Mary went to visit her cousin Elizabeth. The angel Gabriel told Mary that Elizabeth was expecting a baby, too. Mary left Nazareth immediately to go to her cousin to help her.

Elizabeth was filled with the Holy Spirit, and recognized that Mary was to be the mother of the Lord. Elizabeth's baby grew up to be known as John the Baptist, who prepared the way of the Lord – his cousin Jesus!

We repeat the words of Elizabeth when she saw Mary every time we say the Hail Mary.

A reading from the holy gospel according to Luke
**Glory to you, Lord.**

In those days Mary set out
and went with haste
to a Judean town in the hill country,
where she entered the house of Zechariah
and greeted Elizabeth.
When Elizabeth heard Mary's greeting,
the child leapt in her womb.
And Elizabeth was filled
with the Holy Spirit
and exclaimed with a loud cry,
"Blessed are you among women,
and blessed is the fruit of your womb.
And why has this happened to me,
that the mother of my Lord comes to me?

For as soon as I heard the sound
of your greeting,
the child in my womb leapt for joy.
And blessed is she who believed
that there would be a fulfilment
of what was spoken to her by the Lord."

The gospel of the Lord.
**Praise to you, Lord Jesus Christ.**

Let us pray:
Most holy and gracious God,
Mary, your servant,
left her home to go to her cousin
because she knew Elizabeth
would need help
with the baby that was soon to be born.
Help us to be like Elizabeth and her baby,
recognizing with joy
the presence of Jesus.
We ask this through Christ our Lord.
**Amen.**

In honour of the Visitation, we pray:
**Hail Mary…**

✠ **In the name of the Father, and of the Son, and of the Holy Spirit. Amen.**

Note: Today's reading is Luke 1:39-44.

## JUNE
## SOLEMNITY OF THE SACRED HEART OF JESUS*

✠ **In the name of the Father, and of the Son, and of the Holy Spirit. Amen.**

Introduction: Today is the Solemnity of the Sacred Heart of Jesus. We honour Jesus' sacred heart, the symbol of his threefold love: human love, spiritual love and divine love. We remember his great and merciful love for us.

Jesus gave St. Margaret Mary the task of promoting this feast. He wants everyone to remember the great love he has for us.

A reading from the holy gospel according to Matthew
**Glory to you, Lord.**

At that time Jesus said, "I thank you, Father,
Lord of heaven and earth,
because you have hidden these things
from the wise and the intelligent
and have revealed them to infants;
yes, Father, for such was your gracious will.
All things have been handed over to me
by my Father;
and no one knows the Son
except the Father,
and no one knows the Father except the Son
and anyone to whom the Son chooses
to reveal him.
Come to me, all you that are weary
and are carrying heavy burdens,
and I will give you rest.
Take my yoke upon you, and learn from me;
for I am gentle and humble in heart,
and you will find rest for your souls.
For my yoke is easy, and my burden is light."

The gospel of the Lord.
**Praise to you, Lord Jesus Christ.**

Let us pray:
Most Sacred Heart of Jesus,
in imitation of St. Margaret Mary,
we consecrate and dedicate ourselves
to you.
May we always be united to you,
love you and serve you
with our whole being –
body, soul, mind and heart.
Grant that we may always do your most
holy will.
**Amen.**

Let us pray the prayer that Jesus taught us:
**Our Father...**

✠ **In the name of the Father, and of the Son, and of the Holy Spirit. Amen.**

Note: Today's reading is Matthew 11:25-30.

* This feast is celebrated on the Friday following the Solemnity of the Body and Blood of Christ.

## JUNE 1
## FEAST OF ST. JUSTIN, MARTYR

✠ **In the name of the Father, and of the Son, and of the Holy Spirit. Amen.**

Introduction: Today is the feast of St. Justin, who was born almost 1900 years ago! He became a Christian when he was 30, and devoted himself to teaching and explaining the faith. He opened a school of philosophy in Rome. Arrested and brought to trial because he was a Christian, he was killed for his beliefs.

Justin was the first Christian, and first layperson (meaning he was not a member of the clergy), to write about Christianity at length. Some of his writings are still studied by scholars today.

A reading from the first letter of Paul to the Corinthians

For Christ did not send me to baptize
but to proclaim the gospel,
and not with eloquent wisdom,
so that the cross of Christ
might not be emptied of its power.
For the message about the cross
is foolishness to those who are perishing,
but to us who are being saved
it is the power of God.
For since, in the wisdom of God,
the world did not know God
through wisdom,
God decided, through the foolishness
of our proclamation,
to save those who believe.
For God's foolishness is wiser
than human wisdom,
and God's weakness is stronger
than human strength.

The word of the Lord.
**Thanks be to God.**

Let us pray:
Creator God,
your wisdom is beyond our understanding.
Help us to learn what is wise in your eyes,
and do what is right, like St. Justin did,
even if it seems foolish
in the eyes of the world.
We ask this through Christ our Lord.
**Amen.**

Let us pray the prayer that Jesus taught us:
**Our Father...**

✠ **In the name of the Father, and of the Son, and of the Holy Spirit. Amen.**

Note: Today's reading is 1 Corinthians 1:17-18, 21, 25.

## JUNE 3
## FEAST OF ST. CHARLES LWANGA AND COMPANIONS

✠ **In the name of the Father, and of the Son, and of the Holy Spirit. Amen.**

Introduction: Today is the feast of St. Charles Lwanga and companions. St. Charles was master of pages in the court of the king of Uganda. He was also a catechist – one who teaches others about the faith. The king was very angry that some of his pages had become Christians. He had Charles and these pages killed. One of the pages was only 13 years old. They are martyrs – people who died for what they believe.

A reading from the first letter of Peter

Now who will harm you
if you are eager to do what is good?
But even if you do suffer
for doing what is right,
you are blessed.
Do not fear what they fear,
and do not be intimidated,
but in your hearts sanctify Christ as Lord.
Always be ready to make your defence
to anyone who demands from you
an account of the hope that is in you;
yet do it with gentleness and reverence.
Keep your conscience clear,
so that, when you are maligned,
those who abuse you
for your good conduct in Christ
may be put to shame.
For it is better to suffer for doing good,
if suffering should be God's will,
than to suffer for doing evil.

The word of the Lord.
**Thanks be to God.**

Let us pray:
Most holy and loving God,
the Ugandan martyrs
suffered and died because of their belief
in you and your Son, Jesus.
Help us to believe as strongly as they did,
and to do what is right at all times.
We ask this through Christ our Lord.
**Amen.**

Let us pray the prayer that Jesus taught us:
**Our Father…**

✠ **In the name of the Father, and of the Son, and of the Holy Spirit. Amen.**

Note: Today's reading is 1 Peter 3:13-17.

## JUNE 11
## FEAST OF ST. BARNABAS, APOSTLE

✠ **In the name of the Father, and of the Son, and of the Holy Spirit. Amen.**

Introduction: St. Barnabas was a Jew of Cyprus, born in the first century. He sold his property and gave the money to the apostles, then lived with the earliest converts to Christianity in Jerusalem. He worked closely with St. Paul: first they travelled to Antioch to preach, and later were sent to preach to the Gentiles (non-Jewish people). According to tradition, Barnabas also preached in Alexandria and Rome, and was stoned to death at Salamis.

A reading from the Acts of the Apostles

Awe came upon everyone,
because many wonders and signs
were being done by the apostles.
All who believed were together
and had all things in common;
they would sell their possessions and goods
and distribute the proceeds to all,
as any had need.
Day by day,
as they spent much time together
in the temple,
they broke bread at home and ate their food
with glad and generous hearts, praising God
and having the goodwill of all the people.
And day by day
the Lord added to their number
those who were being saved.

The word of the Lord.
**Thanks be to God.**

Let us pray:
Most holy and loving God,
St. Barnabas and the earliest Christians
followed Jesus' commands
to love one another
by sharing all they had with each other.
Help us to be faithful to Jesus' commands
by sharing with others,
and being kind, gentle,
caring and respectful.
We ask this through Christ our Lord.
**Amen.**

Let us pray the prayer that Jesus taught us:
**Our Father…**

✠ **In the name of the Father, and of the Son, and of the Holy Spirit. Amen.**

Note: Today's reading is Acts 2:43-47.

## JUNE 13
## FEAST OF ST. ANTHONY OF PADUA

✠ **In the name of the Father, and of the Son, and of the Holy Spirit. Amen.**

Introduction: Today is the feast of St. Anthony, who was born in Lisbon, Portugal, in 1195. He joined the Canons Regular of St. Augustine and was ordained a priest in 1219, then transferred to the Franciscans in 1221, taking the name Anthony. When he gave a sermon at an ordination, his career as a preacher was launched. He preached all over Italy, and was extremely successful. He became well known as a confessor and for winning converts back to the faith.

After 1226 he settled in Padua, where he attacked wrongdoing and corruption wherever he found it. He completely reformed the city, helping the poor and working constantly and untiringly with heretics. He died on June 13, 1231, at age 36. He was canonized the following year and declared a doctor of the Church in 1946. He was one of the greatest preachers of all times.

St. Anthony accomplished much and has a lot to teach us. He is the patron saint of the poor and oppressed, was faithful to the teachings of Jesus, was a man of prayer and had great faith.

A reading from the holy gospel according to Luke
**Glory to you, Lord.**

Jesus said,
"Do not be afraid, little flock,
for it is your Father's good pleasure
to give you the kingdom.
Sell your possessions, and give alms.
Make purses for yourselves
that do not wear out,
an unfailing treasure in heaven,
where no thief comes near
and no moth destroys.
For where your treasure is,
there your heart will be also."

The gospel of the Lord.
**Praise to you, Lord Jesus Christ.**

Let us pray:
Most all-holy and redeeming God,
St. Anthony preached the Good News of
Jesus tirelessly, unceasingly,
with great love for you
and your divine Son.
He was always ready to help
the poor and oppressed.
Help us to follow his example,
by being faithful to you
and to the teachings of Jesus,
giving alms to the poor,
and standing up for what is right and just.
We ask this through Christ our Lord.
**Amen.**

Let us pray the prayer that Jesus taught us:
**Our Father…**

✠ **In the name of the Father, and of the Son, and of the Holy Spirit. Amen.**

---

Note: Today's reading is Luke 12:32-34.

## JUNE 22
## FEAST OF ST. THOMAS MORE

✠ In the name of the Father, and of the Son, and of the Holy Spirit. Amen.

Introduction: Today is the feast of St. Thomas More. Born in 1478, he later studied law at Oxford, and became a lawyer in 1501. He entered Parliament in 1504 and married Jane Holt. Noted for his learning, intellect and wit, he wrote poetry, history, works against Protestantism, devotional books and prayers. When Jane died, he married Alice Middleton, a widow. Thomas was a tutor of King Henry VIII, who sent him on several diplomatic missions, knighted him, and made him Chancellor of England. When Henry wanted to divorce his wife, which was against Church law, St. Thomas resigned his position and retired penniless. He was arrested because he would not sign the Act of Succession, which he could not agree with, and imprisoned in the Tower of London in 1534. After remaining in prison for 15 months, he was convicted of treason and executed in 1535.

St. Thomas More gave up power and wealth because he upheld the teachings of the Church. Would we be willing to do the same?

A reading from the holy gospel according to Matthew
**Glory to you, Lord.**

Jesus said to the people,
"Blessed are the pure in heart,
for they will see God.
Blessed are the peacemakers,
for they will be called children of God.
Blessed are those who are persecuted
or righteousness' sake,
for theirs is the kingdom of heaven.

Blessed are you when people revile you
and persecute you
and utter all kinds of evil against you falsely
on my account.
Rejoice and be glad,
for your reward is great in heaven."

The gospel of the Lord.
**Praise to you, Lord Jesus Christ.**

Let us pray:
All-just God,
St. Thomas More lost his life
because he was your servant first,
and stood up for what was right.
Help us to stand up for what is right,
even when it is hard.
We ask this through Christ our Lord.
**Amen.**

Let us pray the prayer that Jesus taught us:
**Our Father…**

✠ In the name of the Father, and of the Son, and of the Holy Spirit. Amen.

---

Note: Today's reading is Matthew 5:8-12.

## JUNE 24
## SOLEMNITY OF THE BIRTH OF JOHN THE BAPTIST

✠ **In the name of the Father, and of the Son, and of the Holy Spirit. Amen.**

Introduction: Today is the feast of the birth of John the Baptist. Mary visited John's mother, her cousin Elizabeth, to help her while she was expecting John. Elizabeth and Zechariah named the baby John following the instructions of an angel. When John grew up, he prepared the way for Jesus and the Good News.

Do we prepare the way for Jesus by our actions and words?

A reading from the holy gospel according to Luke
**Glory to you, Lord.**

Now the time came for Elizabeth to give birth, and she bore a son.
Her neighbours and relatives heard that the Lord had shown his great mercy to her, and they rejoiced with her.
On the eighth day
they came to circumcise the child, and they were going to name him Zechariah after his father.
But his mother said,
"No; he is to be called John."
They said to her,
"None of your relatives has this name."
Then they began motioning to his father to find out what name he wanted
to give him.
He asked for a writing-tablet and wrote, "His name is John."
And all of them were amazed.

Immediately his mouth was opened and his tongue freed,
and he began to speak, praising God.
The child grew and became strong in spirit, and he was in the wilderness
until the day he appeared publicly to Israel.

The gospel of the Lord.
**Praise to you, Lord Jesus Christ.**

Let us pray:
Most holy God,
Zechariah lost his speech when he questioned the angel's message to him that Elizabeth was going to have a child in her old age.
Help us to believe the words
you speak to us
through the prophets, the law and Jesus.
Help us to prepare the way of the Lord
like John the Baptist did.
We ask this through Christ our Lord.
**Amen.**

Let us pray the prayer that Jesus taught us:
**Our Father…**

✠ **In the name of the Father, and of the Son, and of the Holy Spirit. Amen.**

---

Note: Today's reading is Luke 1:57-64, 80.

## JUNE 29
## FEAST OF ST. PETER AND ST. PAUL, APOSTLES

✠ **In the name of the Father, and of the Son, and of the Holy Spirit. Amen.**

Introduction: Today we celebrate the feast of the two great apostles, St. Peter and St. Paul. St. Peter is one of the twelve apostles that Jesus chose to help him.

Jesus picked Peter to be the leader of all those who believe in him; Peter was the first pope. St. Paul was chosen by Jesus to make his name known to the Gentiles (non-Jewish people) after Jesus' ascension into heaven.

Both apostles suffered and were killed because they believed in Jesus and spread the Good News to others.

A reading from the holy gospel according to Matthew
**Glory to you, Lord.**

Now when Jesus came into
the district of Caesarea Philippi,
he asked his disciples,
"Who do people say
that the Son of Man is?"
And they said,
"Some say John the Baptist,
but others Elijah,
and still others Jeremiah
or one of the prophets."
He said to them,
"But who do you say that I am?"
Simon Peter answered,
"You are the Messiah,
the Son of the living God."
And Jesus answered him,
"Blessed are you, Simon son of Jonah!
For flesh and blood has not revealed
this to you, but my Father in heaven.

And I tell you, you are Peter,
and on this rock I will build my church,
and the gates of Hades
will not prevail against it.
I will give you the keys
of the kingdom of heaven,
and whatever you bind on earth
will be bound in heaven,
and whatever you loose on earth
will be loosed in heaven."

The gospel of the Lord.
**Praise to you, Lord Jesus Christ.**

Let us pray:
Most loving God,
St. Peter and St. Paul followed you
and did your work here on earth.
Grant that we may spread the Good News,
and be faithful followers of your Son,
following their example.
We ask this through Christ our Lord.
**Amen.**

Let us pray the prayer that Jesus taught us:
**Our Father...**

✠ **In the name of the Father, and of the Son, and of the Holy Spirit. Amen.**

_____

Note: Today's reading is Matthew 16:13-19.

# Special Occasions

## FRIDAY BEFORE THANKSGIVING

✠ **In the name of the Father, and of the Son, and of the Holy Spirit. Amen.**

Introduction: On Monday we will celebrate Thanksgiving. We thank God for all the things we have, and for the people who love us and help us. We thank God for the gift of freedom, and a country where there is peace. We thank God for all the blessings and gifts God showers upon us each and every day.

A reading from the holy gospel according to Luke
**Glory to you, Lord.**

On the way to Jerusalem
Jesus was going through the region
between Samaria and Galilee.
As he entered a village,
ten lepers approached him.
Keeping their distance, they called out,
saying,
"Jesus, Master, have mercy on us!"
When he saw them, he said to them,
"Go and show yourselves to the priests."
And as they went, they were made clean.
Then one of them,
when he saw that he was healed,
turned back, praising God with a loud voice.
He prostrated himself at Jesus' feet
and thanked him.

The gospel of the Lord.
**Praise to you, Lord Jesus Christ.**

Let us follow the example of the one person who came back to thank Jesus as we pray.

The response is:
**Lord, we praise and thank you.**

For our families and our friends,
**Lord, we praise and thank you.**

For our school, our teachers,
and all the staff,
**Lord, we praise and thank you.**

For (*name members of the pastoral team from your parish*),
**Lord, we praise and thank you.**

For all who help us,
**Lord, we praise and thank you.**

For our homes and our food,
**Lord, we praise and thank you.**

For the gifts and blessings we have received,
**Lord, we praise and thank you.**

For the country we live in,
**Lord, we praise and thank you.**

Let us pray the prayer that Jesus taught us:
**Our Father…**

✠ **In the name of the Father, and of the Son, and of the Holy Spirit. Amen.**

Note: Today's reading is Luke 17:11-16a.

## REMEMBRANCE DAY (NOVEMBER 11)

✠ In the name of the Father, and of the Son, and of the Holy Spirit. Amen.

Introduction: Today is Remembrance Day. We remember all those who have died for our country, fighting for peace and justice.

Unfortunately, war has been a part of world history for millennia. In the Old Testament we find many accounts of battles. In the second book of Maccabees, we hear about the Jewish leader Judas Maccabaeus and his followers, who fought for freedom.

A reading from the second book of Maccabees

Then Judas assembled his army
and went to the city of Adullam,
and kept the sabbath there.
On the next day, Judas and his men
went to take up the bodies of the fallen.
They turned to supplication,
praying that the sin that had been
committed might be wholly blotted out.
The noble Judas exhorted the people
to keep themselves free from sin,
for they had seen with their own eyes
what had happened as the result of the sin
of those who had fallen.
He also took up a collection, man by man,
to the amount of two thousand drachmas of
silver, and sent it to Jerusalem
to provide for a sin-offering.
In doing this he acted very well
and honourably,
taking account of the resurrection.
For if he were not expecting
that those who had fallen would rise again,
it would have been superfluous and foolish
to pray for the dead.

But if he was looking to the splendid reward
that is laid up for those
who fall asleep in godliness,
it was a holy and pious thought.
Therefore he made atonement for the dead,
so that they might be delivered from their sin.

The word of the Lord.
**Thanks be to God.**

Let us pray for all those who have died for
freedom in wars and for all those in our
Book of Remembrance:
Eternal rest grant to them, O Lord,
and let perpetual light shine upon them.
May they rest in peace. **Amen.**

Let us pray the prayer that Jesus taught us:
**Our Father…**

✠ In the name of the Father, and of the Son,
and of the Holy Spirit. Amen.

Note: Today's reading is 2 Maccabees 12:38a, 39a, 42-45.

## EARTH DAY (APRIL 22)

✠ In the name of the Father, and of the Son, and of the Holy Spirit. Amen.

Introduction: Today is Earth Day. God has given us the care of the earth and all that is in it.

Are we good stewards of what God has created – the earth, trees, animals and resources of the land? Do we use the gifts of the earth with respect and care?

A reading from the book of Psalms

The response is:
**for his steadfast love endures for ever.**

O give thanks to the Lord, for he is good,
**for his steadfast love endures for ever;**

who by understanding made the heavens,
**for his steadfast love endures for ever;**

who spread out the earth on the waters,
**for his steadfast love endures for ever;**

who made the great lights,
**for his steadfast love endures for ever;**

the sun to rule over the day,
**for his steadfast love endures for ever;**

the moon and stars to rule over the night,
**for his steadfast love endures for ever;**

who gives food to all flesh,
**for his steadfast love endures for ever.**

O give thanks to the God of heaven,
**for his steadfast love endures for ever.**

The word of the Lord.
**Thanks be to God.**

Let us promise God, who gave us the earth and all that is in it, that we will take care of it. Repeat each phrase as it is read aloud:

Creator God,
we the students of

. . . . . . . . . . . . . . . . . . . . . . . . . . . . . . . . .

promise to make our world a better place
by showing care and respect
for the environment.
Help us to be successful in this task.
We ask this through Christ our Lord.
**Amen.**

Let us pray the prayer that Jesus taught us:
**Our Father...**

✠ In the name of the Father, and of the Son, and of the Holy Spirit. Amen.

Note: Today's reading is Psalm 136:1, 5-9, 25-26.

## PRAYER FOR VOCATIONS

✠ **In the name of the Father, and of the Son, and of the Holy Spirit. Amen.**

Introduction: God loves each of us dearly; we are precious in his sight. God calls us by name, and has a specific job for each of us. All Christians, by our baptism, have a vocation to help build the kingdom of God. While some people become priests, religious sisters or brothers, deacons, or consecrated to God to serve God's people in a special way, most live out their vocation as laypeople. We all have gifts to share with the Church and with the world!

In our reading today, Jesus asks us to pray to the owner of the harvest for more workers. The owner of this harvest is God, the harvest is the people of God, and the workers are his helpers. What is God calling us to do?

A reading from the holy gospel according to Matthew
**Glory to you, Lord.**

Then Jesus went about
all the cities and villages,
teaching in their synagogues,
and proclaiming the good news
of the kingdom,
and curing every disease and every sickness.
When he saw the crowds,
he had compassion for them,
because they were harassed and helpless,
like sheep without a shepherd.
Then he said to his disciples,
"The harvest is plentiful,
but the labourers are few;
therefore ask the Lord of the harvest
to send out labourers into his harvest."

The gospel of the Lord.
**Praise to you, Lord Jesus Christ.**

Let us pray:
Most loving and gracious God,
your Son, Jesus, asks us
to pray for more workers for the harvest.
Help each of us to discover
the job God has for us in God's kingdom.
Grant us the courage
to answer God's call with a generous heart
and a willing spirit.
We ask this through Christ our Lord.
**Amen.**

Let us pray the prayer that Jesus taught us:
**Our Father …**

✠ **In the name of the Father, and of the Son, and of the Holy Spirit. Amen.**

---

Note: Today's reading is Matthew 9:35-38.

## PRAYER FOR THE CLERGY OF OUR DIOCESE

✠ **In the name of the Father, and of the Son, and of the Holy Spirit. Amen.**

Introduction: Today we pray for the bishop(s), priests and deacons of our diocese of ................ God has called them to serve God and to be shepherds for God's people. We pray that God will continue to bless, inspire and guide them in their work.

A reading from the book of the prophet Isaiah

The spirit of the Lord God is upon me,
because the Lord has anointed me;
he has sent me
to bring good news to the oppressed,
to bind up the broken-hearted,
to proclaim liberty to the captives,
and release to the prisoners;
to proclaim the year of the Lord's favour,
and the day of vengeance of our God;
to comfort all who mourn;
to provide for those who mourn in Zion –
to give them a garland instead of ashes,
the oil of gladness instead of mourning.

The word of the Lord.
**Thanks be to God.**

Let us pray:
Most loving Father,
you call us by name
and have a special job for each of us.
Give to our bishop (s), priests and
deacons a heart that burns with love
for you and for us.
Give them the grace they need
to be good, holy and faith-filled servants,
to celebrate the sacraments with joy,
and to help us grow
in our faith, love and knowledge of you.
We ask this through Christ our Lord.
**Amen.**

Let us pray the prayer that Jesus taught us:
**Our Father...**

✠ **In the name of the Father, and of the Son, and of the Holy Spirit. Amen.**

Note: Today's reading is Isaiah 61:1-3a.

# FURTHER READING

Ascough, Richard S. *Miracles of Jesus*. Ottawa: Novalis, 2003.

Barclay, William. *The Gospel of John*, Volume 2. (The Daily Study Bible Series.) Louisville, KY: Westminster Press, 1975.

————. *The Gospel of Luke*. (The Daily Study Bible). Perrysburg, OH: Welch Publishing Company, 1975.

Batten, Alicia. *Teachings of Jesus*. Ottawa: Novalis, 2005.

Bick, Margaret. *Preparing to Celebrate in Schools*. (Preparing for Liturgy series). Ottawa: Novalis, 1996.

Brown, Raymond E., S.S., Joseph A. Fitzmeyer, S.J., Roland E. Murphy, O. Carm, eds. *Jerome Biblical Commentary*. New Jersey: Prentice-Hall, 1968.

*Catechism of the Catholic Church*. Ottawa: Canadian Conference of Catholic Bishops, 1994.

Cocks, Nancy. *Growing up with God: Using Stories to Explore a Child's Faith and Life*. Ottawa: Novalis, 2003.

Cooper, Noel. *Language of the Heart: How to Read the Bible (A User's Guide for Catholics)*. Ottawa: Novalis, 2003.

Delaney, John J. *Pocket Dictionary of Saints*. New York: Doubleday, 1983.

*Dictionary of Mary*. New York: Catholic Book Publishing Company, 1985.

Eddy, Corbin. *Who Knows the Colour of God? Homilies and Reflections for Year C*. Ottawa: Novalis, 2000.

————. *Who Knows the Reach of God? Homilies and Reflections for Year A*. Ottawa: Novalis, 2001.

————. *Who Knows the Shape of God? Homilies and Reflections for Year B*. Ottawa: Novalis, 2002.

Foley, Leonard, O.F.M., ed. *Saint of the Day*. Chicago: St. Anthony Messenger Press, 1990.

Halmo, Joan. *Celebrating the Church Year with Young Children*. Ottawa: Novalis, 1988.

Knox, Ian. *Theology for Teachers* (revised edition). Ottawa: Novalis, 1999.

Lang, (Rev.) Jovian P., OFM. *Dictionary of Liturgy*. New York: Catholic Book Publishing Company, 1989.

*The Holy Bible* (New Revised Standard Version - Catholic Edition). Toronto: Canadian Bible Society, 1993.

Levy, Rosalie Marie. *Heavenly Friends*. Boston: Daughters of St. Paul, 1984.

*Liturgical Calendar*. Ottawa: Canadian Conference of Catholic Bishops, 1999.

*Liturgy of the Hours*, 4 volumes. New York: Catholic Book Publishing Company, 1975.

MacKenthun, Carole, R.S.M. *Saints Alive: Blessed Kateri Tekakwitha*. New York: William H. Sadlier, 1987.

Marsh, John. *Saint John*. (The Pelican New Testament Commentaries). London: Penguin Books, 1971.

McKenzie, John L., S.J. *Dictionary of the Bible*. New York: The Bruce Publishing Company, 1965.

McLaughlin, John L. *The Questions of Jesus*. Ottawa: Novalis, 2001.

————. *Parables of Jesus*. Ottawa: Novalis, 2004.

National Bulletin on Liturgy. *The Liturgical Year: Its Story*. Volume 33, Number 163, Winter 2000.

Richards, James. *Preparing Morning and Evening Prayer*. (Preparing for Liturgy series). Ottawa: Novalis, 1997.

Spicer, J.E., CSsR. *Preparing for Sunday: Exploring the Readings for Year A*. Ottawa: Novalis, 2004.

————. *Preparing for Sunday: Exploring the Readings for Year B*. Ottawa: Novalis, 2002.

————. *Preparing for Sunday: Exploring the Readings for Year C*. Ottawa: Novalis, 2003

Sweet, Marilyn J. *Preparing to Celebrate with Youth* (Preparing for Liturgy series). Ottawa: Novalis, 1997.

Vogels, Walter. *Words of Wisdom: Proverbs for Everyday Living*. Ottawa: Novalis, 1999.

————. *Becoming Fully Human: Living the Bible with God, Each Other and the Environment*. Ottawa: Novalis, 2003.

Lectionary – Weekdays A and Lectionary – Weekdays B. Study editions. Ottawa: Canadian Conference of Catholic Bishops, 1994.

# APPENDIX 1 — INDEX OF BIBLICAL READINGS

# APPENDIX 1 - INDEX OF BIBLICAL READINGS

| | |
|---|---|
| 11:29-30, 32 | Twenty-eighth Week of OT, Monday |
| 12:6-7 | Twenty-eighth Week of OT, Friday |
| 12:32-34 | St. Anthony of Padua, June 13 |
| 12:35-38 | Twenty-ninth Week of OT, Tuesday |
| 13:18-21 | Thirtieth Week of OT, Tuesday |
| 14:12-14 | Thirty-first Week of OT, Monday |
| 15:8-10 | Thirty-first Week of OT, Thursday |
| 17:11-16a | Friday Before Thanksgiving |
| 17:11-19 | Thirty-second Week of OT, Wednesday |
| 18:35-43 | Thirty-third Week of OT, Monday |
| 19:1-6, 8 | Thirty-third Week of OT, Tuesday |
| 19:45-46 | Thirty-third Week of OT, Friday |
| 21:1-4 | Thirty-fourth Week of OT, Monday |
| 21:12,13 | Thirty-fourth Week of OT, Wednesday |
| 21:29-33 | Thirty-fourth Week of OT, Friday |
| 24:25-31 | Wednesday Within the Octave of Easter |
| 24:36-48 | Thursday Within the Octave of Easter |

**John**

| | |
|---|---|
| 3:1-8 | Second Week of Easter, Monday |
| 3:11-15 | Second Week of Easter, Tuesday |
| 3:13-17 | Triumph of the Cross, September 14 |
| 3:16-21 | Second Week of Easter, Wednesday |
| 3:31-36 | Second Week of Easter, Thursday |
| 4:46-53 | Fourth Week of Lent, Monday |
| 5:1-8 | Fourth Week of Lent, Tuesday |
| 5:16-20a | Fourth Week of Lent, Wednesday |
| 5:31-37a | Fourth Week of Lent, Thursday |
| 5:33-35 | Third Week of Advent, Friday |
| 6:5b-10a, 11-15 | Second Week of Easter, Friday |
| 6:22-29 | Third Week of Easter, Monday |
| 6:30-35 | Third Week of Easter, Tuesday |
| 6:35-40 | Third Week of Easter, Wednesday |
| 6:43-45, 47-51 | Third Week of Easter, Thursday |
| 6:52-59 | Third Week of Easter, Friday |
| 7:1-2, 10, 25-28a, 30 | Fourth Week of Lent, Friday |
| 8:25-30 | Fifth Week of Lent, Tuesday |
| 8:31-38a, 40 | Fifth Week of Lent, Wednesday |
| 8:51-55a,d, 56-59 | Fifth Week of Lent, Thursday |
| 10:11-16 | Fourth Week of Easter, Monday |
| 10:22-30 | Fourth Week of Easter, Tuesday |
| 10:31-36, 39 | Fifth Week of Lent, Friday |
| 11:17, 20-27 | All Souls, November 2 |
| 12:44-50 | Fourth Week of Easter, Wednesday |
| 13:2-4, 6-8, 12-15 | Holy Thursday |
| 13:16-20 | Fourth Week of Easter, Thursday |
| 13:21-28, 30 | Tuesday In Holy Week |
| 14:1-6 | Fourth Week of Easter, Friday |
| 14:6-11a | Sts. Philip and James, May 3 |
| 14:21-24 | Fifth Week of Easter, Monday |
| 14:27-31 | Fifth Week of Easter, Tuesday |
| 15:1-8 | Fifth Week of Easter, Wednesday |
| 15:9-11 | Fifth Week of Easter, Thursday |
| 15:12-17 | Fifth Week of Easter, Friday |
| 15:26–16:4 | Sixth Week of Easter, Monday |

**Philippians**

| | |
|---|---|
| 1:1-7a | Thirtieth Week of OT, Friday |
| 4:4-9 | St. Marguerite D'Youville, October 16 |

**Colossians**

| | |
|---|---|
| 3:12-14 | Friday, First Week of School |
| 3:14-15, 17, 23-24 | St. Joseph the Worker, May 1 |

**1 Thessalonians**

| | |
|---|---|
| 5:16-23a | Last Day of the School Year |

**1 Timothy**

| | |
|---|---|
| 2:1-6a, 8 | Twenty-fourth Week of OT, Monday |
| 4:12-14a, 15 | Twenty-fourth Week of OT, Thursday |
| 6:11-12 | Twenty-fourth Week of OT, Friday |

**2 Timothy**

| | |
|---|---|
| 1:1-2, 5-8 | Sts. Timothy and Titus, January 26 |
| 1:3, 5a, 6-9 | Ninth Week of OT, Wednesday |
| 1:13-14, 2:3-4 | St. Francis De Sales, January 24 |
| 3:10-12, 14-17 | Ninth Week of OT, Friday |
| 3:14-17 | St. Jerome, September 30 |
| 4:1-5 | St. Philip Neri, May 26 |

**James**

| | |
|---|---|
| 3:13-18 | Seventh Week of OT, Monday |
| 3:13, 17 | St. Theresa of Jesus, October 15 |
| 5:9-12 | Seventh Week of OT, Friday |
| 5:14-15 | Our Lady of Lourdes, February 11 |

**1 Peter**

| | |
|---|---|
| 3:13-17 | St. Charles Lwanga and Companions, June 3 |

**2 Peter**

| | |
|---|---|
| 1:2-4a, 5-8a | Ninth Week of OT, Monday |

**1 John**

| | |
|---|---|
| 4:7-10 | Tuesday After Epiphany |
| 4:11-13, 15-16, 18a | Wednesday After Epiphany |
| 4:19–5:3 | Thursday After Epiphany |

**Revelation**

| | |
|---|---|
| 7:9, 13-15 | St. Agnes, January 21 |
| 19:1, 5-8 | St. Marguerite Bourgeoys, January 12 |

314

# APPENDIX 2 - INDEX OF FEAST DAYS

Feast days are ranked according to the following order, from the most important to the least:

S – Solemnity

F – Feast

M – Memorial

OM – Optional Memorial

Prayers for solemnities and feasts should be used, as they are important feast days.

## September

| | |
|---|---|
| 8 | Birth of Mary (F) |
| 12 | Holy Name of Mary (OM) |
| 14 | Triumph of the Cross (F) |
| 15 | Our Lady of Sorrows (M) |
| 21 | Matthew, Apostle and Evangelist (F) |
| 26 | John de Brébeuf and Isaac Jogues, Priests and Martyrs, and companions, martyrs, secondary patrons of Canada (F) |
| 27 | Vincent de Paul, Priest (M) |
| 29 | Michael, Gabriel and Raphael, Archangels (F) |
| 30 | Jerome, Priest and Doctor (M) |

## October

| | |
|---|---|
| 1 | Theresa of the Child Jesus, Virgin and Doctor (M) |
| 2 | Guardian Angels (M) |
| 4 | Francis of Assisi (M) |
| 7 | Our Lady of the Rosary (M) |
| 15 | Theresa of Avila, Virgin and Doctor (M) |
| 16 | Marguerite D'Youville (M) |
| 16 | Margaret Mary (OM) |
| 18 | Luke, Evangelist (F) |
| 28 | Simon and Jude, Apostles (F) |

## November

| | |
|---|---|
| 1 | All Saints (S) |
| 2 | Commemoration of the Faithful Departed |
| 9 | Dedication of St. John Lateran (F) |
| 11 | Martin of Tours, Bishop (M) |
| 21 | Presentation of Mary (M) |
| 22 | Cecilia, Virgin and Martyr (M) |
| 30 | Andrew, Apostle (F) |

## December

| | |
|---|---|
| 3 | Francis Xavier, Priest (M) |
| 6 | Nicholas, Bishop (OM) |
| 8 | Immaculate Conception (S) |
| 12 | Our Lady of Guadalupe (F) |
| 14 | St. John of the Cross, Priest and Doctor (M) |

## January

Baptism of the Lord (F) (Note: This feast is usually celebrated on the Sunday following the Solemnity of Epiphany. When Epiphany is January 7 or later, Baptism of the Lord is celebrated the next day, on Monday.)

| | |
|---|---|
| 12 | Marguerite Bourgeoys, Religious (M) |
| 21 | Agnes, Virgin and Martyr (M) |
| 24 | Francis de Sales, Bishop and Doctor (M) |
| 25 | Conversion of Paul, Apostle (F) |
| 26 | Timothy and Titus, Bishops (M) |
| 28 | Thomas Aquinas, Priest and Doctor (M) |

## February

| | |
|---|---|
| 2 | Presentation of the Lord (F) |
| 11 | Our Lady of Lourdes (M) |
| 22 | Chair of Peter, Apostle (F) |

## March

| | |
|---|---|
| 17 | Patrick, Bishop (OM) |
| 19 | Joseph, Husband of Mary (S) |
| 25 | Annunciation of the Lord (S) |

## April

| | |
|---|---|
| 17 | Blessed Kateri Tekakwitha, Virgin (OM) |
| 25 | Mark, Evangelist (F) |
| 29 | Catherine of Siena, Virgin and Doctor (M) |

## May

| | |
|---|---|
| 3 | Philip and James, Apostles (F) |
| 14 | Matthias, Apostle (F) |
| 26 | Philip Neri, Priest (M) |
| 31 | Visitation (F) |

## June

Friday following the the Solemnity of the Body and Blood of the Christ:
Sacred Heart (S)

| | |
|---|---|
| 1 | Justin, Martyr (M) |
| 3 | Charles Lwanga and companions, Martyrs (M) |
| 11 | Barnabas, Apostle (F) |
| 13 | Anthony of Padua, Priest and Doctor (M) |
| 22 | Thomas More, Martyr (OM) |
| 24 | Birth of John the Baptist (S) |
| 29 | Peter and Paul, Apostles (S) |

# APPENDIX 3 - TRADITIONAL PRAYERS

## Lord's Prayer I

Our Father, who art in heaven,

hallowed be thy name;

thy kingdom come;

thy will be done on earth as it is in heaven.

Give us this day our daily bread;

and forgive us our trespasses

as we forgive those who trespass against us;

and lead us not into temptation,

but deliver us from evil. Amen.

∞∞∞∞∞∞∞

## Lord's Prayer II

*from Catholic Book of Worship III, inside front cover*

Our Father in heaven,

hallowed be your name,

your kingdom come, your will be done,

on earth as in heaven.

Give us today our daily bread.

Forgive us our sins

as we forgive those who sin against us.

Save us from the time of trial

and deliver us from evil.

For the kingdom, the power

and the glory are yours,

now and forever. Amen.

∞∞∞∞∞∞∞

## Hail Mary

Hail Mary, full of grace,

the Lord is with you.

Blessed are you among women

and blessed is the fruit of your womb, Jesus.

Holy Mary, Mother of God,

pray for us sinners,

now and at the hour of our death. Amen.

∞∞∞∞∞∞∞

## Glory

Glory to the Father,

and to the Son,

and to the Holy Spirit.

As it was in the beginning,

is now, and will be forever. Amen.

## Angel of God

Angel of God, my guardian dear,

to whom God's love entrust me here.

Ever this day be at my side

to light and guard,

to rule and guide.

Amen.

∞∞∞∞∞∞∞

## Angelus

The angel of the Lord declared unto Mary, and she conceived of the Holy Spirit. Hail Mary…

Behold, the handmaid of the Lord; be it done to me according to your word. Hail Mary…

And the word was made flesh, and dwelt among us. Hail Mary…

Pray for us, O holy Mother of God; that we may be made worthy of the promises of Christ.

Pour forth, we beseech you, O Lord, your grace into our hearts that we, to whom the incarnation of your Son was made known by the message of an angel, may by his passion and cross be brought to the glory of his resurrection. We ask this through the same Christ, our Lord. Amen.

∞∞∞∞∞∞∞

## Come, Holy Spirit

Come, Holy Spirit,

fill the hearts of your faithful

and kindle in them the fire of your love.

Send forth your Spirit, O Lord,

and renew the face of the earth.

O God, on the first Pentecost

you instructed the hearts of those

who believed in you

by the light of the Holy Spirit:

under the inspiration of the same Spirit,

give us a taste for what is right and true

and a continuing sense of his joy-bringing presence and power,

through Jesus Christ our Lord. Amen.

# APPENDIX 3 - TRADITIONAL PRAYERS

## Magnificat

My soul magnifies the Lord,

and my spirit rejoices in God my Saviour,

for he has looked with favour

on the lowliness of his servant.

Surely, from now on all generations

will call me blessed;

for the Mighty One has done great things for me,

and holy is his name.

His mercy is for those who fear him

from generation to generation.

He has shown strength with his arm;

he has scattered the proud

in the thoughts of their hearts.

He has brought down the powerful

from their thrones,

and lifted up the lowly;

he has filled the hungry with good things,

and sent the rich away empty.

He has helped his servant Israel,

in remembrance of his mercy,

according to the promise he made to our ancestors,

to Abraham and to his descendants forever.

*Luke 1:46-55*

∞∞∞∞∞∞∞∞

Eternal rest grant unto them, O Lord,

and let perpetual light shine upon them.

May they rest in peace. Amen.

## Penitential Rite

I confess to almighty God,

and to you, my brothers and sisters,

that I have sinned through my own fault,

in my thoughts and in my words,

in what I have done,

and in what I have failed to do;

and I ask blessed Mary, ever virgin,

all the angels and saints,

and you, my brothers and sisters,

to pray for me to the Lord our God.

∞∞∞∞∞∞∞∞

## Kyrie eleison

Lord, have mercy. Lord, have mercy.

Christ, have mercy. Christ, have mercy.

Lord, have mercy. Lord, have mercy.

# APPENDIX 4 - TABLE OF MOVEABLE DATES AND WEEKS IN ORDINARY TIME

## Table of Moveable Dates

| Year | Ash Wednesday | Easter Sunday | Pentecost Sunday |
|------|---------------|---------------|------------------|
| 2005 | Feb. 9 | Mar. 27 | May 15 |
| 2006 | Mar. 1 | Apr. 16 | June 4 |
| 2007 | Feb. 21 | Apr. 8 | May 27 |
| 2008 | Feb. 6 | Mar. 23 | May 11 |
| 2009 | Feb. 25 | Apr. 12 | May 31 |
| 2010 | Feb. 17 | Apr. 4 | May 23 |
| 2011 | Mar. 9 | Apr. 24 | June 12 |
| 2012 | Feb. 22 | Apr. 8 | May 27 |
| 2013 | Feb. 13 | Mar. 31 | May 19 |
| 2014 | Mar. 5 | Apr. 20 | June 8 |
| 2015 | Feb. 18 | Apr. 5 | May 24 |

## Weeks in Ordinary Time

| Year | BEFORE LENT # of weeks | Last date before Lent | AFTER LENT OT resumes | Resuming week # | First Sunday of Advent |
|------|-----------|------------------|------------|-----------------|------------------------|
| 2005 | 5 | Feb. 8 | May 16 | 7 | Nov. 27 |
| 2006 | 8 | Feb. 28 | June 5 | 9 | Dec. 3 |
| 2007 | 7 | Feb. 20 | May 28 | 8 | Dec. 2 |
| 2008 | 4 | Feb. 5 | May 12 | 6 | Nov. 30 |
| 2009 | 7 | Feb. 24 | June 1 | 9 | Nov. 29 |
| 2010 | 6 | Feb. 16 | May 24 | 8 | Nov. 28 |
| 2011 | 9 | Mar. 8 | June 13 | 11 | Nov. 27 |
| 2012 | 7 | Feb. 21 | May 28 | 8 | Dec. 2 |
| 2013 | 5 | Feb. 12 | May 20 | 7 | Dec. 1 |
| 2014 | 8 | Mar. 4 | June 9 | 10 | Nov. 30 |
| 2015 | 6 | Feb. 17 | May 25 | 8 | Nov. 29 |